IMAGES
of America

WASHINGTON COUNTY

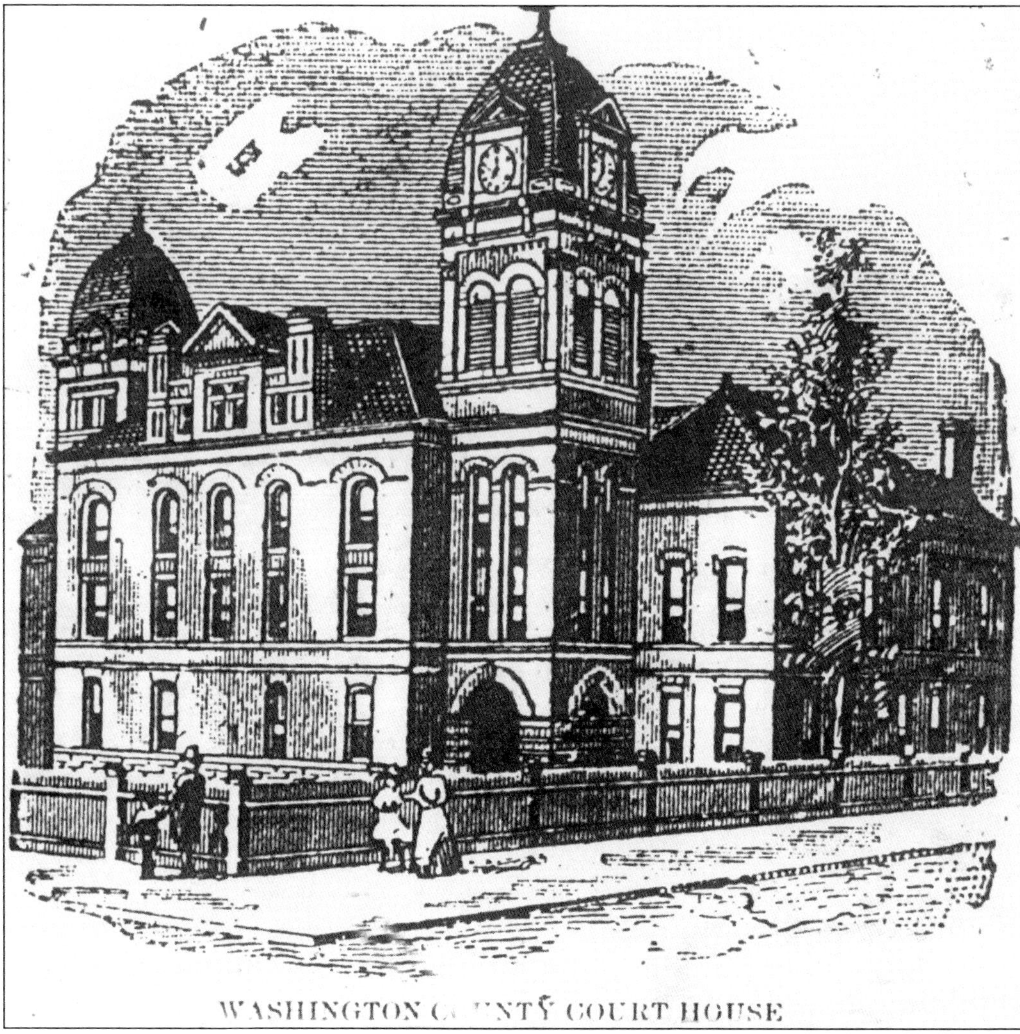

The third courthouse was built in 1868 and extensively renovated in 1898 into a more Victorian style. This building, with a 1938 addition, still serves the county today.

(on the cover) The Coca-Cola Bottling Company was situated on Malone Street, north of the courthouse, 1916. One gentleman in the center is W.L. Williams, owner, who sold the plant to O.L. Hudson in the early 1920s.

IMAGES of America

WASHINGTON COUNTY

Washington County Historical Society

ARCADIA PUBLISHING

ISBN 978-0-7385-1567-0

Published by Arcadia Publishing
Charleston, South Carolina

Printed in the United States of America

Library of Congress Catalog Card Number: 2003107851

For all general information contact Arcadia Publishing at:
Telephone 843-853-2070
Fax 843-853-0044
E-mail sales@arcadiapublishing.com
For customer service and orders:
Toll-Free 1-888-313-2665

Visit us on the Internet at www.arcadiapublishing.com

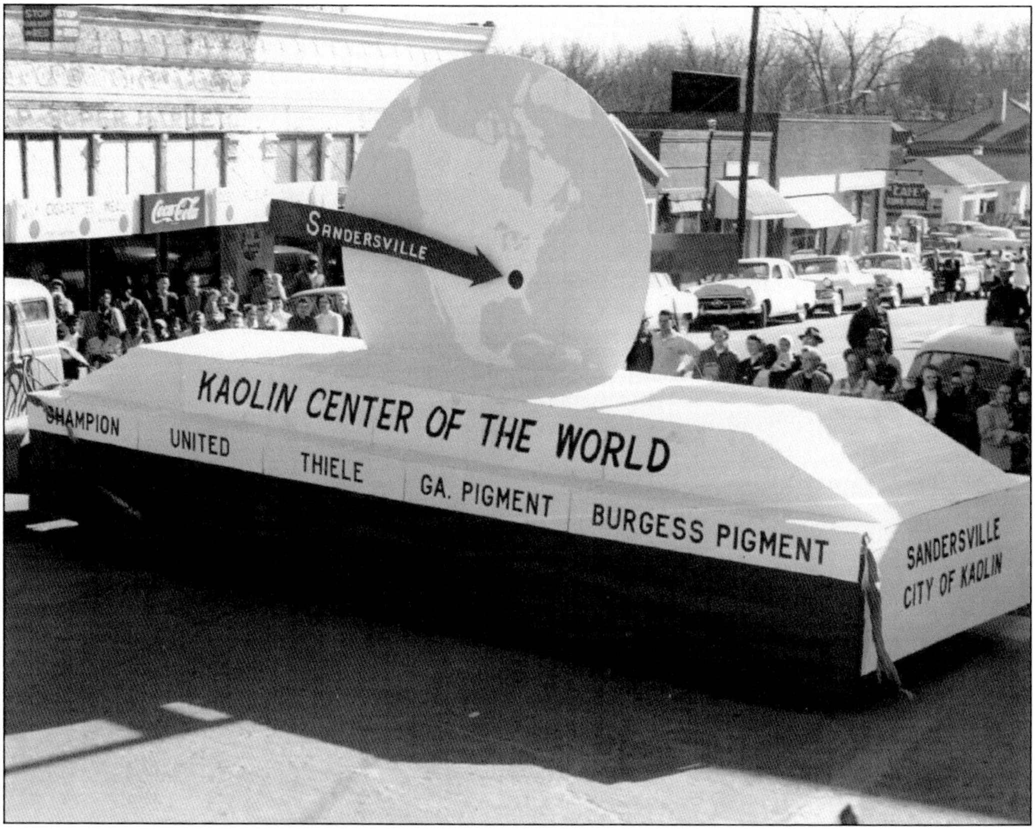

This 1956 Kaolin Parade float lists all of the kaolin processing companies in town. This was the first year for the Kaolin Festival, which has become an annual event.

Contents

ACKNOWLEDGMENTS

We hope this book of pictures will bring a feeling of nostalgia, remembrance, and appreciation for our heritage in Washington County, Georgia. These photographs reflect the history of many of the county's people as they attended school, worked, worshiped, and played.

Look carefully and you will see how people lived and dressed following the styles and mores of the times. This collection covers about 100 years from the mid-19th to the mid-20th centuries. Unfortunately, we have few pictures of our county's very early days.

This is not a history book, but a pictorial glimpse of times past. If you want to see more of our history, read our book, *Cotton to Kaolin, A History of Washington County*, which incidentally also includes 191 other photographs not used in this book.

Proceeds from this book, prepared by members of the Washington County Historical Society, will help support the work of the society, formed on July 4, 1976. The society opened a museum on the courthouse square in 1978 in the 1891 sheriff's residence and jail. That building now is our Genealogical Research Center. In 1999, the Brown House Museum was opened, which also serves as the headquarters for the society. The c. 1850 structure is a significant part of the area's history and played an important role in the Civil War.

In 1979 the Georgia Archives had a program called "Vanishing Georgia," where photographers visited each county, and residents would bring in their old pictures to share and preserve. Some of our pictures are from that collection.

We are grateful to all those who searched, researched to identify, and brought in their pictures for inclusion in the book. We regret we could not use all those brought in, but they will be added to the archives of the museum, creating a valuable resource.

I am especially grateful to Betty Kicklighter who chaired this project; Mary Alice Jordan, museum and archives director; and to my husband Ray, who scanned all of the pictures. The museum docents were wonderful help, and we appreciate the computer expertise at Sandersville Tech and from Shaun Veal.

Brenda Hollingsworth, 2003 President
Washington County Historical Society

Note: Pictures labeled "Georgia Archives" are courtesy of the Georgia Division of Archives and History, office of Secretary of State.

Introduction

Imagine 60,000 soldiers with their horses and equipment plus followers descending upon a village of 500, where most men were off fighting. That was the weekend of November 25, 1864 when Gen. William T. Sherman and his troops came through Sandersville and Washington County on his "March to the Sea." It was a time of hardship for everyone in the area.

Georgia's Legislature defined Washington County in February 1784 and settlers came claiming land grants. Warthen was the first settlement, where the Superior Courts met, and a jail was built. Constructed of hand-hewn logs, that jail has been restored and is considered the oldest log jail in Georgia. It and the entire village of Warthen are listed on the National Register.

Sandersville (originally Saunders Crossroads), at the crossing of two Indian trails, was named county seat by the Legislature in 1796. Seven counties and portions of nine more were eventually cut from the original Washington County. Many early post office communities grew and faded with time while railroads determined several villages. Presently there are Davisboro, Deepstep, Harrison, Oconee, Riddleville, Sandersville, Tennille, and Warthen.

As a frontier county, self-contained farms and plantations were common.

Religion had an impact even in the early times. The first church was constituted in 1790. First came Baptist, then Methodist organized, and by 1856, Christian churches were established followed by Catholic and Episcopal around 1900. Today there are 120 churches of various denominations, many descending from early ones.

During his "visit," Sherman selected the Brown House as his headquarters. Sunday, November 27, as Sherman left Sandersville, he ordered the courthouse and jail burned. In Tennille, railroad tracks were pulled up, heated, and twisted into "bowties."

The following May, in 1865, President (of the Confederacy) Jefferson Davis came through Warthen and Sandersville and the last official act of the Confederacy occurred in Sandersville. The act provided for distribution of the treasury.

A new courthouse was completed in 1868 and enlarged to a Victorian style in 1899. Before the turn of the 20th century, brick store buildings replaced wooden ones that had burned.

Medicine played a key role in the county's history. The first Dr. William Rawlings, a famous surgeon, opened a hospital about 1895. Nurses were taught at Rawlings Nurses Training School from 1903 to 1932. Operating on the Sandersville Square for 65 years, the Rawlings Sanitarium moved to a new facility in 1961. First called Memorial Hospital, it is now the Washington County Regional Medical Center.

During the time from about 1890 to the mid-1920s, stable cotton prices brought prosperity and fine homes, many existing today. From a concentration on cotton as a major money crop, farmers diversified. Other agricultural products flourished, but later began to fail. A prosperous lumber industry grew.

Fortunately for Washington County, kaolin lay dormant, waiting to fill its role in the economy. Kaolin, a white, alumina silicate clay, is used in papermaking, medicines, paints, and many other products. Processed kaolin products are shipped around the world. As the industry grew, the county became the largest refiner of kaolin, becoming the "Kaolin Capital of the World." In 2003, there are five processing companies and numerous mines attracting college-educated personnel, scientists, and geologists from many countries. An annual Kaolin Festival celebrates the importance of the resource. At the end of the 20th century, kaolin was Georgia's largest volume export.

Organized in 1976, the Washington County Historical Society operates two museums, one in the old county jail and sheriff's home, now the Genealogical Research Museum, and the Brown House Museum, which serves as Society headquarters. Four districts are on the National Register of Historic Places, and the Old City Cemetery and several structures are listed, too. An exhibit dedicated to Charles Edward Choate is in the Chamber of Commerce.

Two Georgia governors came from Washington County: Jared Irwin, Revolutionary War soldier and frontier Indian fighter, and Thomas Hardwick, formerly a U.S. Senator and Congressman. Also notable are Louis Cohen, who started many businesses—the first Sandersville Railroad, a bank, and mercantile stores; Ben Tarbutton, Sr. of the later Sandersville Railroad, who welcomed the kaolin industry in the mid-20th century; Elijah Poole Mohammed, leader of the National of Islam, was born near Deepstep; the Gordys of Motown Music fame; and McHenry Boatright, who won fame as a concert singer.

At the turn of the 21st century, Washington County has Sandersville Technical College plus a local campus for Georgia Military College; a new, comprehensive library, excellent schools, good recreational facilities, and a lively cultural life of local and nationally affiliated clubs. In the area there is a functioning agriculture industry, a fledgling nursery industry, a healthy timber business, a number of manufacturing plants, and a district Department of Transportation complex. In 2002 and 2003, two peak power plants were built.

Washington County is a diversified yet rural community comprised of people who appreciate their past and work for the future.

One

Family Together Time

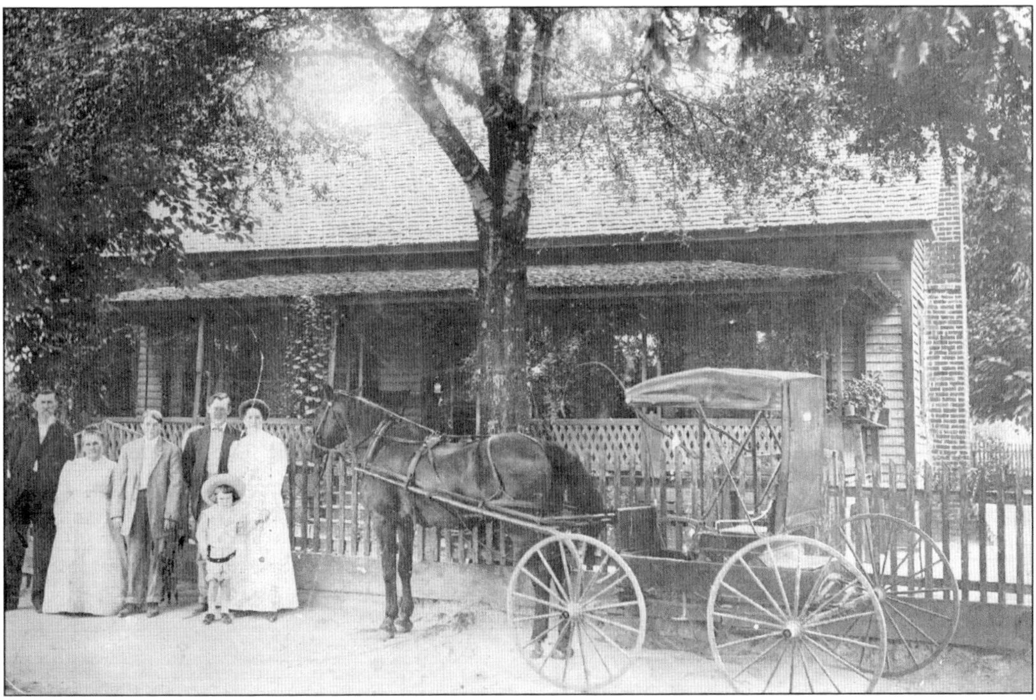

The home of the William Jasper Taylor family was located three miles from Davisboro. Pictured c. 1910, from left to right, are William Jasper Taylor; his wife Jane Jones; their sons, William Grady Taylor and John Harrison Taylor; John's wife Eunice Wilson Taylor; and John and Eunice's son William. (Georgia Archives.)

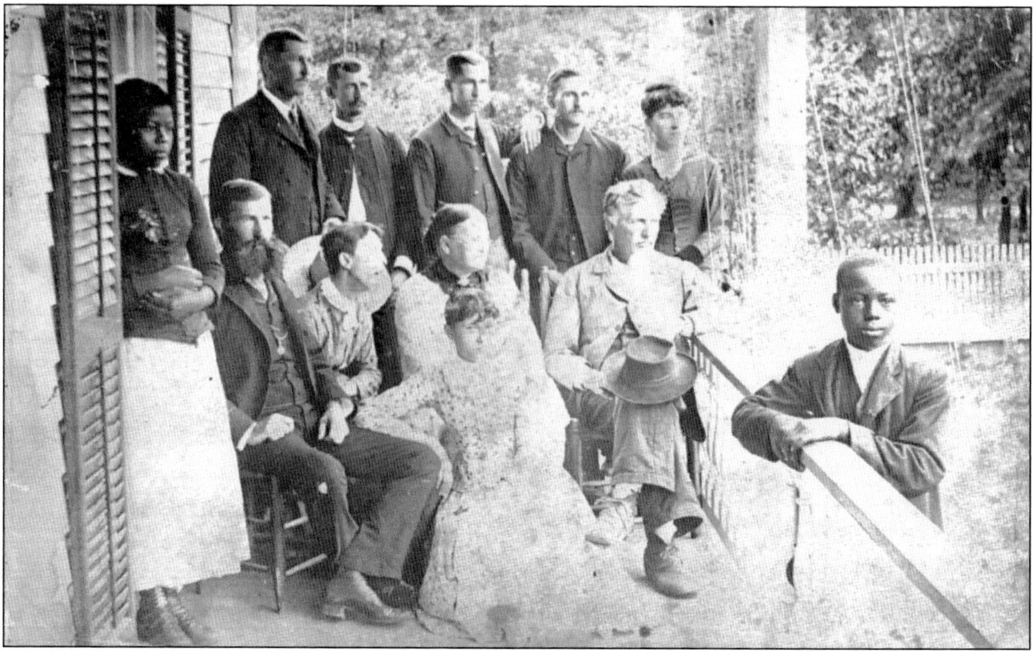

The Kelly family and their servants gathered on the porch for the visiting photographer. Pictured from left to right are (front row) maid Carrie Hooks, Dr. Tom J. Kelly, Jane Kelly, Elizabeth Kelly, Ella Kelly, Robert Kelly, and butler Peter John Hooks; (back row) Robert Allen Kelly, an unidentified visitor, William Marion Kelly, James L. Kelly, and Francis Qudie Kelly, c. 1910. (Georgia Archives).

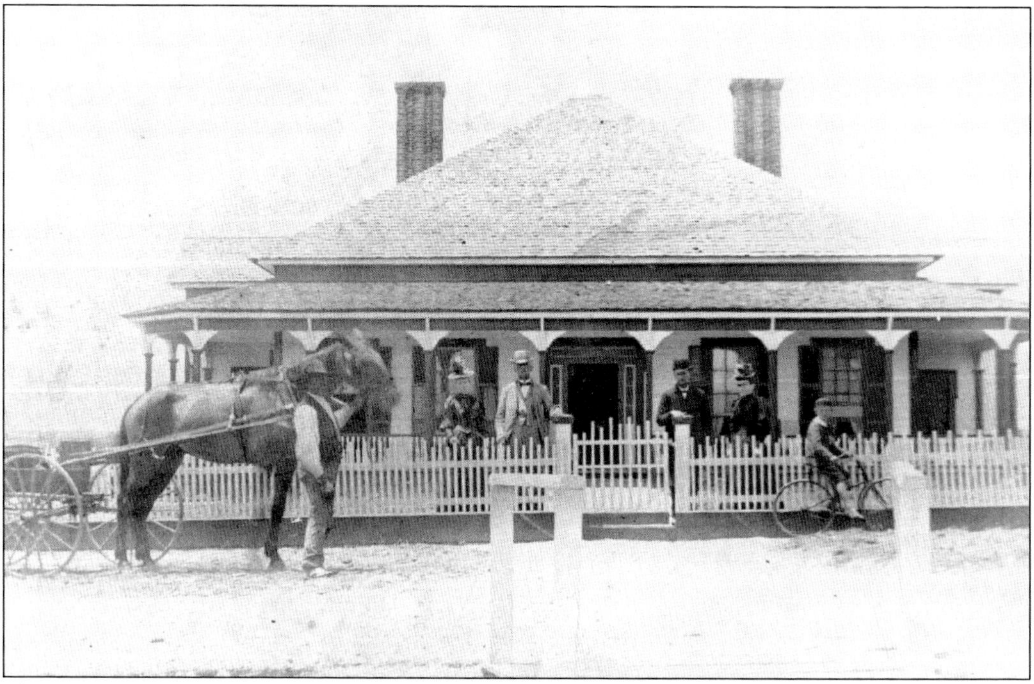

Shown here are Mr. and Mrs. J.B. Newsom and Mr. and Mrs. N.J. Newsom. Riding the bicycle is N.J. Newsom Jr., who grew up to become a prominent Washington County physician.

The Braswell family of Harrison is out for a drive in a Ford truck equipped with roll-up window shades, *c.* 1918. They are, from left to right, Helen, Tom, Grady, and Robert. (Georgia Archives.)

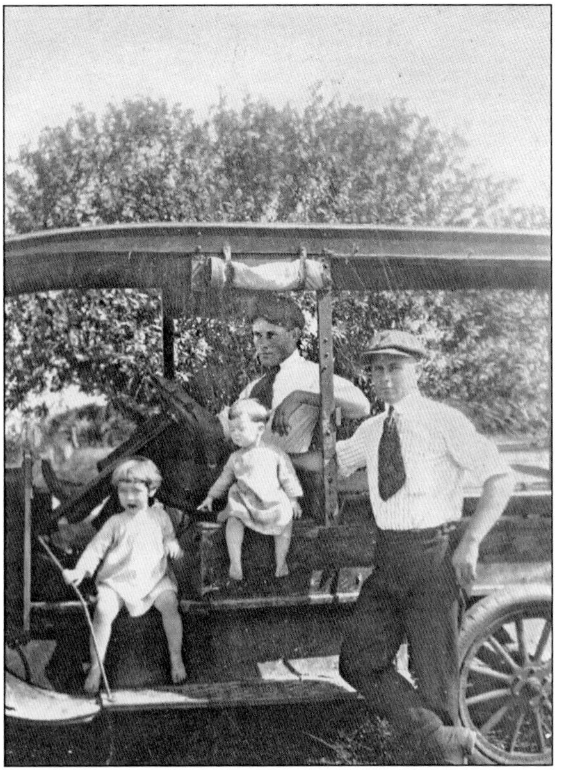

Gathered at the Jordan homeplace in Davisboro are A.W.H. Jordan and his family. Jordan died in 1919 and his wife Nannie Taylor Jordan preceded him in 1909. (Georgia Archives.)

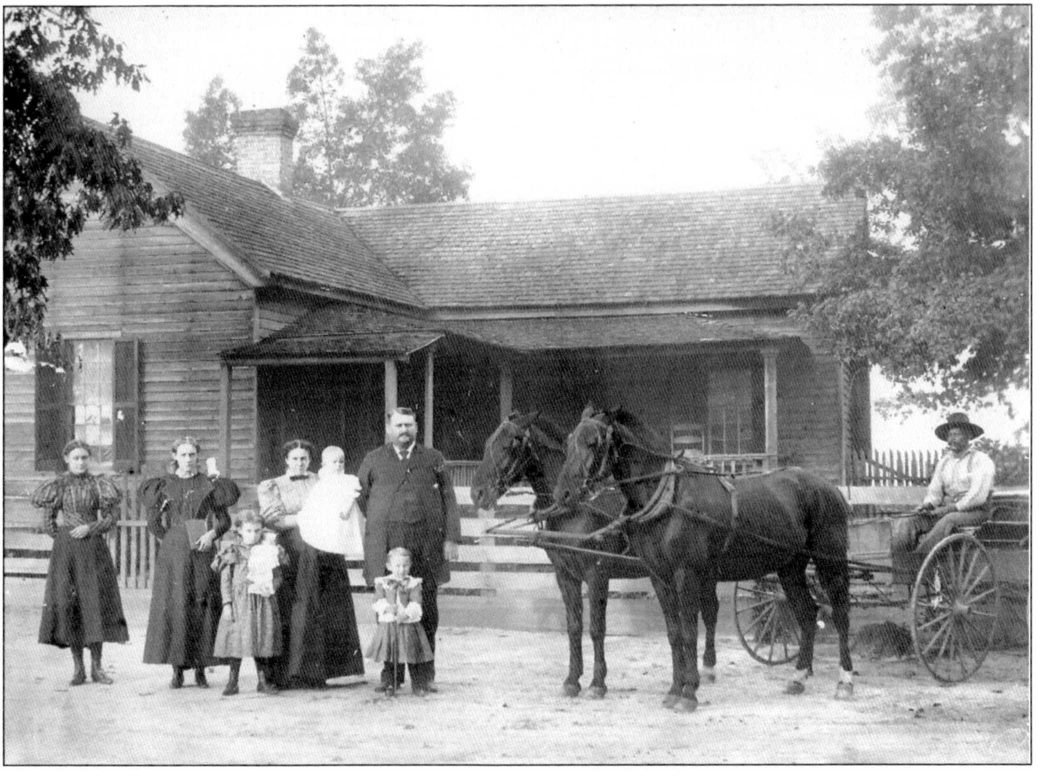

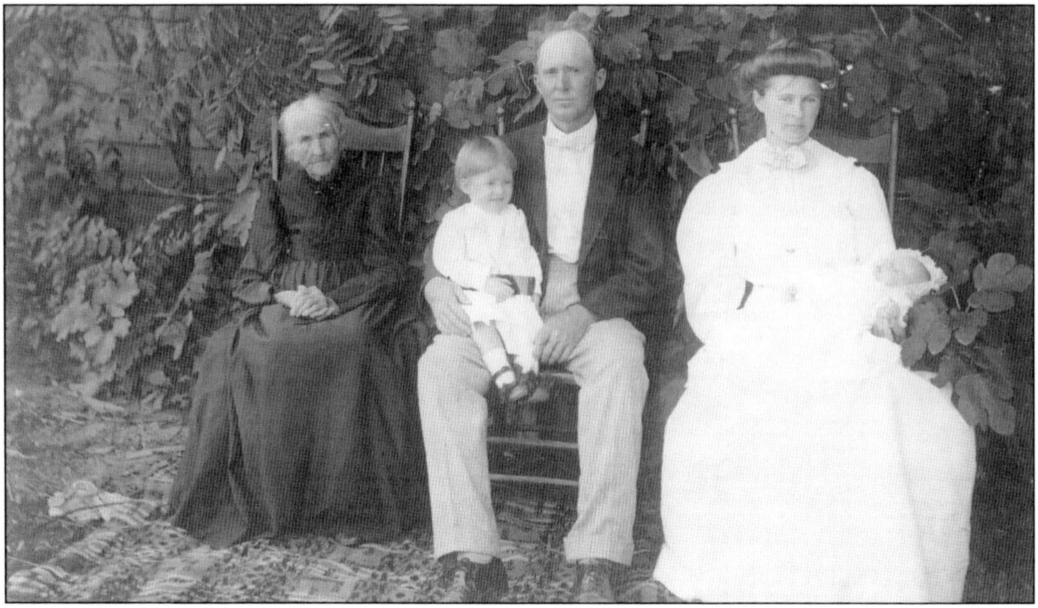

A traveling photographer captured Samson B. Davis, his wife Lillie, their sons, Earl and Elmer, and Samson's mother, Effie Ann Walters Davis in 1908.

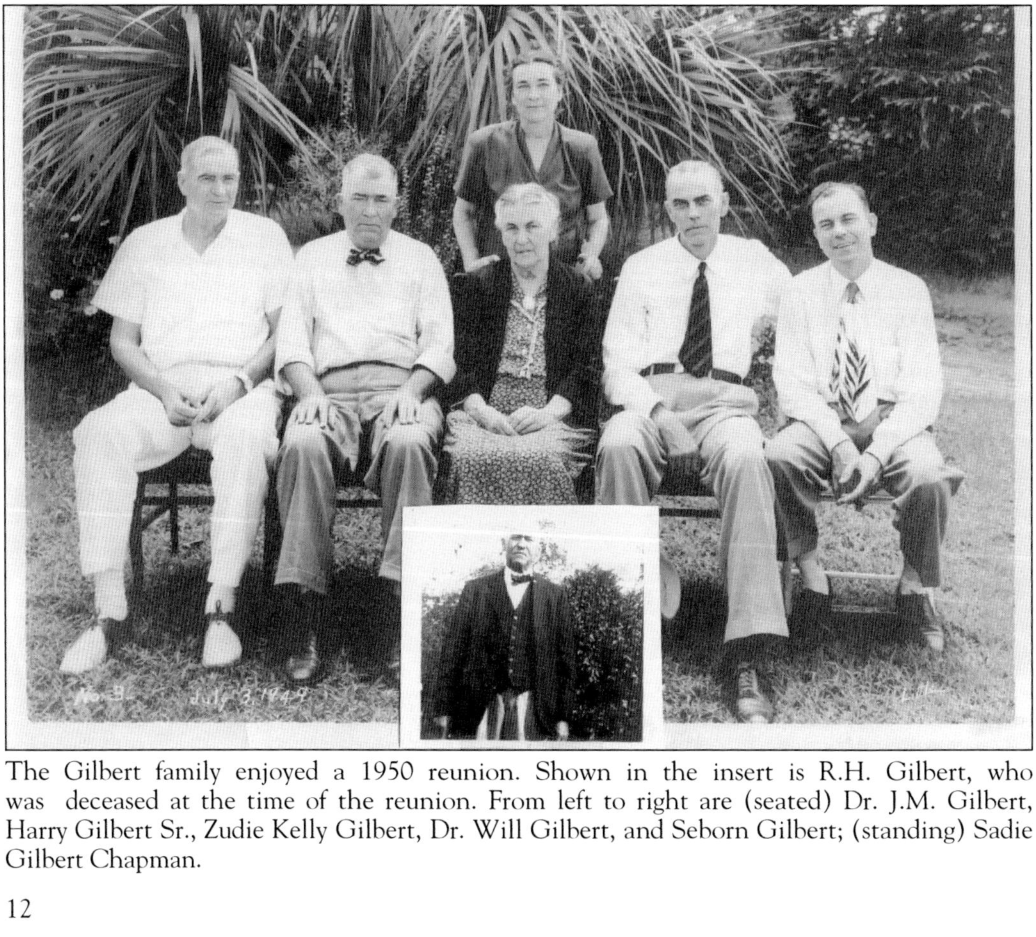

The Gilbert family enjoyed a 1950 reunion. Shown in the insert is R.H. Gilbert, who was deceased at the time of the reunion. From left to right are (seated) Dr. J.M. Gilbert, Harry Gilbert Sr., Zudie Kelly Gilbert, Dr. Will Gilbert, and Seborn Gilbert; (standing) Sadie Gilbert Chapman.

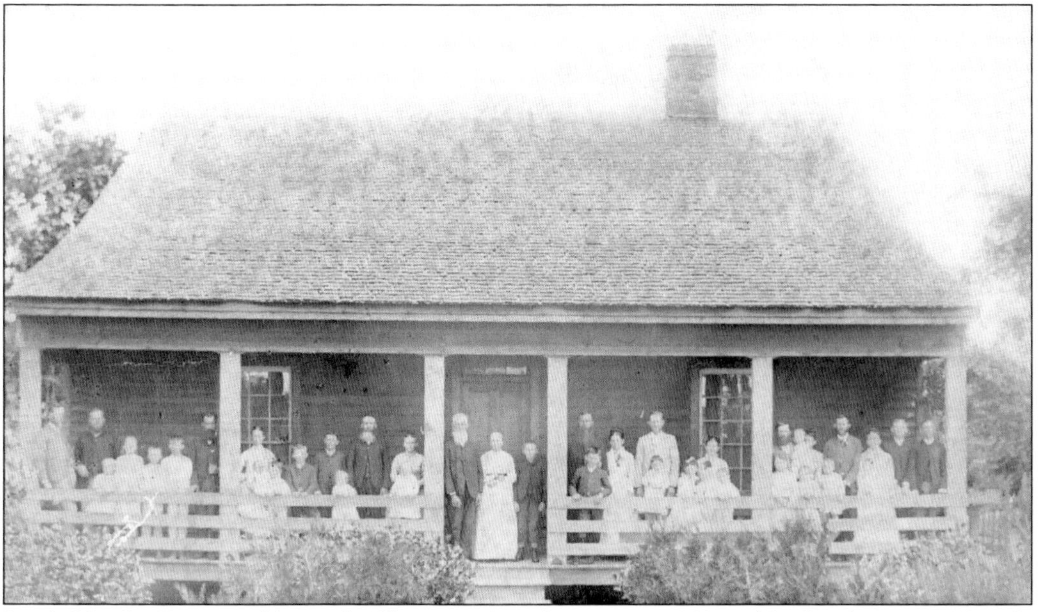

Jacob Rhodes Davis and his wife Effie moved to the area in 1850 and built a home on Heard's Bridge Road, where they raised 12 children. On August 28, 1888, the family gathered for a reunion and this photo was taken. The couple is standing in the doorway.

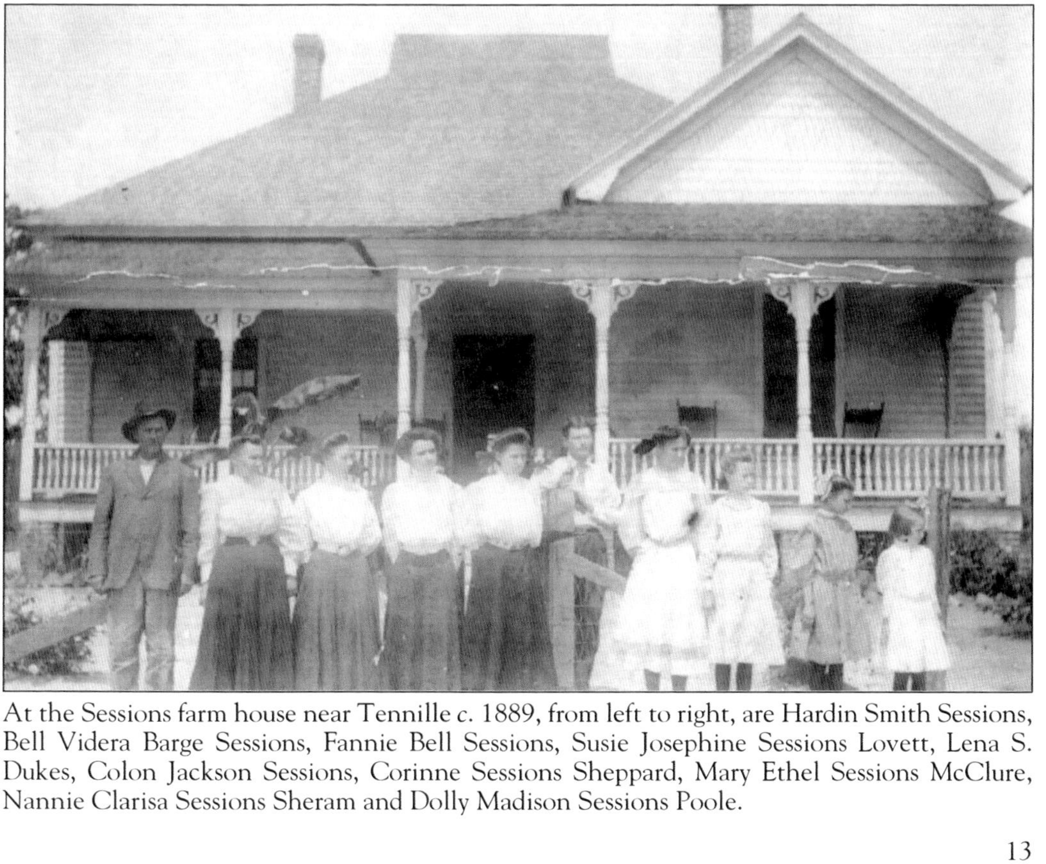

At the Sessions farm house near Tennille *c.* 1889, from left to right, are Hardin Smith Sessions, Bell Videra Barge Sessions, Fannie Bell Sessions, Susie Josephine Sessions Lovett, Lena S. Dukes, Colon Jackson Sessions, Corinne Sessions Sheppard, Mary Ethel Sessions McClure, Nannie Clarisa Sessions Sheram and Dolly Madison Sessions Poole.

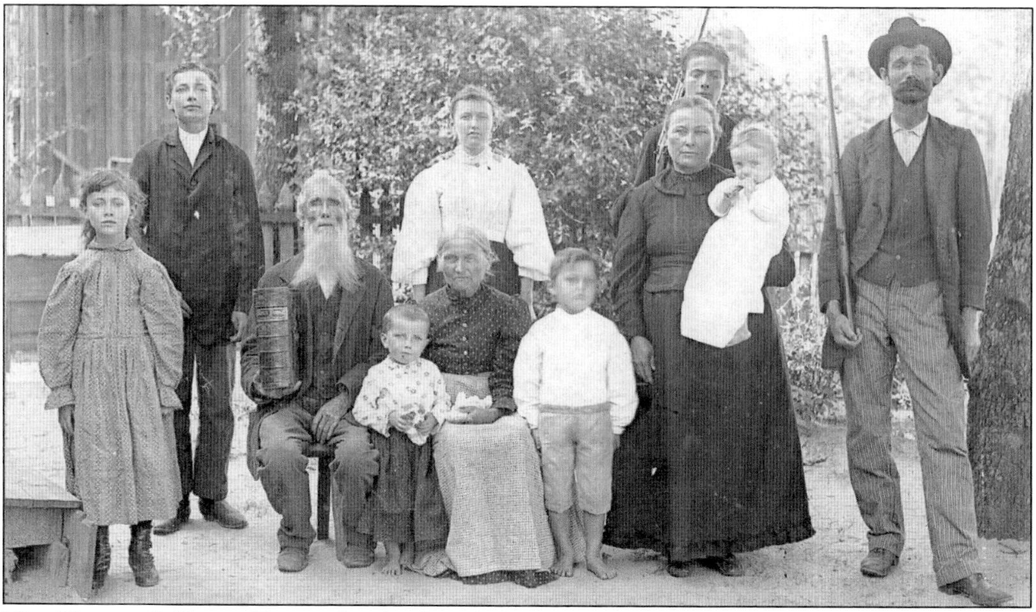

The Thomas Jefferson Frazier family, from left to right, are Lizzie, Gordon, Thomas Jefferson Frazier, Talmadge, Mary Swint Frazier, Daisy, Sam, Laura Frazier (holding baby Napoleon), Baxter (behind her), and John G. Fazier. Thomas Jefferson Frazier is holding the family Bible.

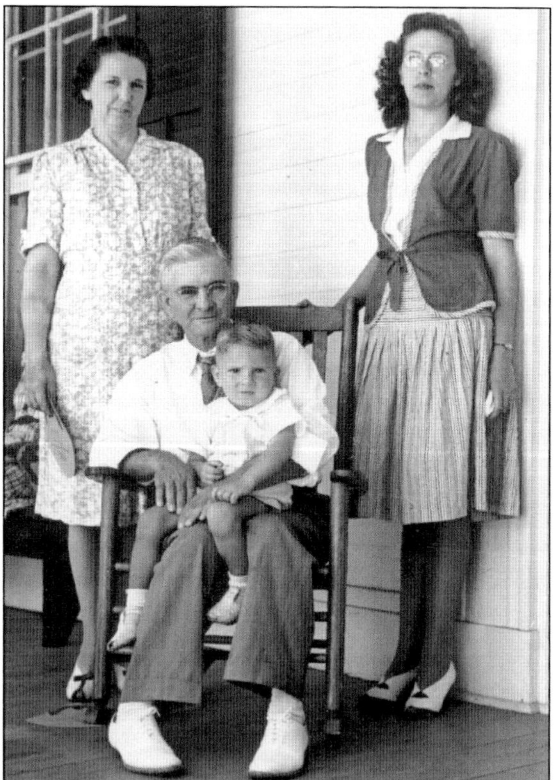

W.B. Francis Sr. holds his grandson, James C. "Jimmy" Francis Jr, c. 1941. Standing are his wife Geraldine and Harriett (Mrs. Cordy) Francis.

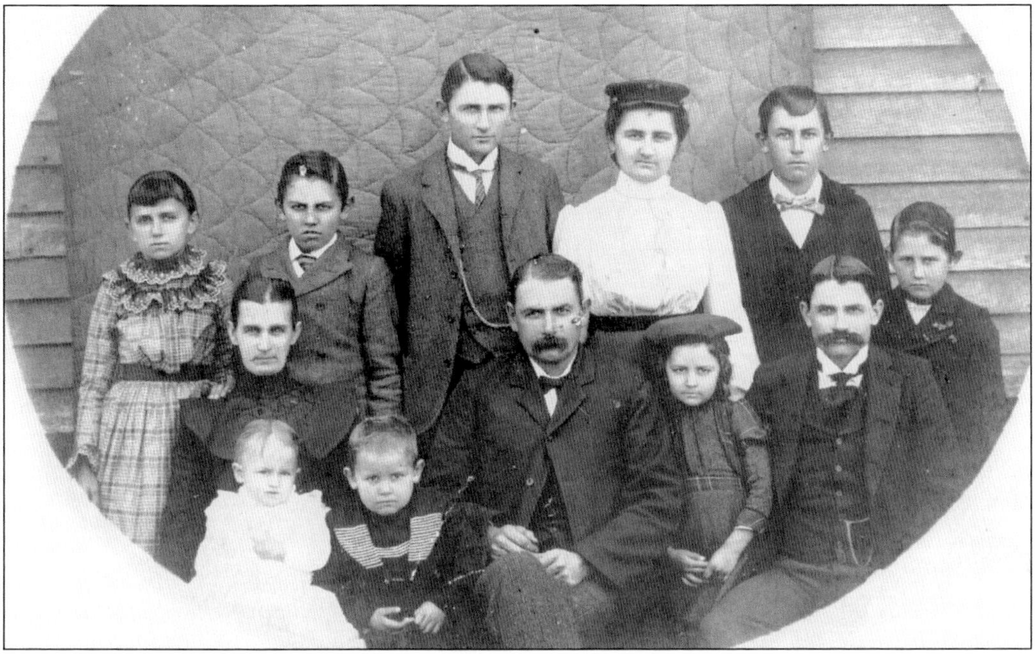

Son Wade, (center, back) took this picture of the Absolom William Jordan Wood family of Harrison in 1900–1901 by pulling a string to trip the camera. Family members, from left to right, are (front row) Waldo Emerson sitting on his mother, Dora Eulalie's lap; Thomas Lanier; A.W.J. "Papa" Wood; Lurline; and Martin Luther; (back row) Ethel, Charles Lewis, Wade Hampton, Maude, Arthur Wellesley, and James Raiford.

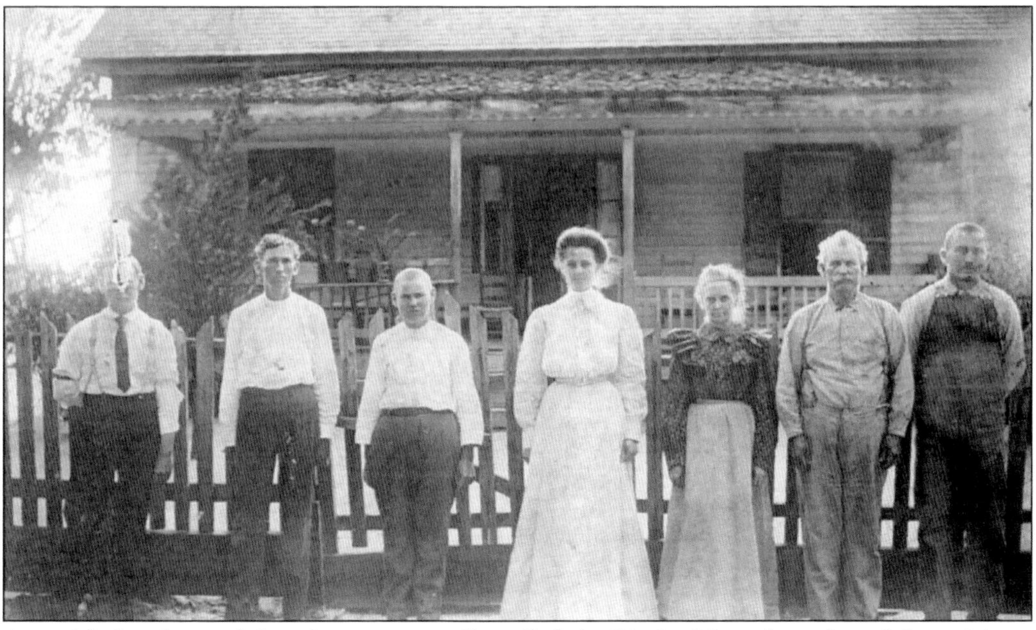

Assembled in front of their home, originally called the Taylor Hart place, from left to right *c.* 1910, are T. Clinton Jones, Melton T. Jones I, Addison Vickers Jones, Fannie Smith (J.T.'s stepdaughter), Mamie Smith Jones (J.T.'s second wife), John Thomas "J.T." Jones I, and Ed Smith (J.T.'s stepson.)

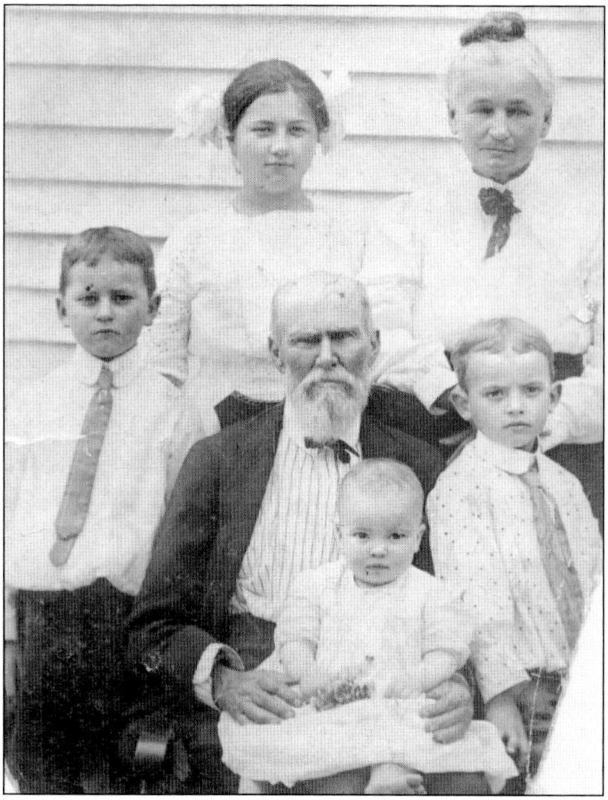

Sol Pittman shared this 1903 photo of his Grandpa and Grandma Gladin, Aunt Mollie, Roy, Ineas, and Baby Rawlings Gladin.

Mary Tanner Moye (front, center) was proud to have her photograph made with family surrounding her, c. 1900. From left to right, they are (front row) Solomon Matthew Moye and James T. Moye; (back row) Duran Griffin Moye, John L. Moye, Jim Pate, Sally Moye McNeely, Isaac Nathan Moye, Mary Moye Hitt, Tom Miles, Winnifred Moye McNeely, and Saphronia Moye Hartley. Not pictured are Charles Moye and Eula Moye.

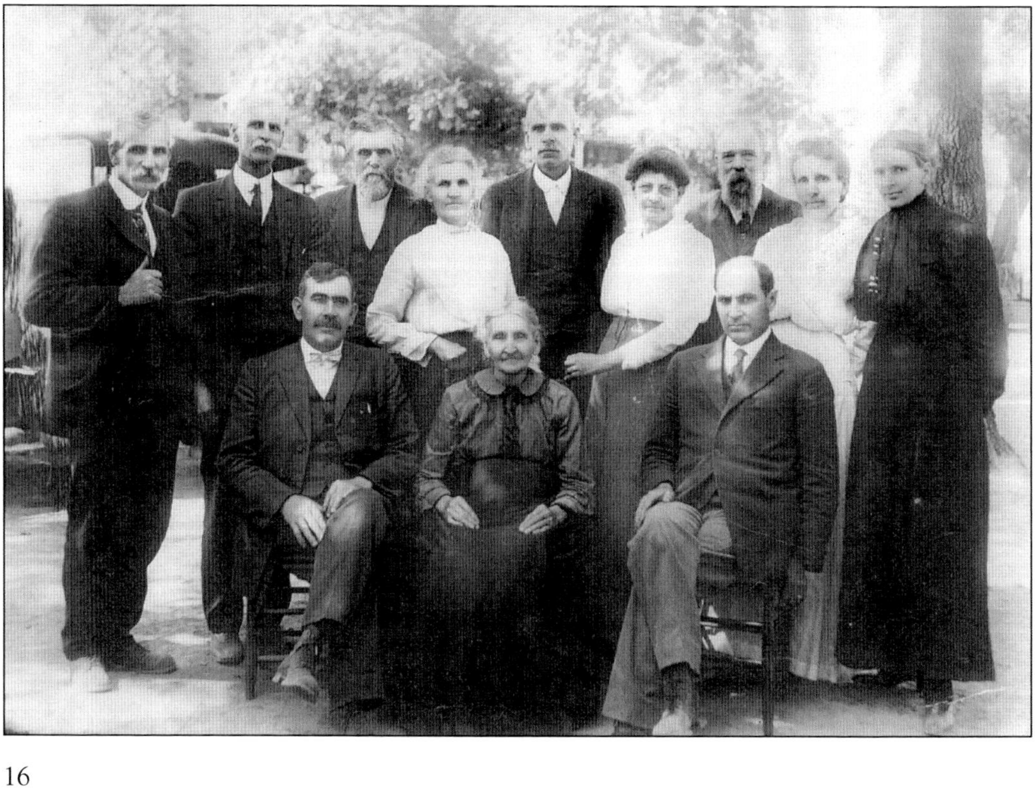

The daughters of George Columbus Walker, from left to right are (front row) Lucile Walker, age 9 and Jessie Walker, age 15; (back row) Clem Walker, age 21; Mattie Lou Walker, age 23; and Pink Walker, age 25. The photo may have been taken during the event of Clem Walker's marriage to Horatio Hollifield Newman.

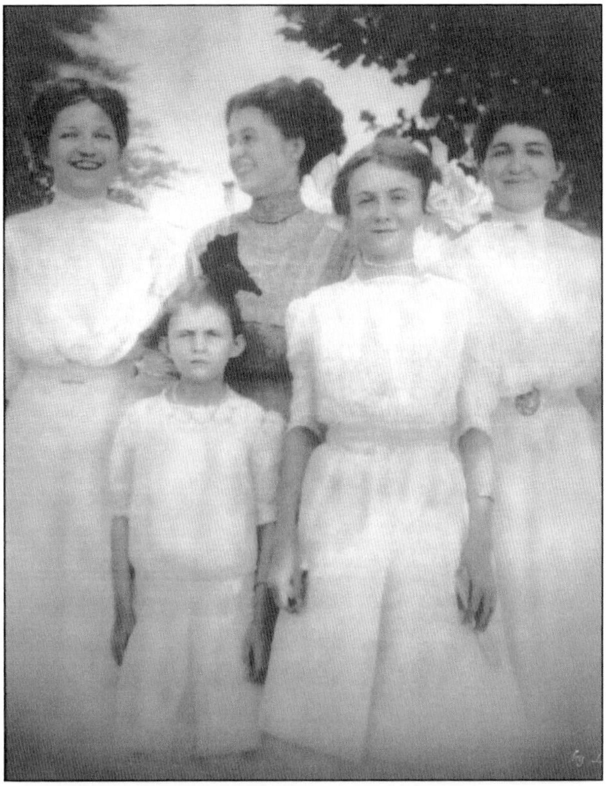

The Jesse Mercer Tanner family included, from left to right, (first row) Annie Claire Tanner, Velma Tanner Duggan, and Will Dunham Duggan; (second row) Ruby Tanner, Jesse Mercer Tanner, Zimmie Jordan Tanner holding Anita Tanner West, and Mae Young Tanner; (third row) Marion Tanner Carswell (child), Stanley K. Tanner, Ivy Robert Tanner, Sadye Tanner, Annie Wade Tanner, Mell J. Tanner (lived to be 102), and G.W. Duggan (child); (fourth row) Eva Tanner and Archie Tanner.

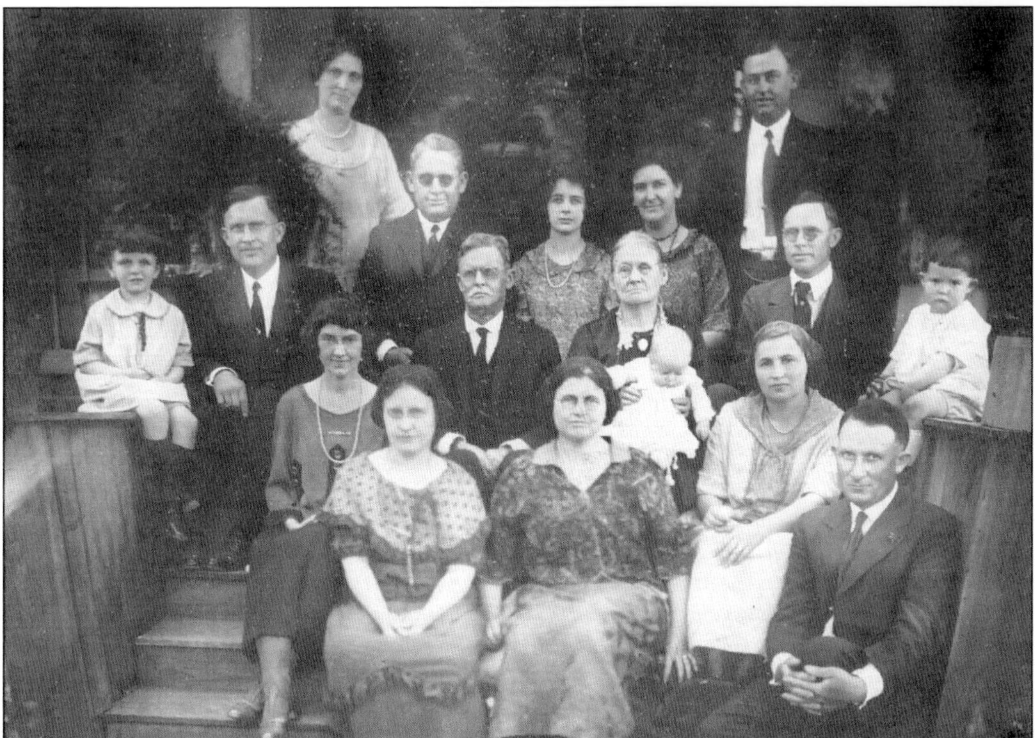

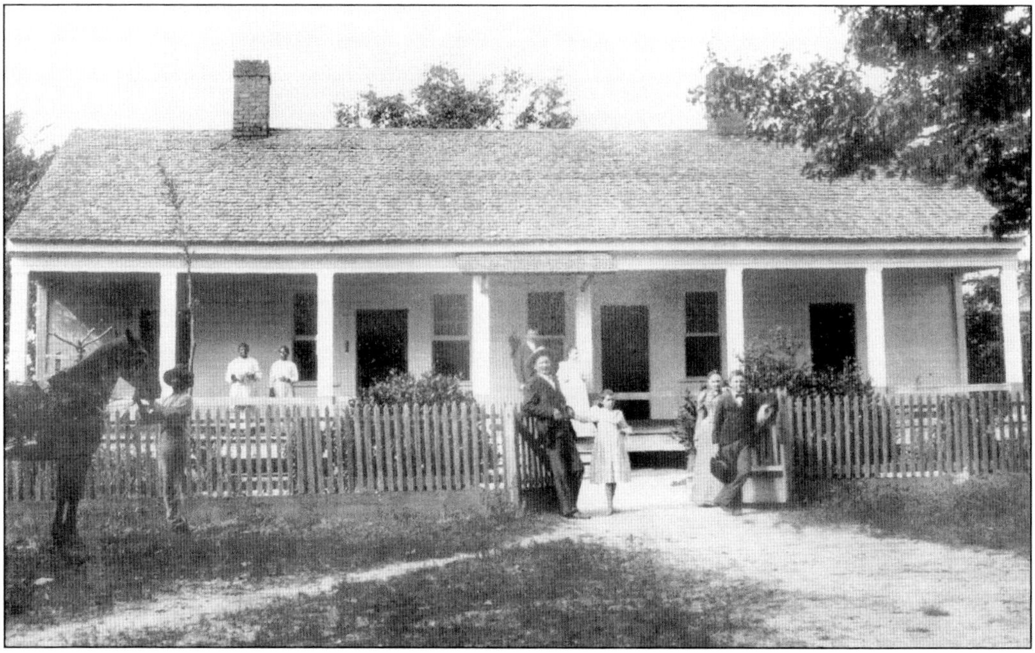

Members of the Wilkerson household are in front of their home, called Forest Grove, just east of Sandersville in 1894. Pictured from left to right are Ephraim Stubbs (with horse); Mandy the cook; her daughter Telia; the Rev. A.B. Herring, a long-time boarder; John B. Wilkerson, proprietor of the farm; niece Mattie Carter; grand-niece Annie Lou Russell; Tommie Warthen Wilkerson, wife of John; and Julian Lyle "Jack" Wilkerson at age 13.

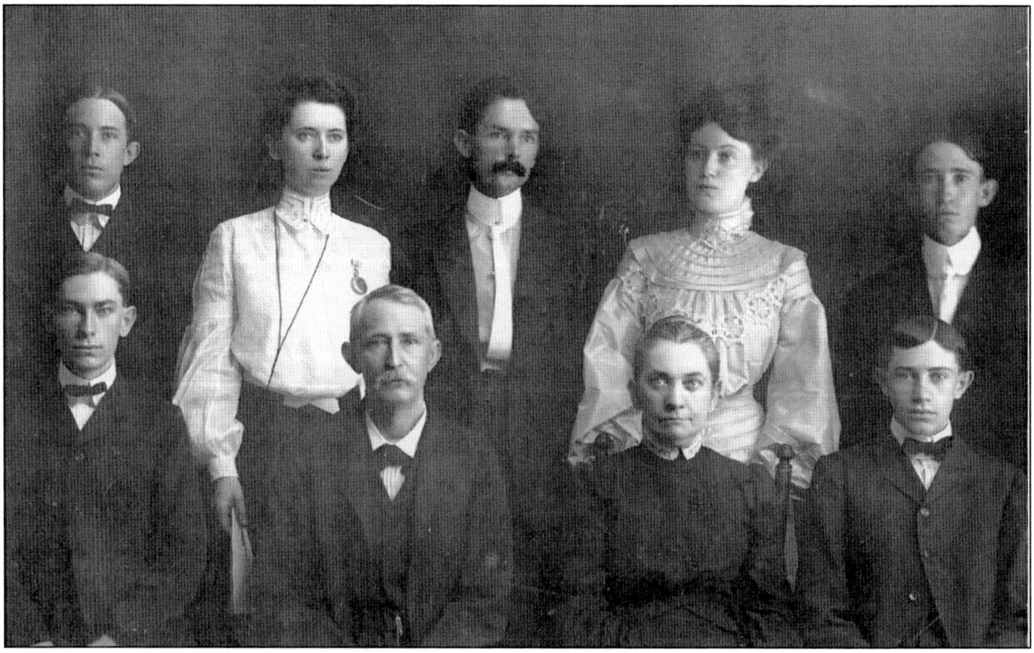

The Thomas Harris Sparks family are pictured *c.* 1900. From left to right, they are (front row) Battle Sparks, Mr. and Mrs. Thomas Harris Sparks, and Andrew Sparks Sr.; (back row) Thomas Mathis Sparks, Bessie Aldred, Jack Aldred, Mamie Sparks, and Aylsee Sparks.

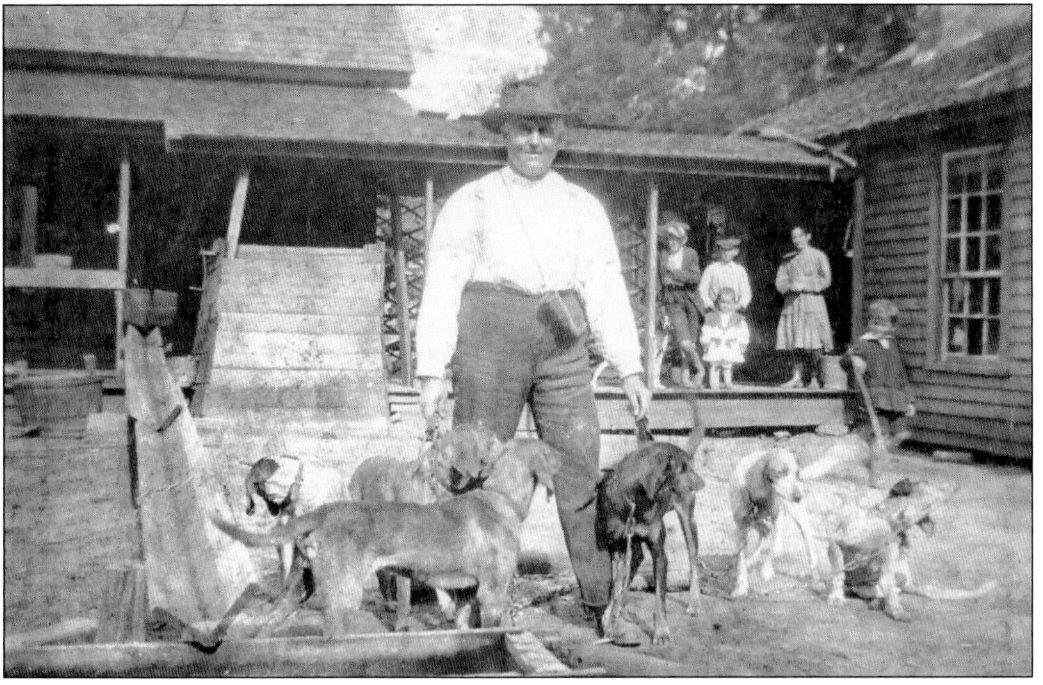

Thomas J. Davis was superintendent of the Washington County School System and was a teacher. He loved to hunt and is shown in 1906 with his pack of dogs at his home, located three miles east of Tennille toward Riddleville. (Georgia Archives.)

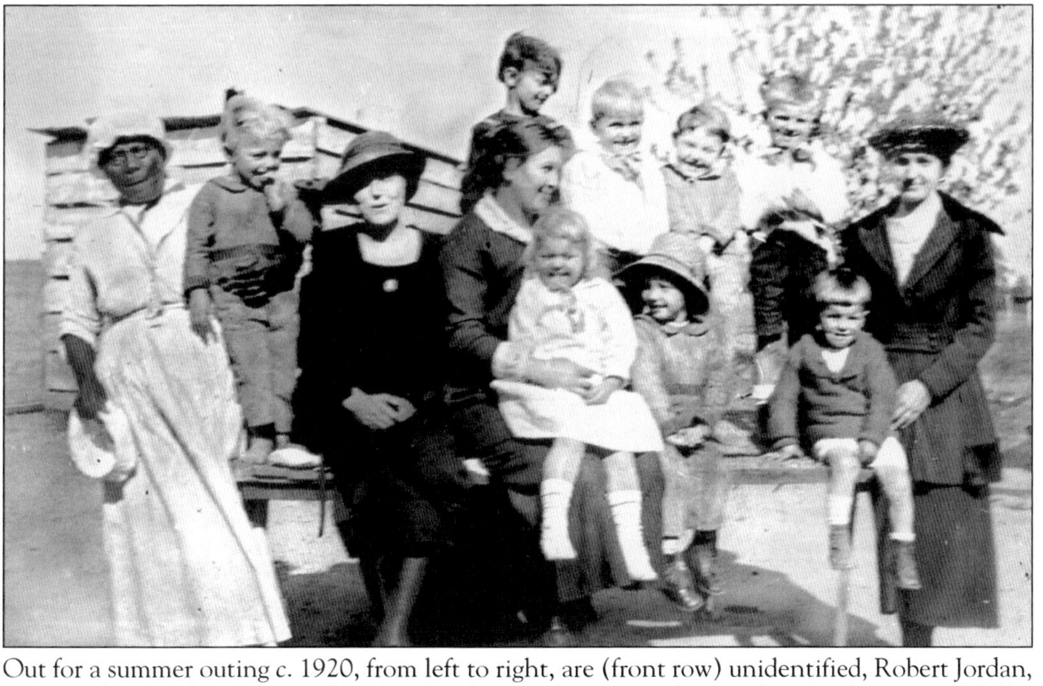

Out for a summer outing *c.* 1920, from left to right, are (front row) unidentified, Robert Jordan, Mrs. Nathan Jordan Sr., Cynthia Cox Taylor, Catherine Taylor, Nathan Jordan Jr., and Billie Francis; (back row) Audrey Jordan, Raborn Taylor, Richard Jordan, Cordy Francis, and Sallie Maude Thompson Francis.

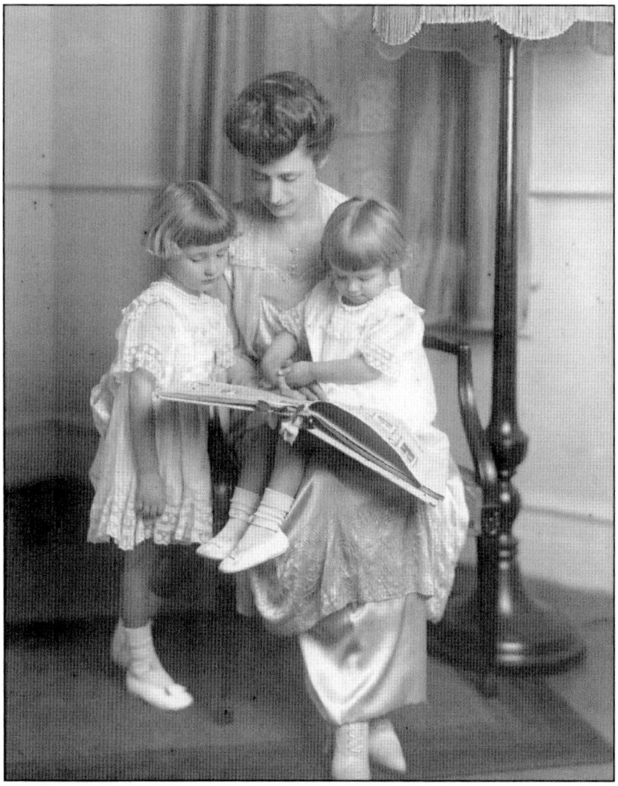

Minnie Blitch Harris, shown in 1918, loved to read to her daughters, Marianne Harris Leonard and Laura Ashley Harris Evans. (Georgia Archives.)

Macon Warthen is shown with his wife Aunt Tami, c. 1875. The cook to the left is Aunt Mahalia, noted for making the "best tea cakes in Warthen."

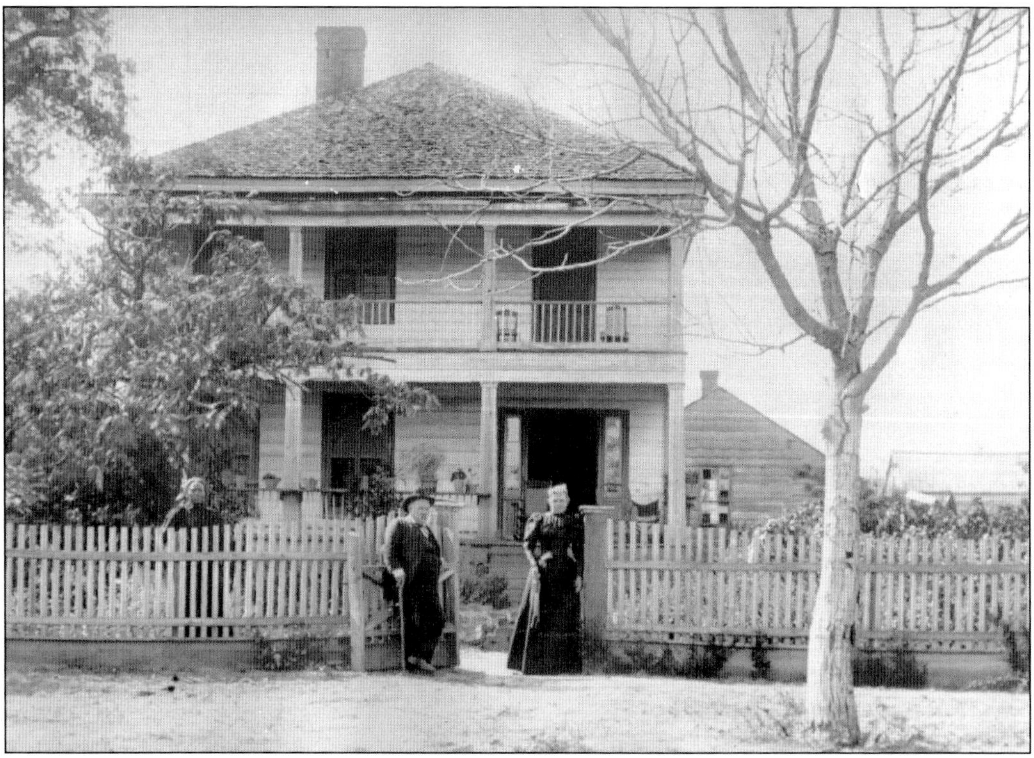

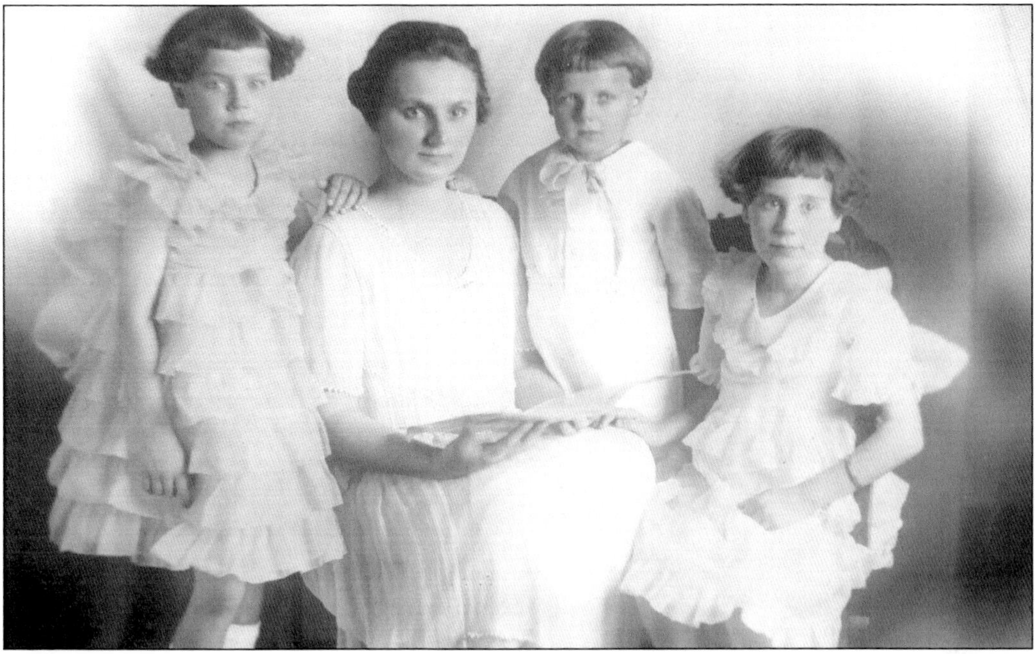

Dressed in their best finery *c.* 1919 are Sallie Mae Vickers Gilbert and her children, from left to right, Ruth, Harry Jr., and Helen Gilbert.

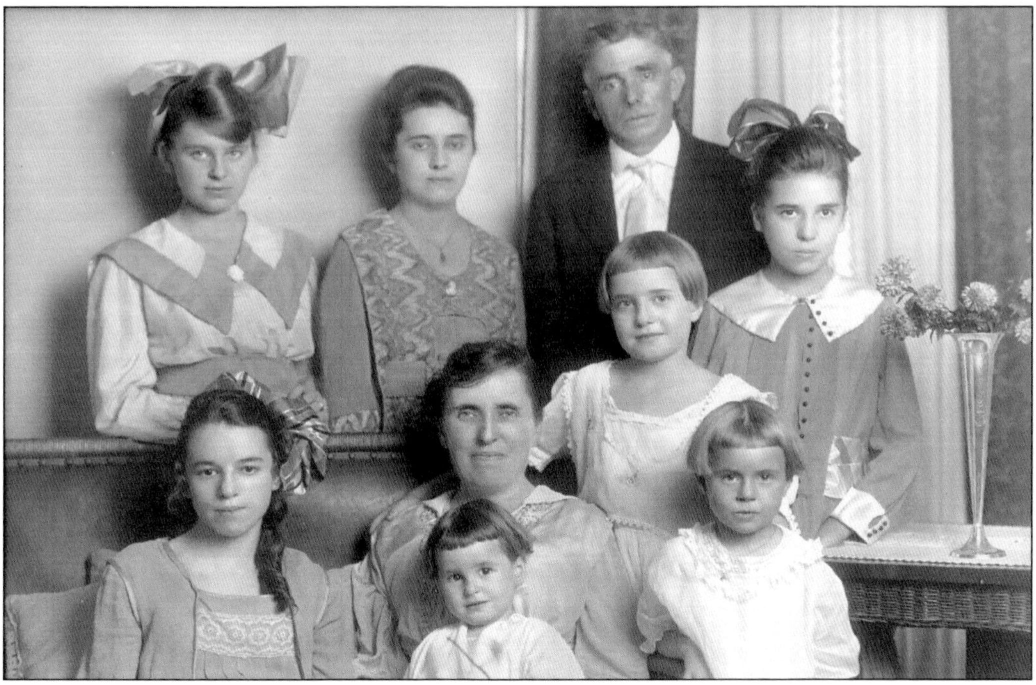

The William Walter Harris family are pictured *c.* 1918. From left to right, they are (front row) Elizabeth Harris Covington, Wiley Harris Davis, mother Fannie Bell Harris, Fannie Bell Harris DeBeaugrine, and Ellen Harris West; (back row) Mildred Harris Dunlap, Mattie Harris Williams, father William Walter Harris, and Eugenia Harris Harper. Mrs. Harris had made the dresses for all six daughters.

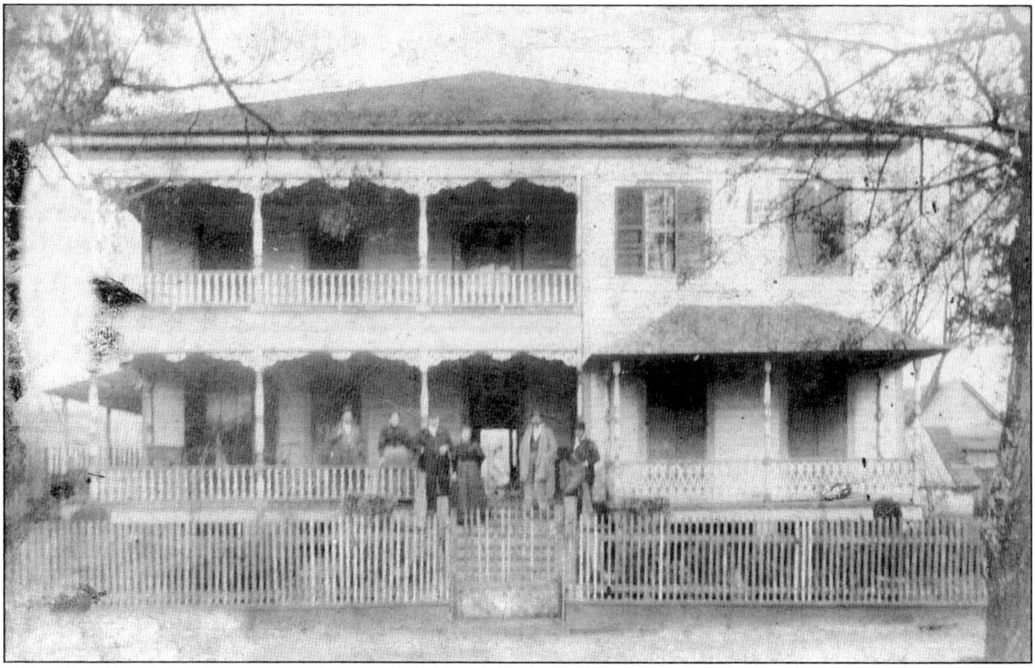

The Summerlin House was an imposing structure on South Harris Street, between Magnolia Inn and the Schub House, in 1905.

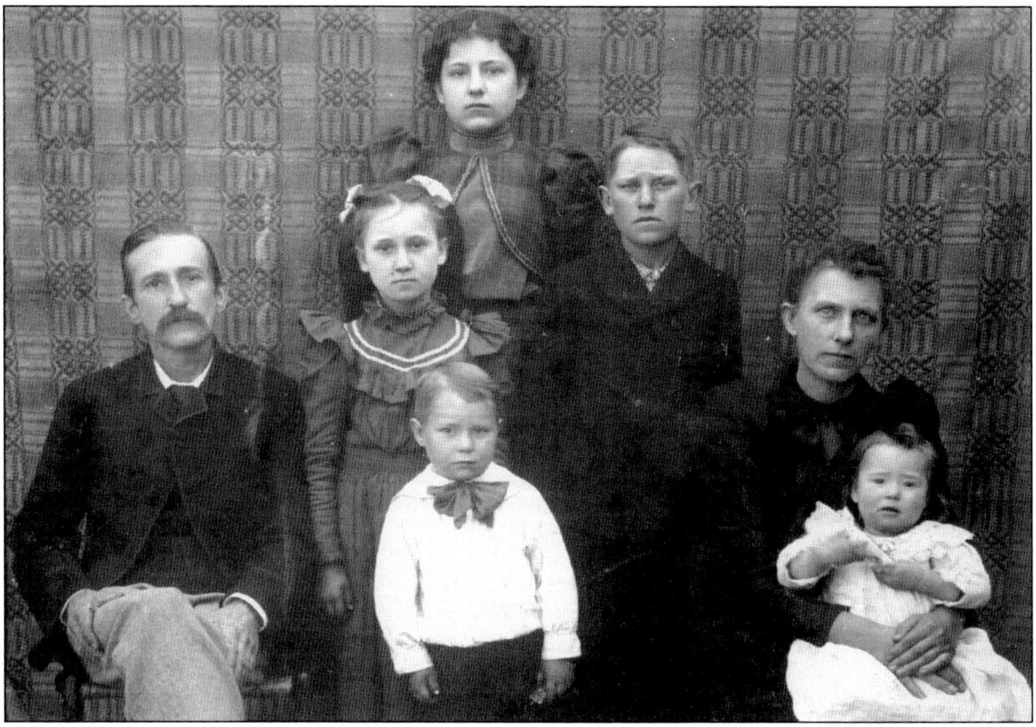

Can you identify this unknown family?

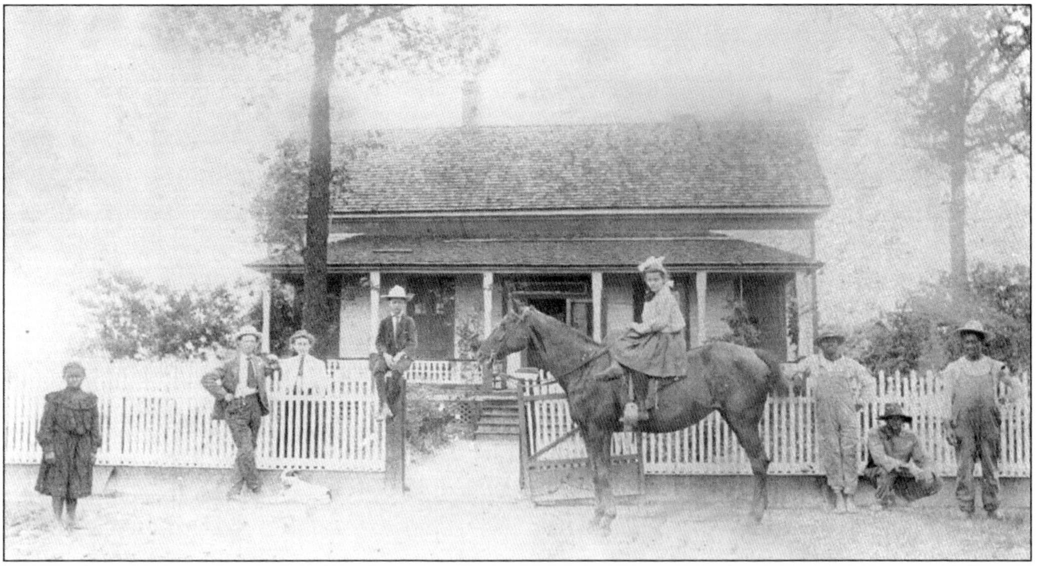

Ella Smith (1887–1973) is astride the horse in front of the Smith home place. The daughter of John English Smith Jr. and Mattie G. Wood Smith, Ella later married Brevard Cooley.

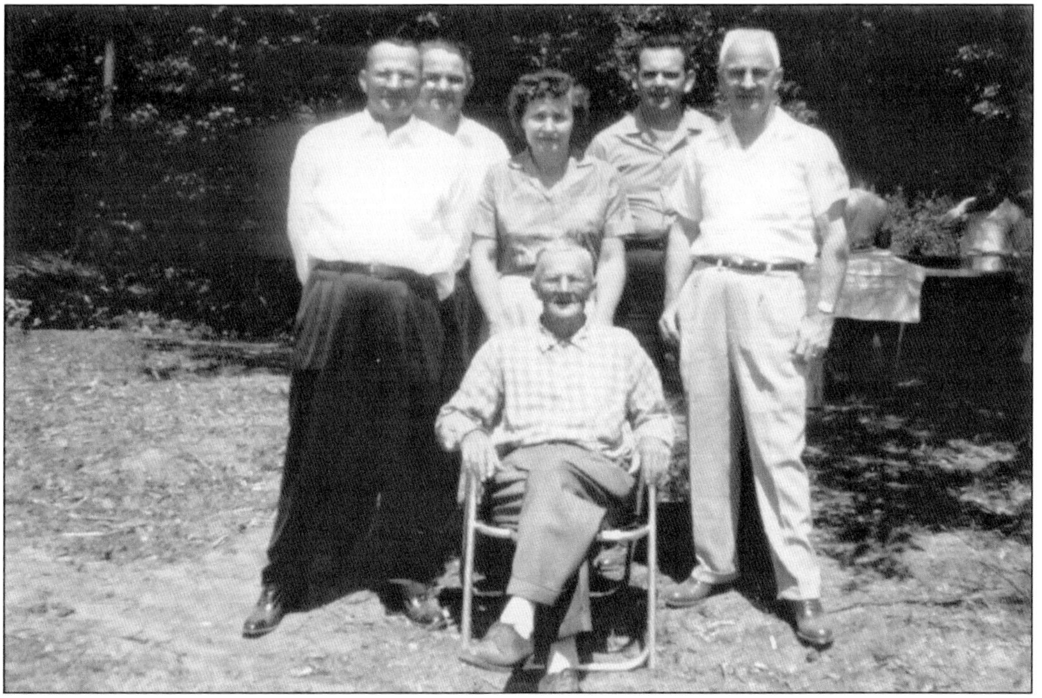

It was a sunny day for this picture featuring, from left to right, (front row) Joseph Edgar Cooper; (back row) Quinton Cooper, Sam Cooper, Loree Cooper Davis, Hugh Cooper, and Carlus Cooper in 1950.

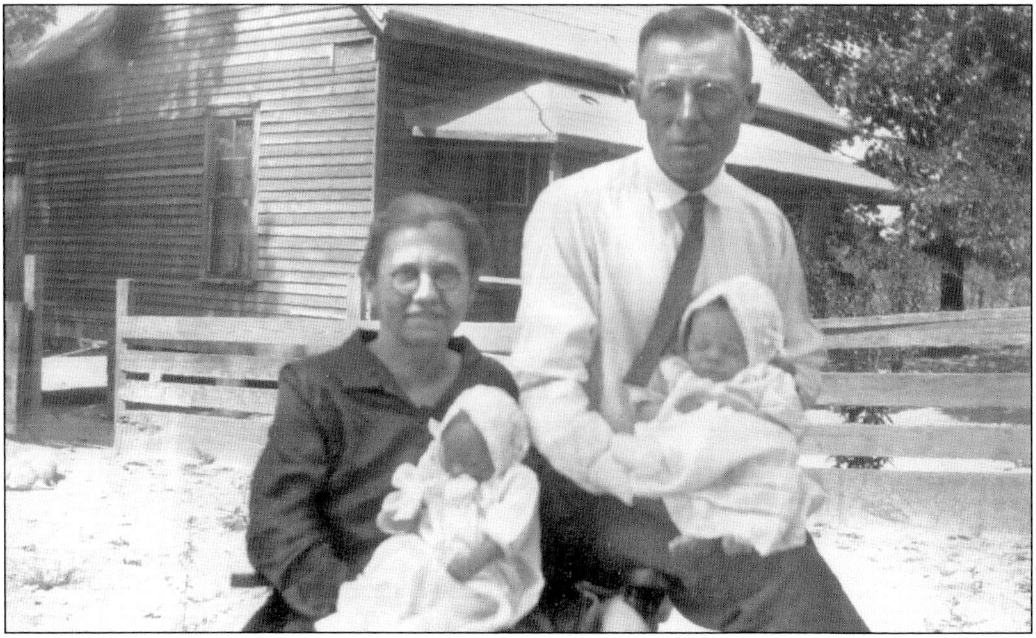

Mattie and Luther Veal had twin babies Edwina and Edwin in 1927.

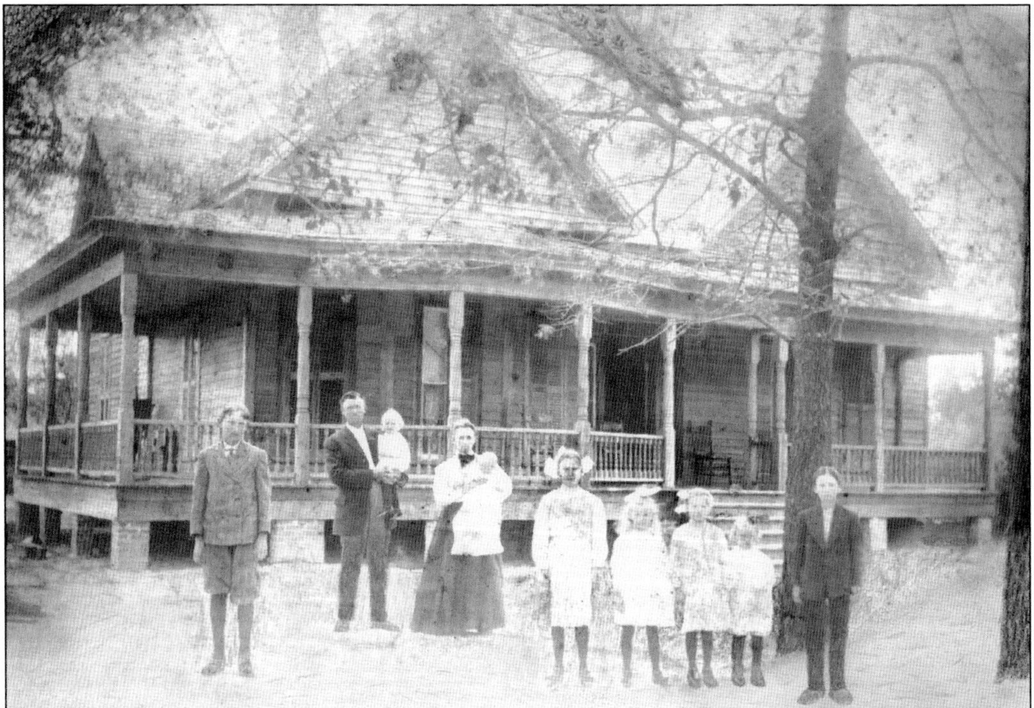

The B. Frank Chambers Sr. family was photographed in 1911 in front of the family home on Deepstep Road. From left to right are Bennie Frank, Mr. Chambers holding Jessie, Mrs. Chambers holding Dock, Rubye, Maude, Emma, Bertie, and Fred. Children born later included Minnie Belle, Zelma, and Elizabeth.

Two

Church Chimes and Wedding Bells

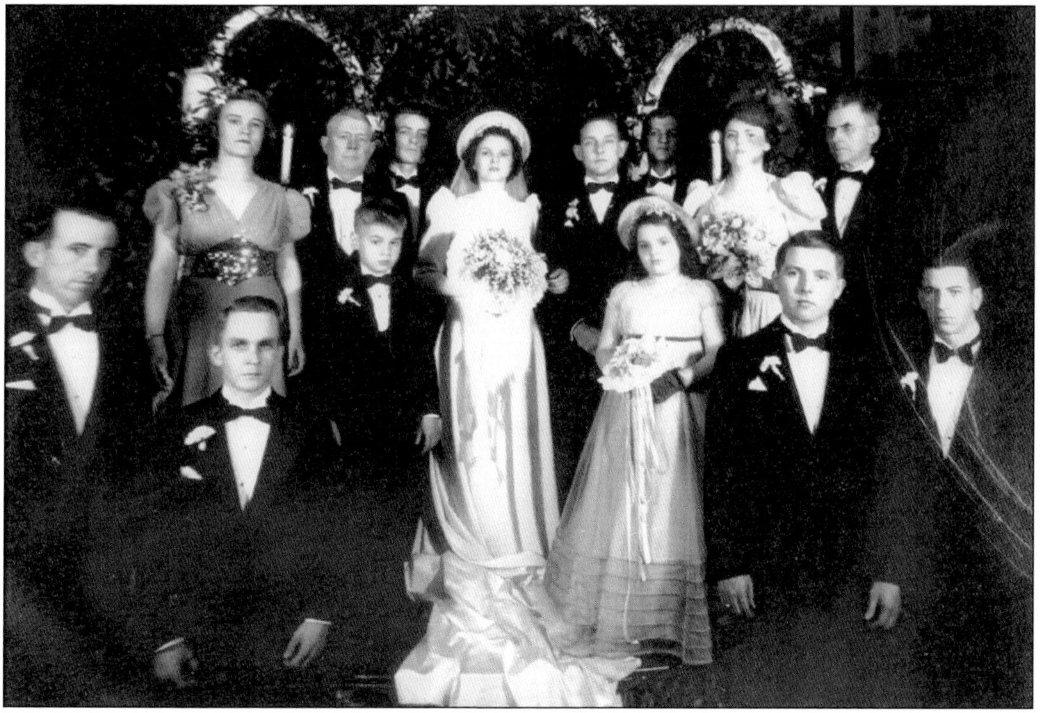

For the February 1939 wedding of Nelle Cooley and Orran Edward "Dick" Hudson, participants were Alton Avant, Richard Irwin, Oscar Rogers, O.J. May, Mary Lozier Rogers Irwin, O.L. Hudson, Mike Summerlin, Warren Newman, Martha Cooley Pearl, and C. Brevard Cooley. Ben Tarbutton Jr. and Mary Jane McElrath Bowling are the two children.

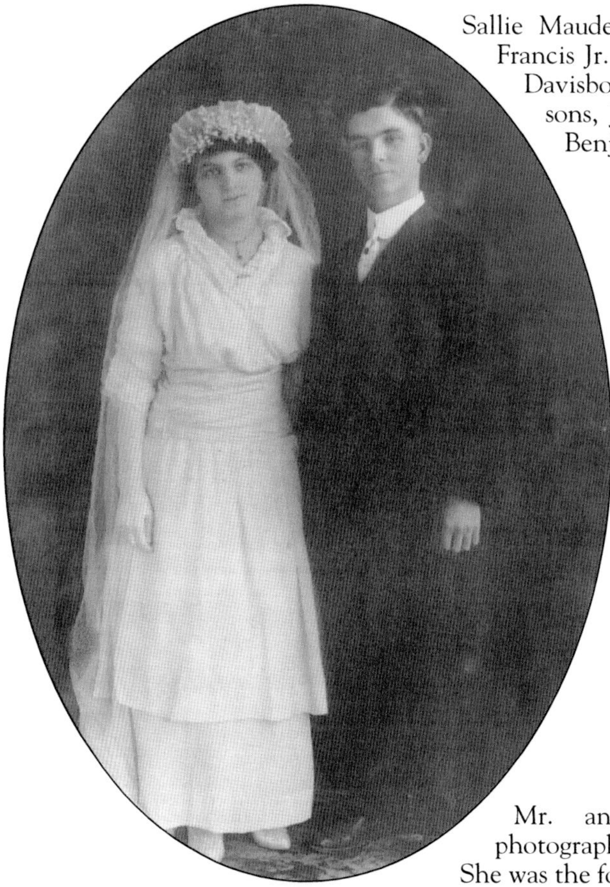

Sallie Maude Thompson and William Benjamin Francis Jr. were married October 6, 1914 at the Davisboro Baptist Church. They had two sons, James Cordy Francis Sr. and William Benjamin Francis III.

Mr. and Mrs. Arthur Lee Giles are photographed on their honeymoon in 1912. She was the former Matress Doolittle.

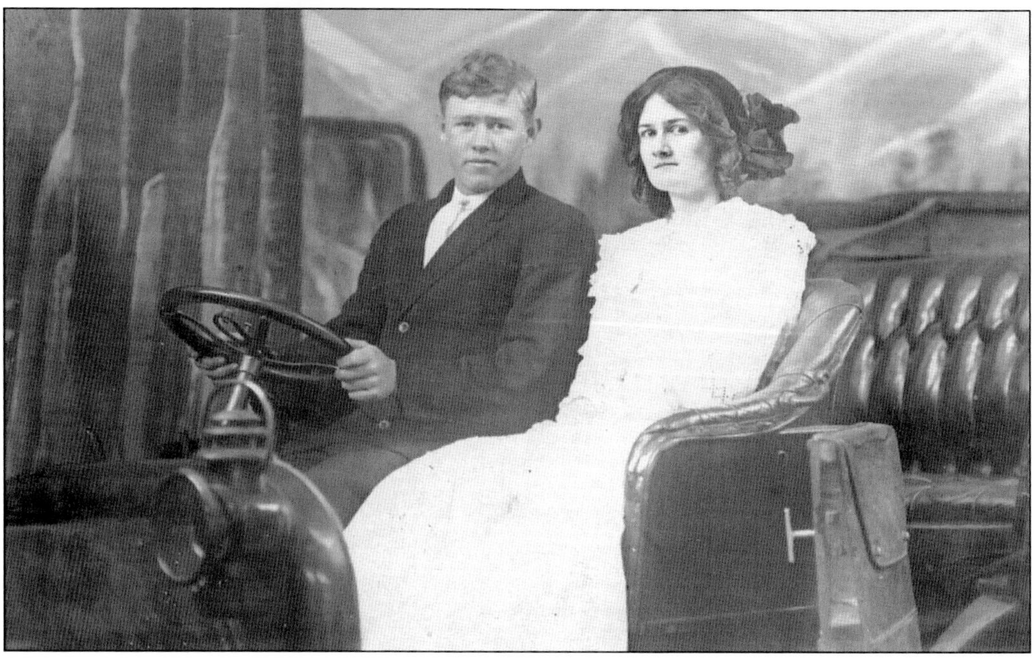

This is the wedding photo of Addie Lee Renfroe when she married Julian Gerome Giles in September 1894.

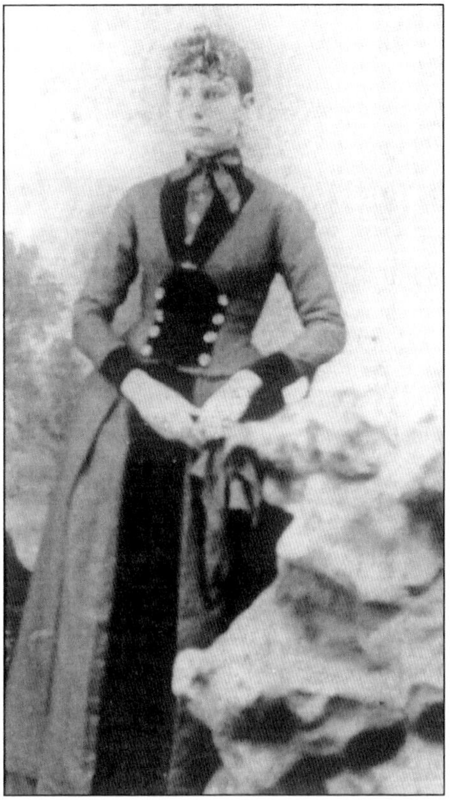

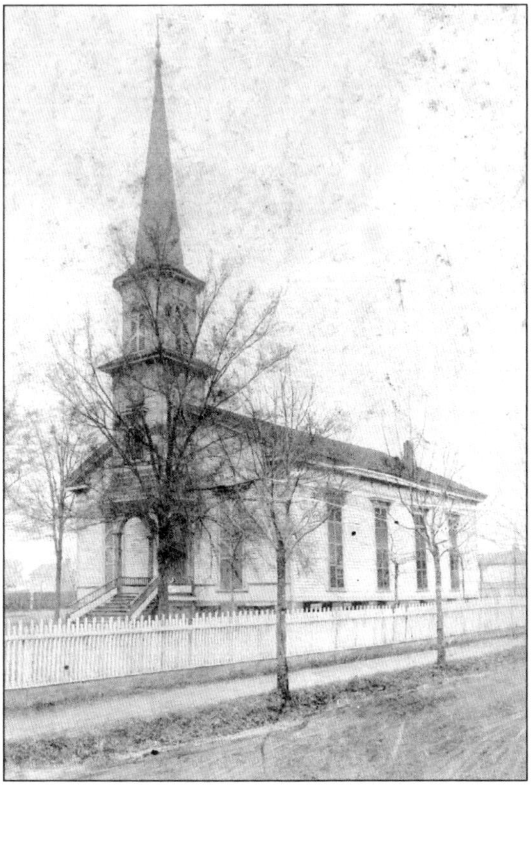

The Sandersville Methodist Church was first located in the Old City Cemetery. Its second structure, this wooden building was constructed in 1859 at the corner of West Church and Brookins Streets. In 1901, it was moved to Floyd Street to make room for the first brick church on that site. The wooden building burned sometime in the 1930s.

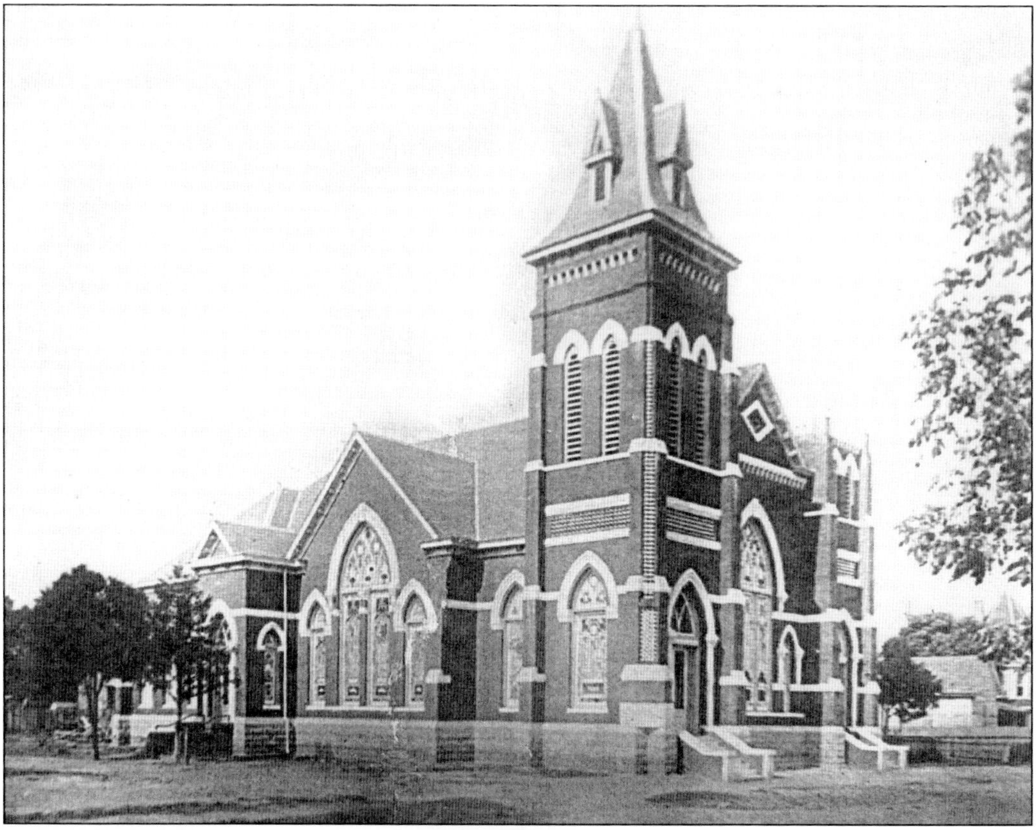

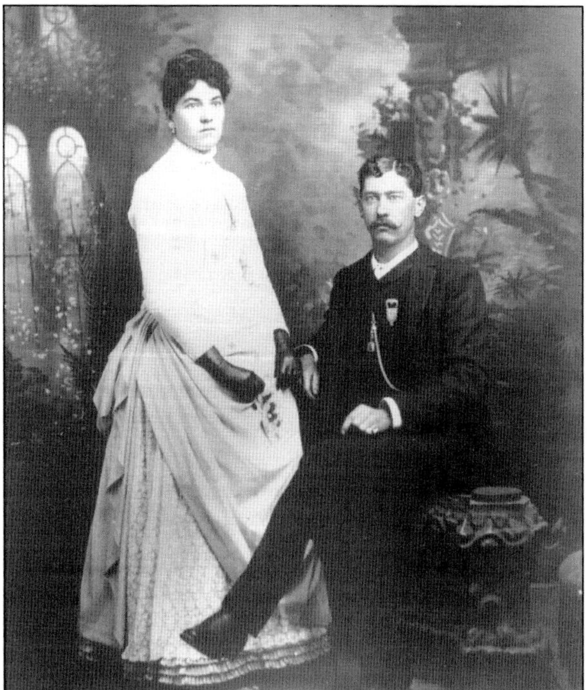

Constructed in 1905, the Sandersville Baptist Church was torn down in 1962 when the congregation constructed new buildings on Mathis Circle. This building of detailed Victorian architecture stood on the corner of South Harris and West Church Streets.

Robert Henry Gilbert and Missouri Frances Kelley were married on February 26, 1887.

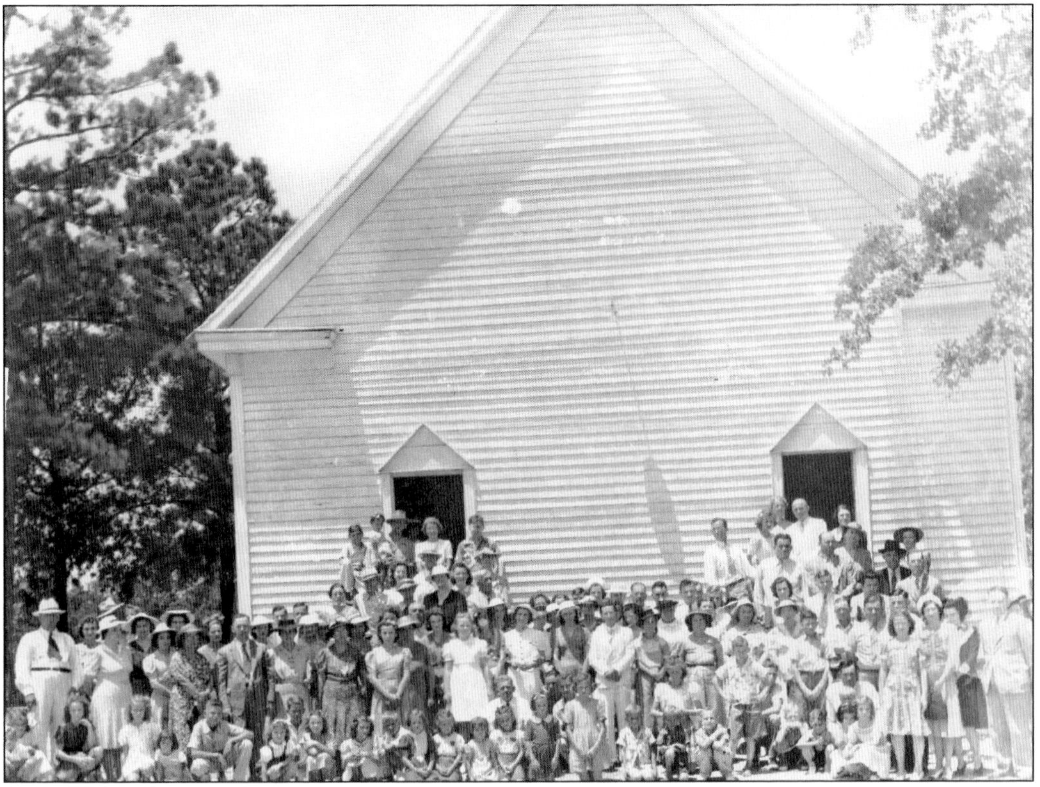
Pine Hill Methodist Church held a dinner on the grounds on the first Sunday of August 1930.

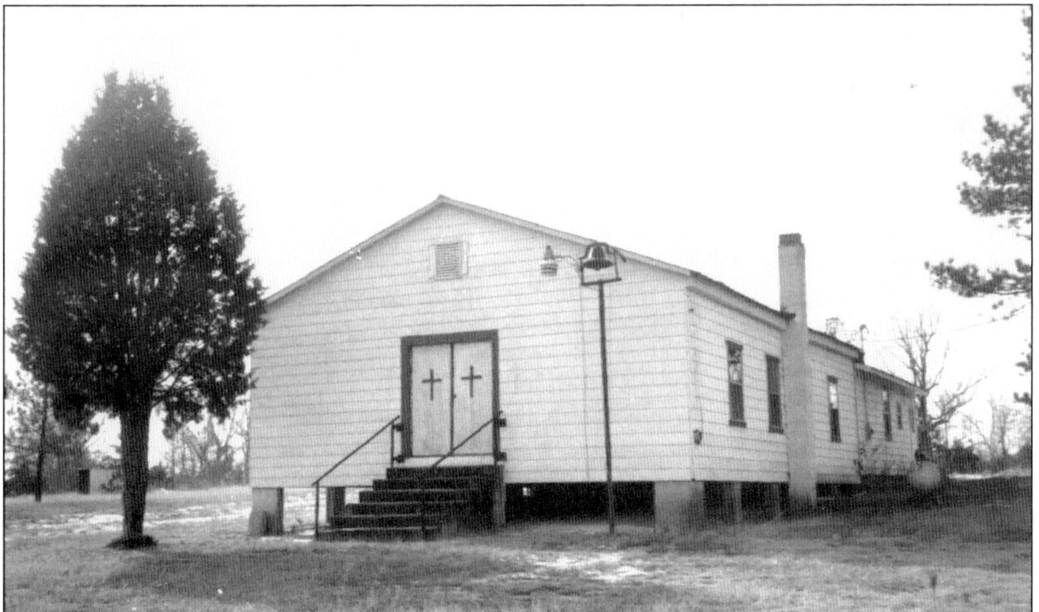
The members of the St. Luke A.M.E. Church in Riddleville used the bell out front to call them to worship. The church began in 1902.

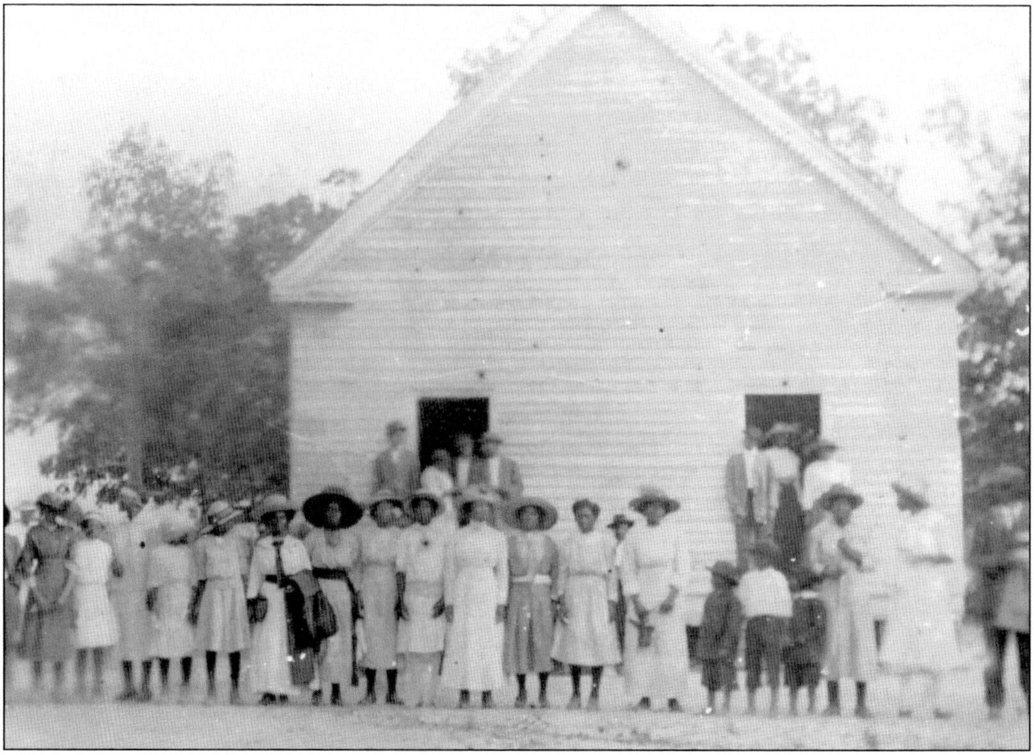

Members of Piney Mount Baptist Church gathered c. 1925 for a photo. The building is located northwest of Warthen.

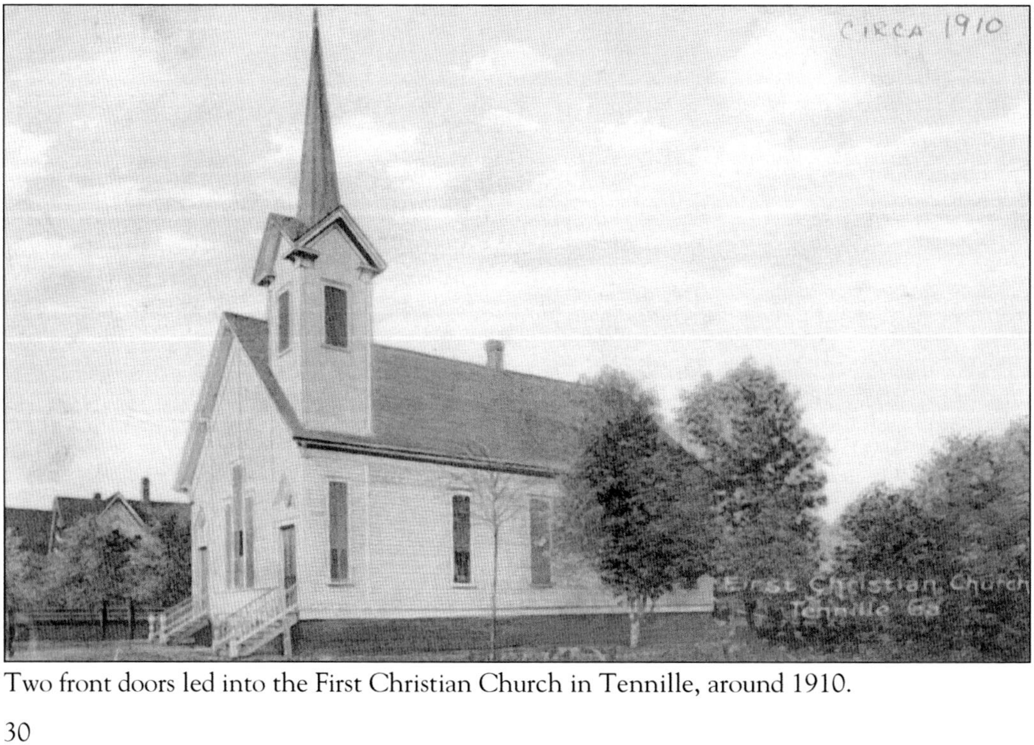

Two front doors led into the First Christian Church in Tennille, around 1910.

Mary Cooley is pictured in her wedding dress in 1905 when she married Edward Tarver Averett.

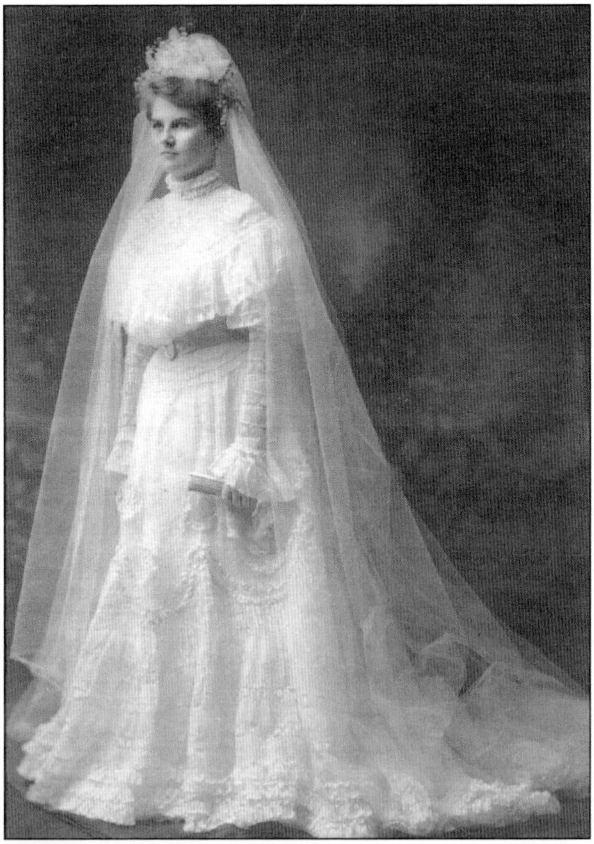

The sanctuary of the Sandersville First Methodist Church was beautifully decorated for the wedding of Mary C. Cooley to Edward Tarver Averett in 1905. This building was struck by lightning in August 1938 and burned.

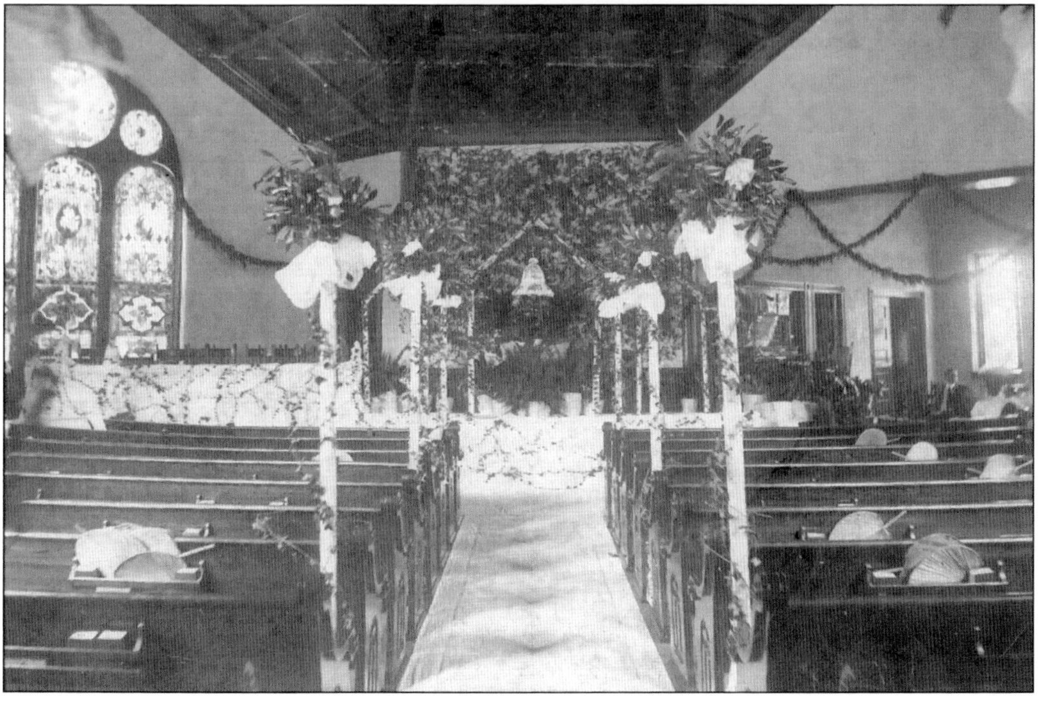

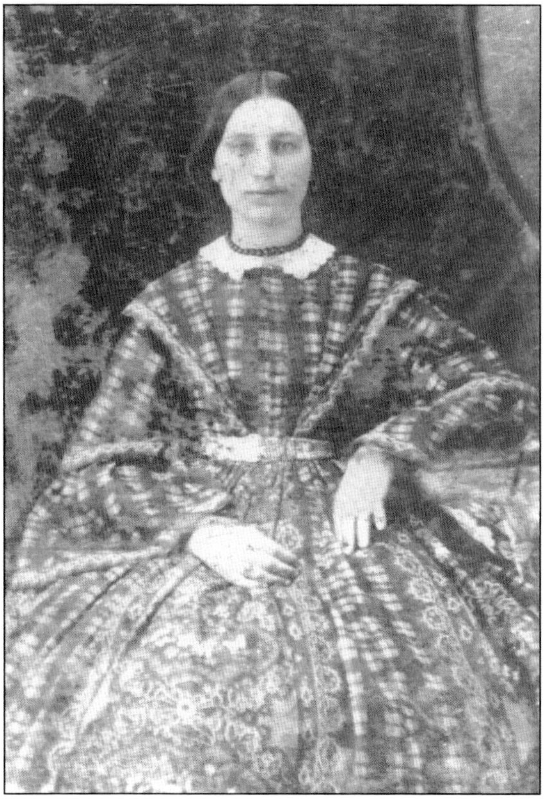

Melissa Hall married John Irwin Giles in March 1862 while he was on furlough from the Confederate Army. She is wearing her wedding dress.

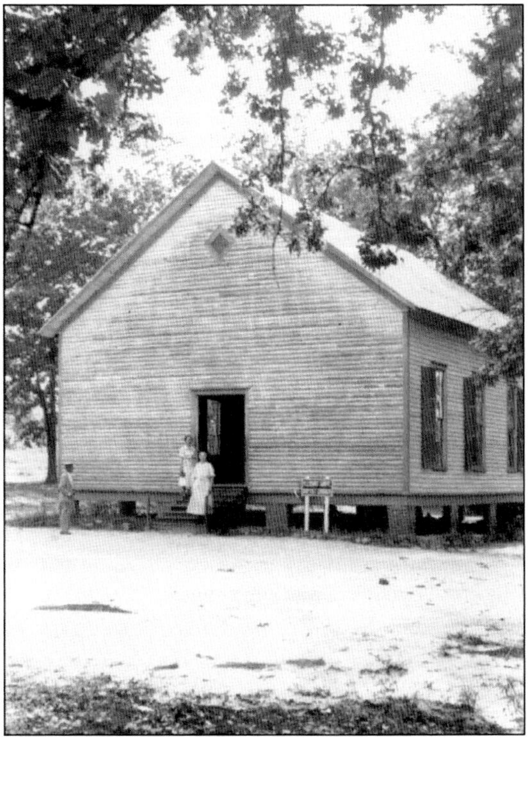

Founded in 1891 at the Pine Hill school house, the Pleasant Grove Baptist Church was constructed by its members in 1893 on land donated by Arnold Harris, an African American. His only request was a pew on the back row reserved for his use. This picture was taken *c.* 1930s.

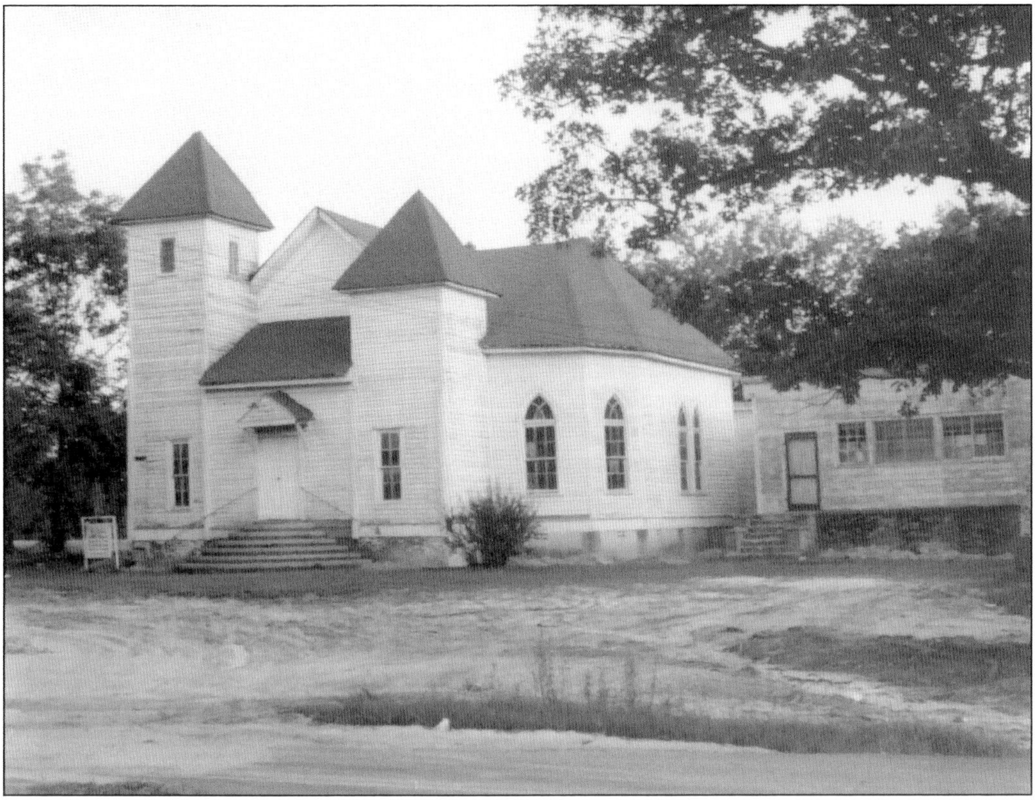

Organized in 1874, the St. James A.M.E. Church originally was a wooden structure built in 1897. In 1958 an education building was added and then the entire structure was bricked in 1981.

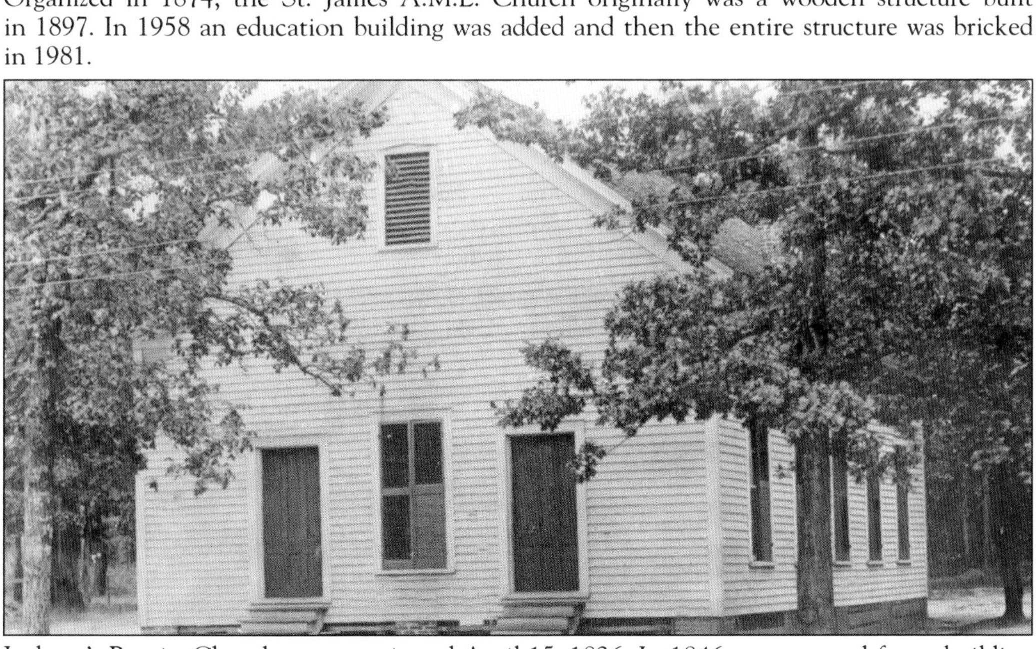

Jackson's Baptist Church was constituted April 15, 1826. In 1846, a new wood-frame building was constructed, which is this building, shown about 1914. In 1923 the building currently in place was built.

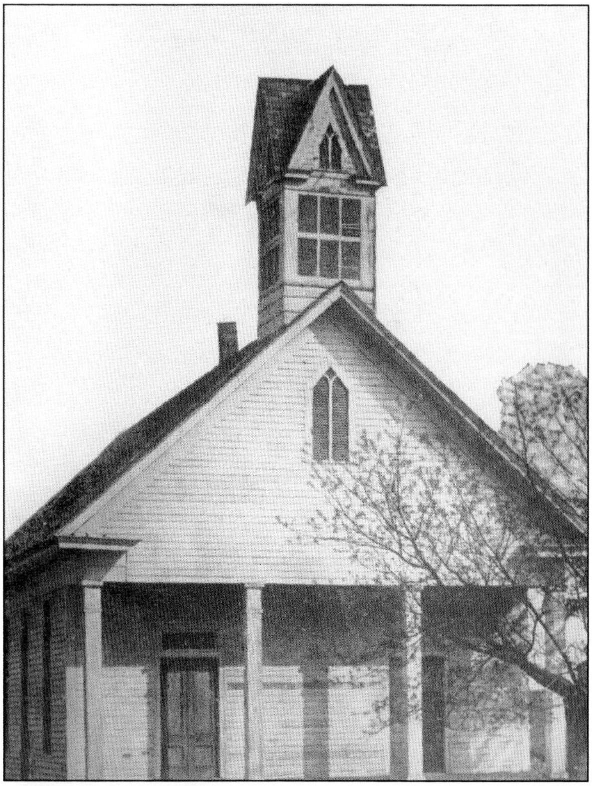

In 1884, Davisboro Methodists organized with the help of New Hope Methodist Pastor J.M. Lovett. In 1885, this one-room church was built. Sunday school rooms were built in the 1920s. By 1926, the congregation had outgrown the church and plans were made for a new building.

James Hartwell Holmes and Annie Wood had a double wedding with Tarver Averett and Mary Cooley. Attending the first couple were ? Renfroe, John Lovett, Mary Tarbutton, Pierce Wood, Mary E. Robinson, E.A. Harris, Irwin Bridges, Sam Deveraux, and Katharyne Hale as flower girl. Attendants for the Averett-Cooley couple were Annie Cooley, W.M. Goodrich, Mayfield Cole, Brevard Cooley, Corinna Shelley, Mercer Richards, Ed Sullivan, Ben Brown, and Mary Harrison as flower girl.

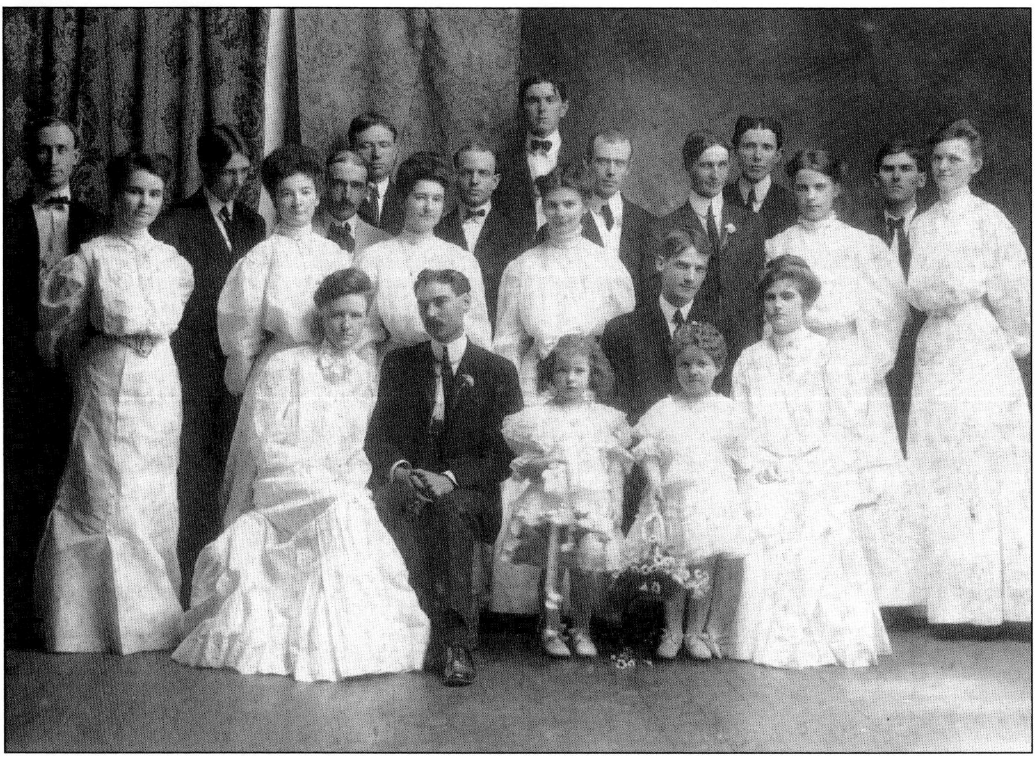

Three

Children's Hour

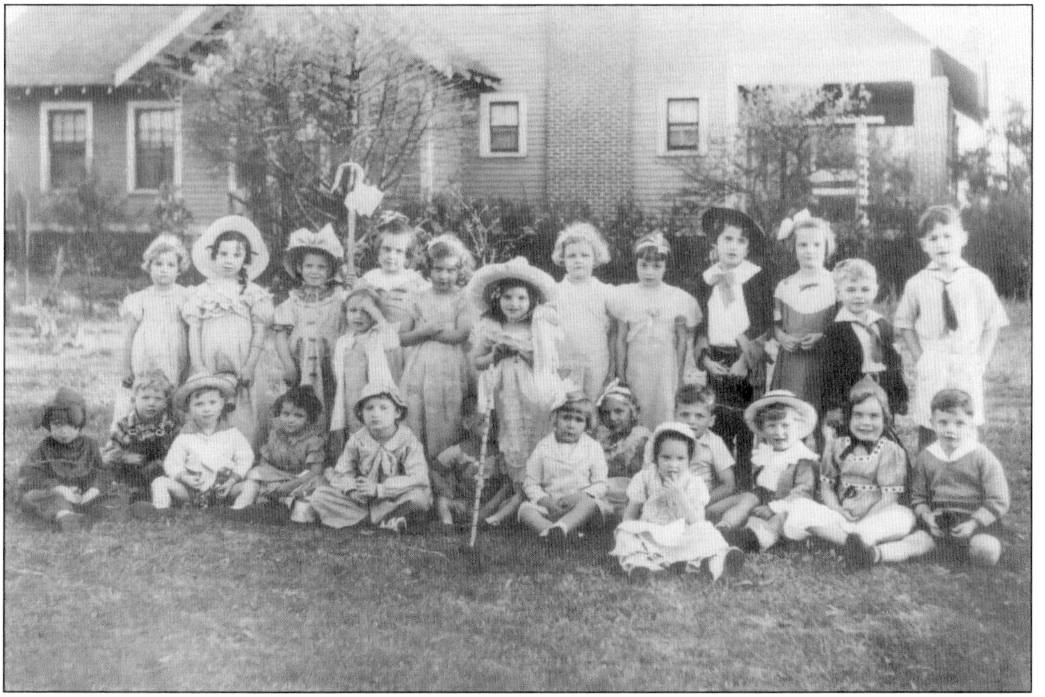

Mary Jane McElrath invited her friends to dress as nursery rhyme characters for her March 27, 1935 birthday party. Attending, from left to right, were (seated) Charles McMichael, Powell Lang Jr., William Hitchcock, Jane May Brooker, Levi Hill, unidentified, Beverly Brown, Ann McElrath Stewart, Baby Pat Greer Summerlin, John McElrath, Margaret Lovell, and Ned Daniel; (standing) Martha Lang Williams, Patricia Mathis, Martha Sheppard Tanner, Frances Armstrong Worst, Martha Lozier Riner, Dorothy Jean Harrison King, Mary Jane McElrath Bowling, Jane Cason, Betty Rogers Mix, Jane Boatright, Mary Ann Weisg Folley, Ben Tarbutton Jr., and Jack Brooker.

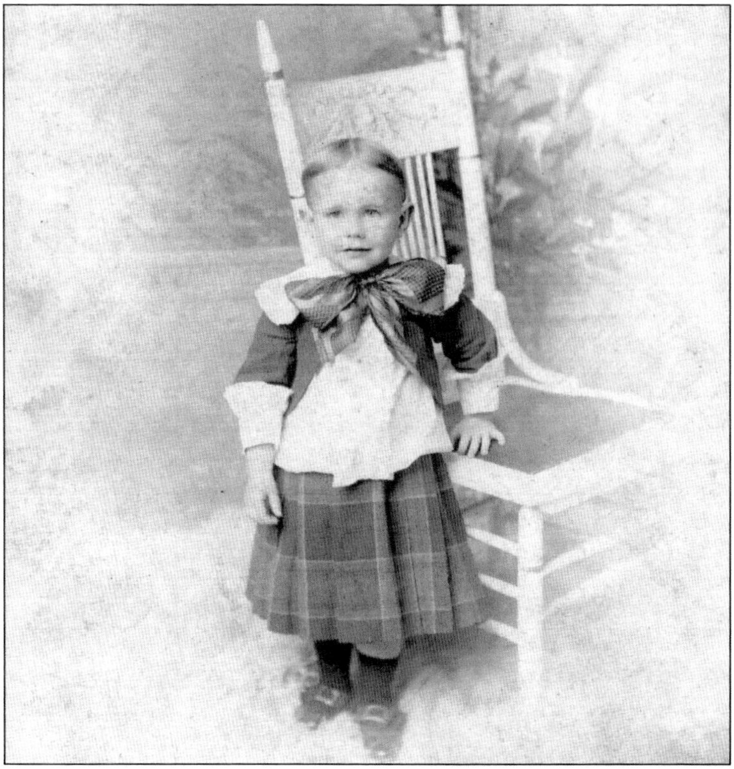

C.A. Adams Jr. is pictured in 1896.

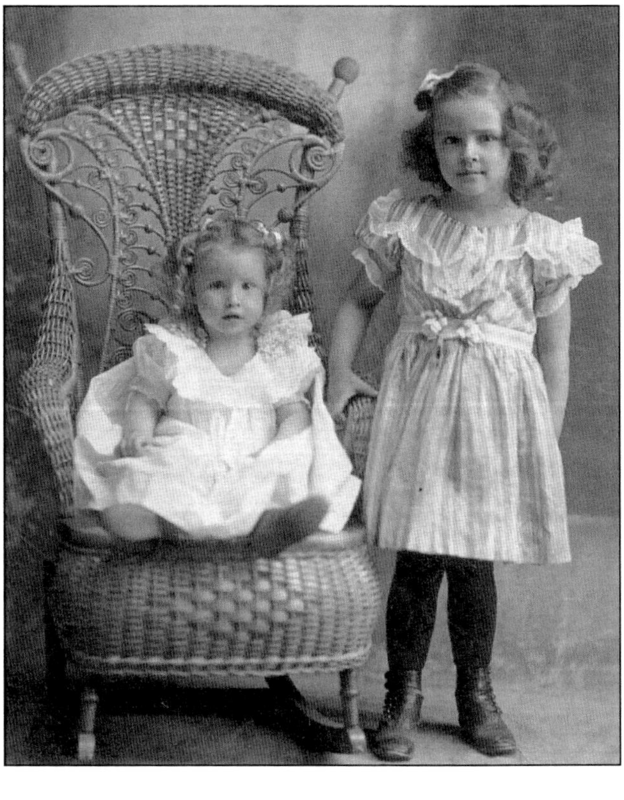

Pat Smith (Hodges) was about two years old when she posed with her sister Annie Mary Smith (Stevens) around 1902.

Mary Tarbutton Freeman and Ben J. Tarbutton Sr. are pictured *c.* 1889.

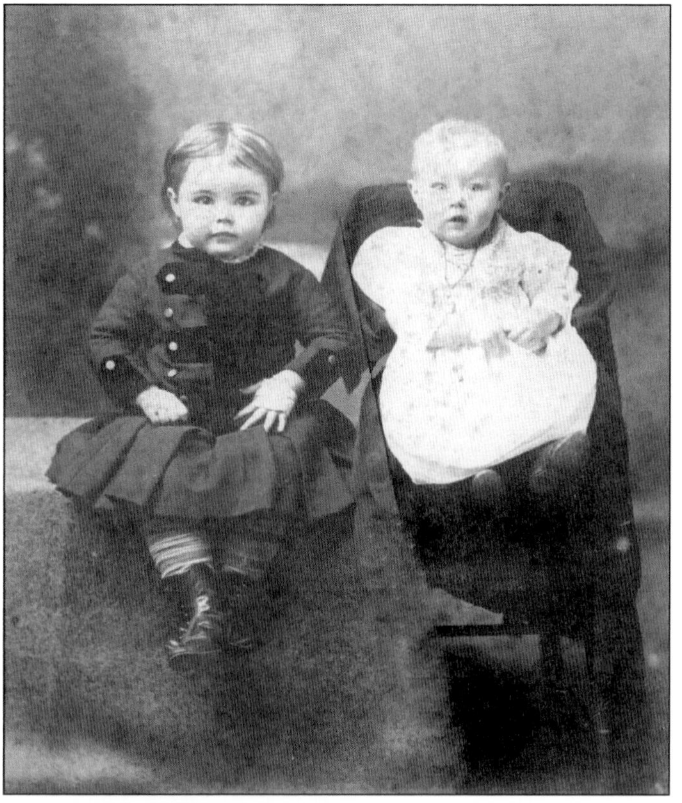

Marie Harrison Brown (Peterson) and Henry "Hal" Wiley Brown were very stylish, *c.* 1900, with their long curls. Marie was the last resident of the Brown House, now operated by the historical society as a museum.

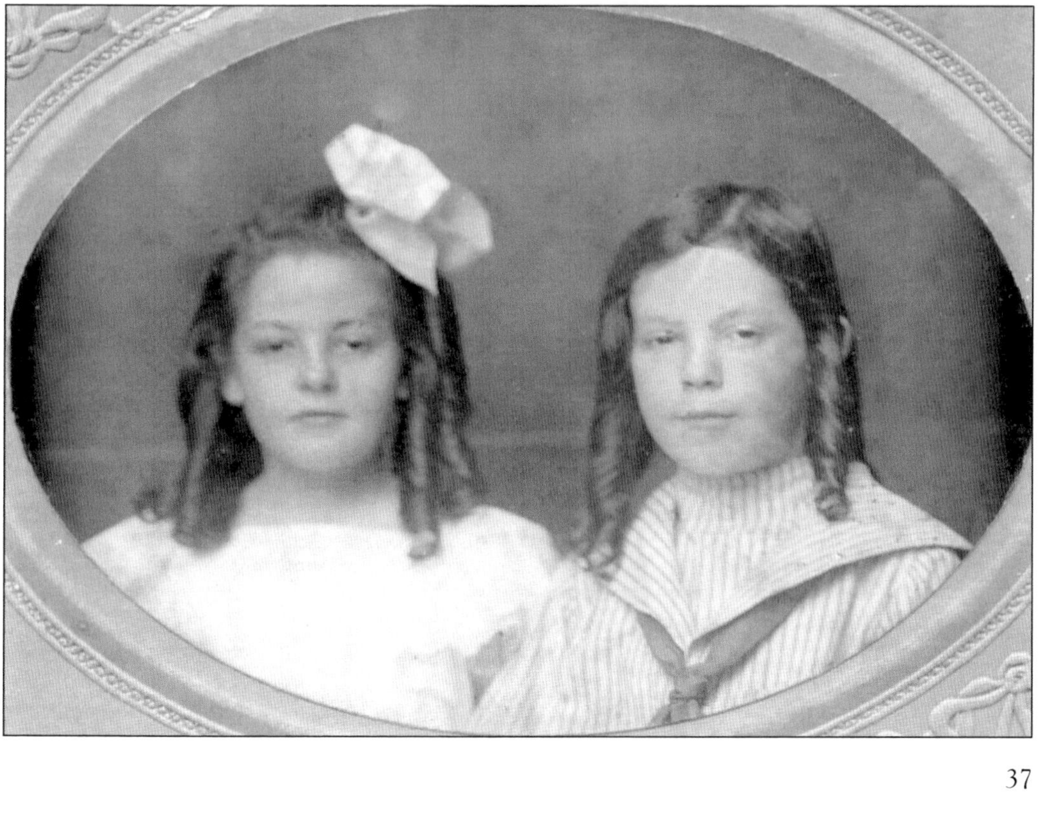

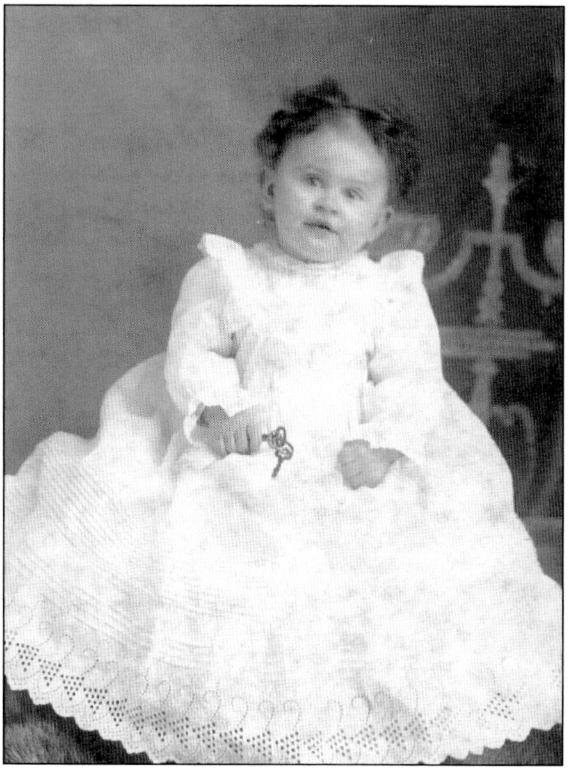

Ten-month-old Mary Rachel Burns holds keys tightly for the photographer.

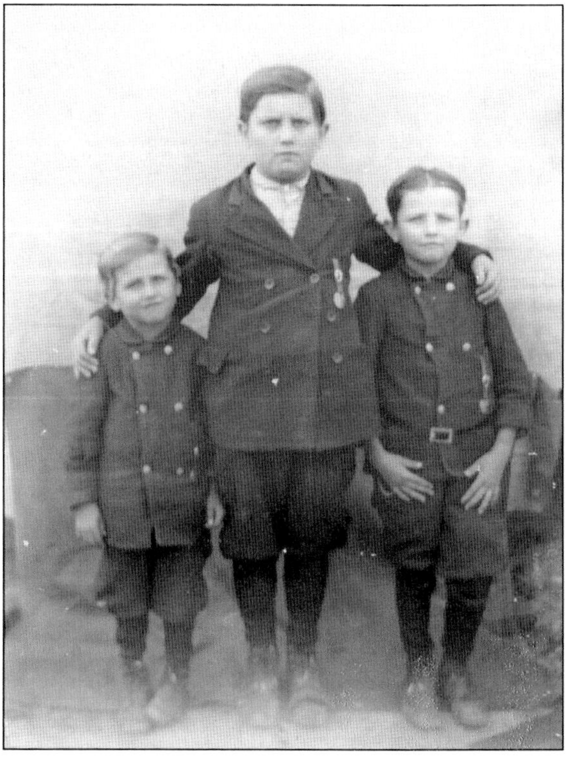

The Brown brothers, Jenning, Pete, and Johnnie, wore similar jackets in 1915.

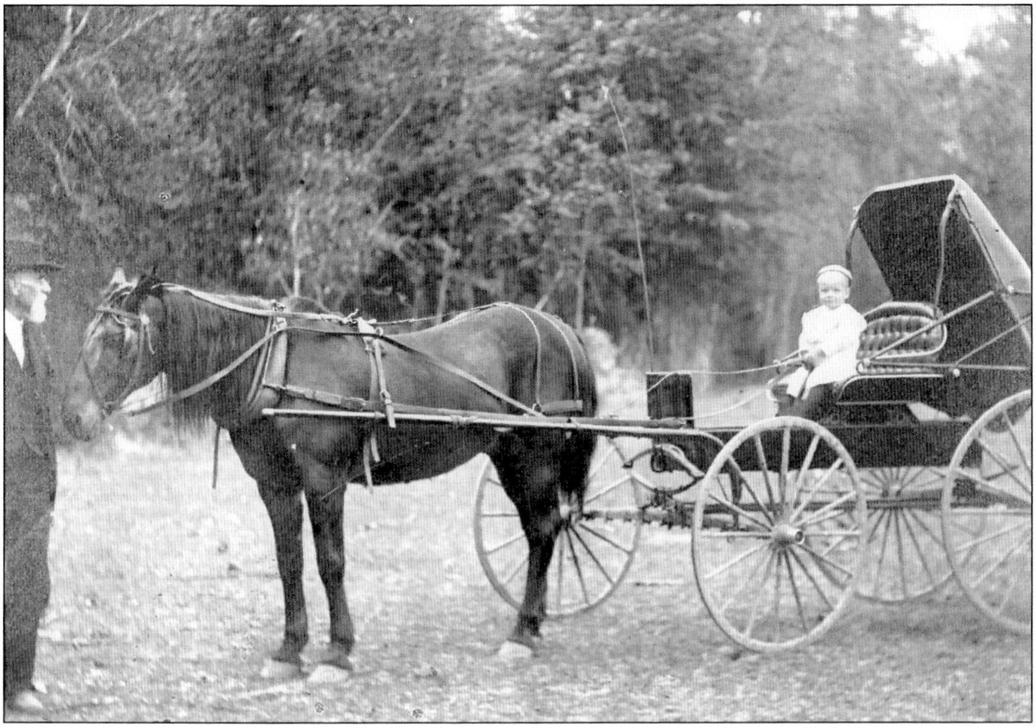

Carlos Steed Avant is a "big boy" driving the buggy led by Augusta S. Avant, c. 1910. (Georgia Archives.)

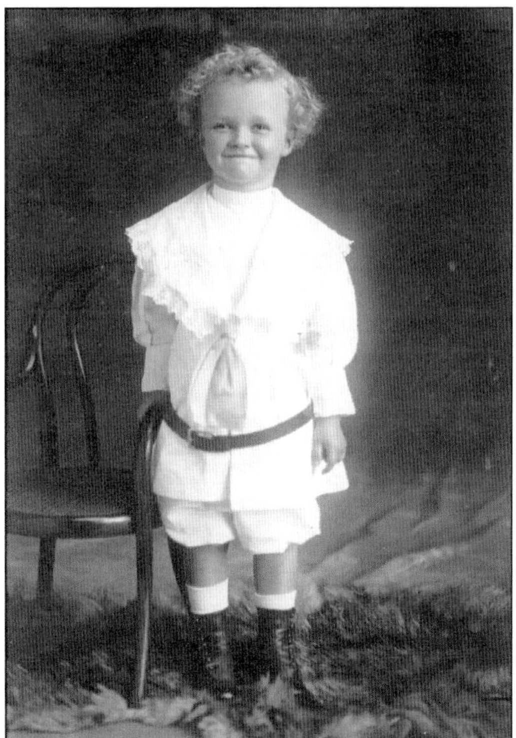

Jesse Strickland Newsom is dressed up for his father's wedding in 1912.

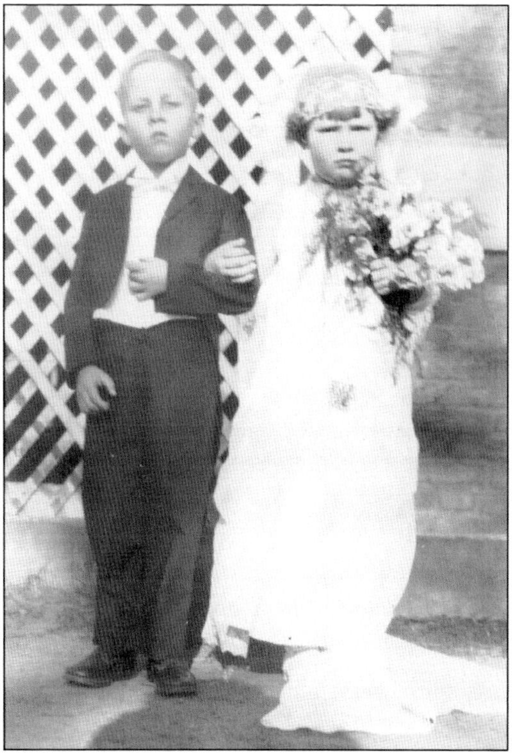

Frances Odom played the bride and Richard Irwin the groom in a Tom Thumb wedding in 1924.

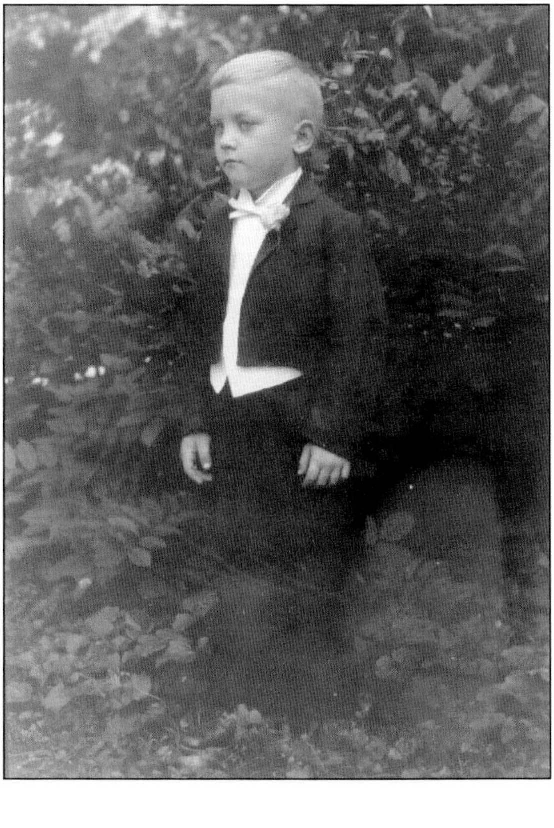

Findlay Irwin Jr. dressed up for a wedding in 1924.

In 1922, Reba Smith (Butler), left, wears a dress made by her mother, Claude Smith. That dress has been worn by every child in the family in a baby photograph since that time. Rhunelle Smith Peterman is seated at the table.

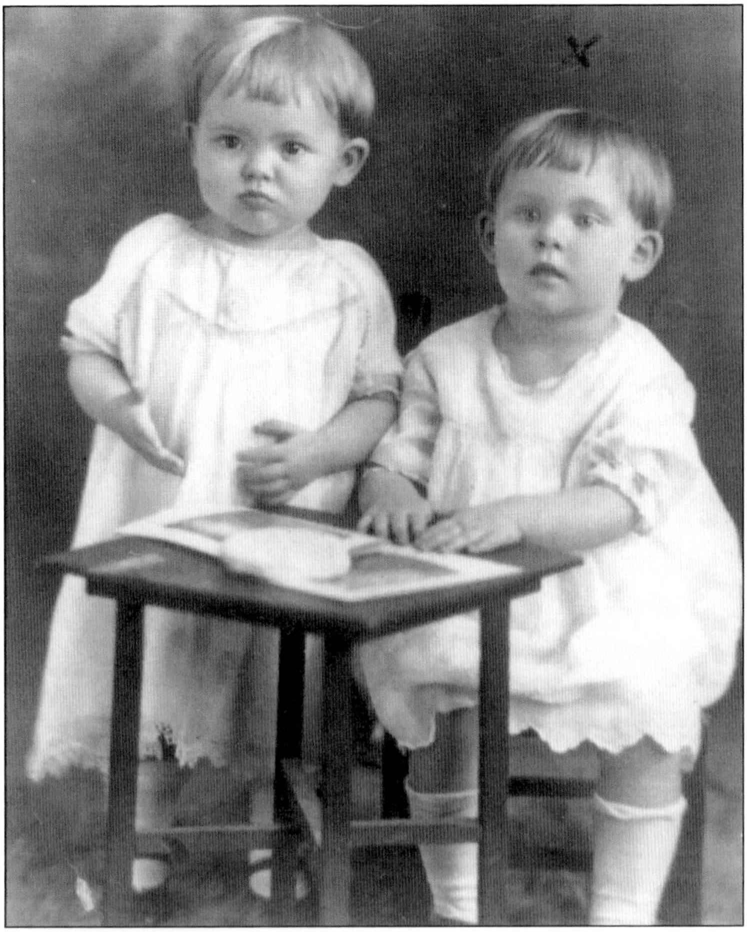

This unidentified child and dog were featured on a greeting card.

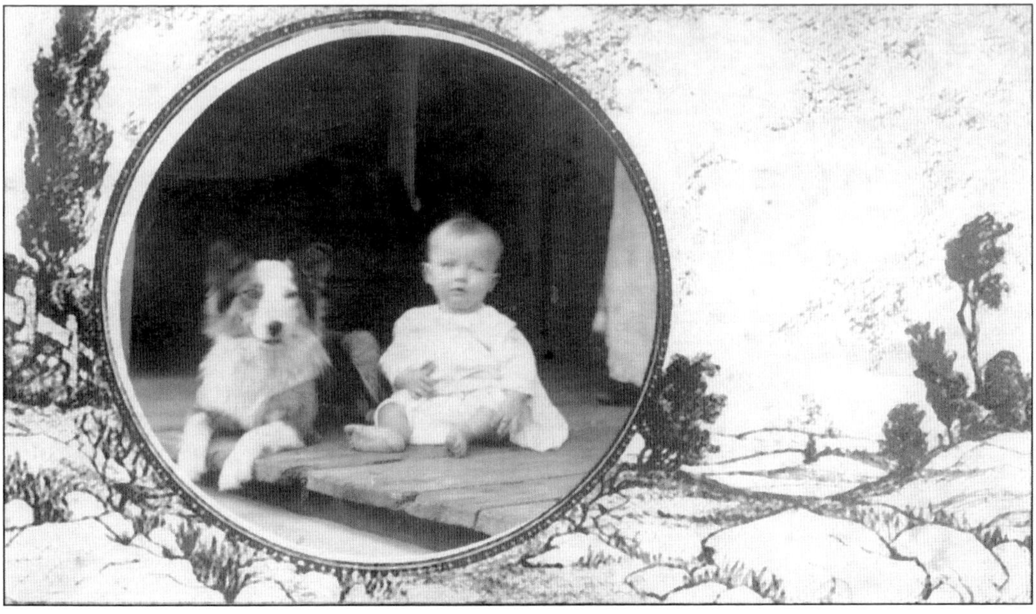

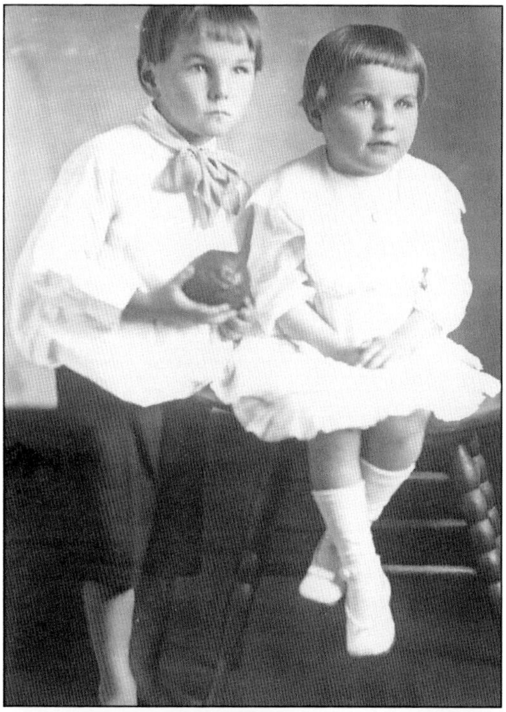

John Thomas Jr. and Ann Gibson of Pringle are pictured in 1920.

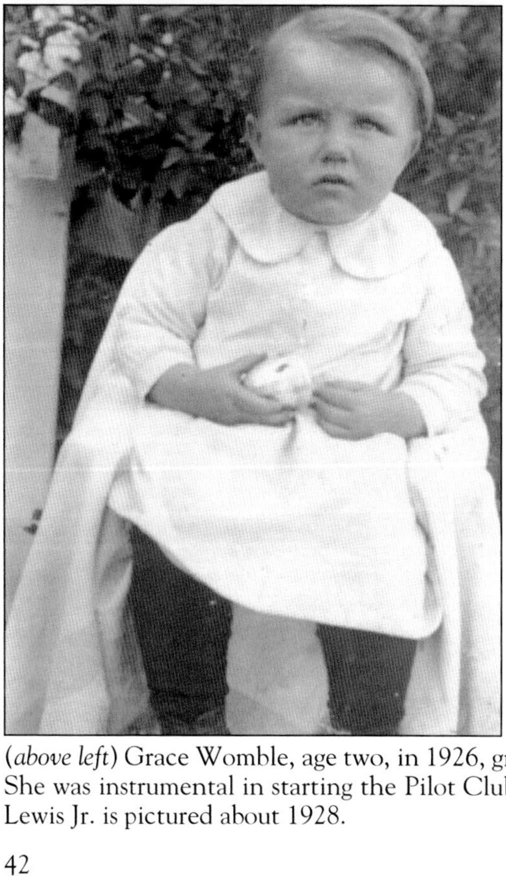

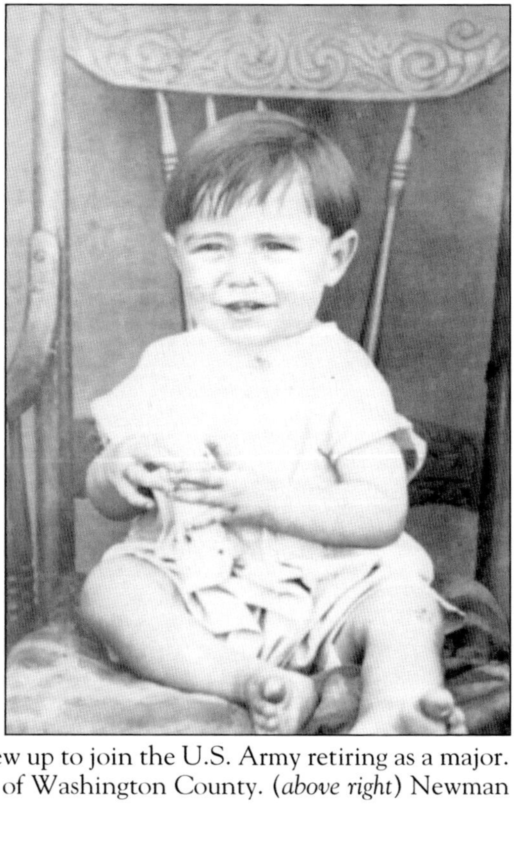

(*above left*) Grace Womble, age two, in 1926, grew up to join the U.S. Army retiring as a major. She was instrumental in starting the Pilot Club of Washington County. (*above right*) Newman Lewis Jr. is pictured about 1928.

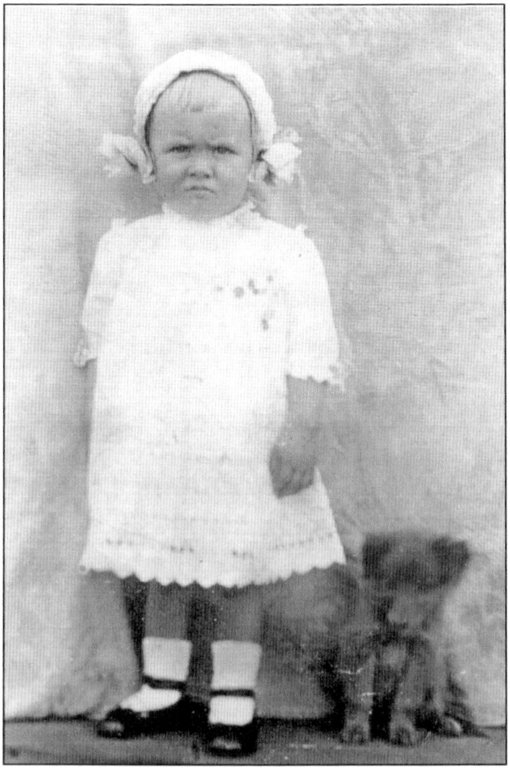

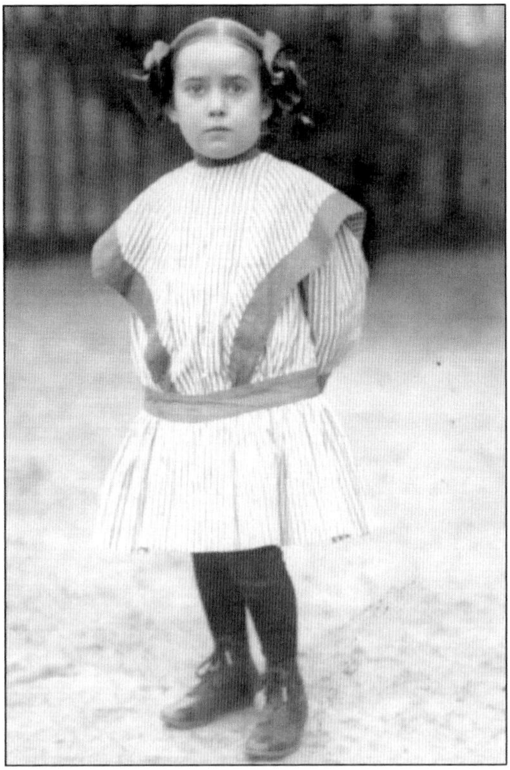

(*above left*) Often young boys wore dresses such as Cecil Giles in this 1915 photo. (*above right*) An unidentified child makes a fashion statement with a stylish dress and hairdo.

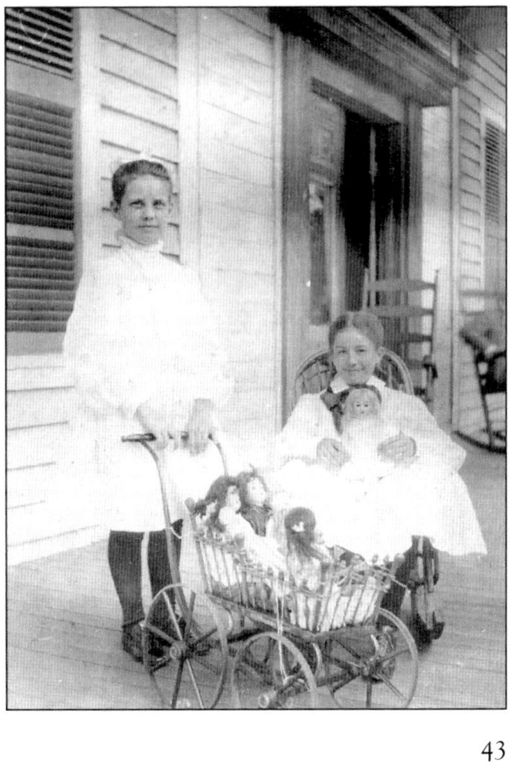

Jennie Adams, left, and Louise Cheatham play with their dolls on the front porch of the Smith-Adams-Cummings home on South Smith Street, c. 1907. (Georgia Archives.)

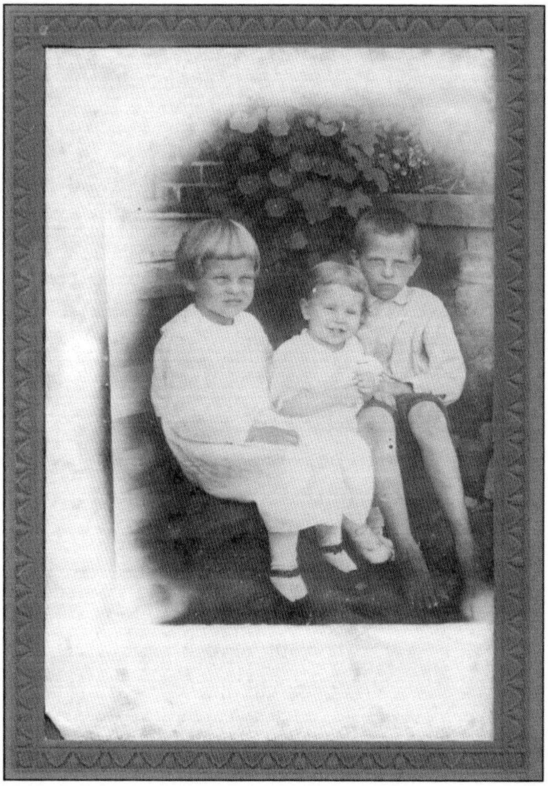

One happy child and two unhappy ones posed for the photographer *c.* 1922. They are Valeria, Harrietta, and Lanier Jr., the children of Vesta Wommack and Lonnie J. Moye Sr.

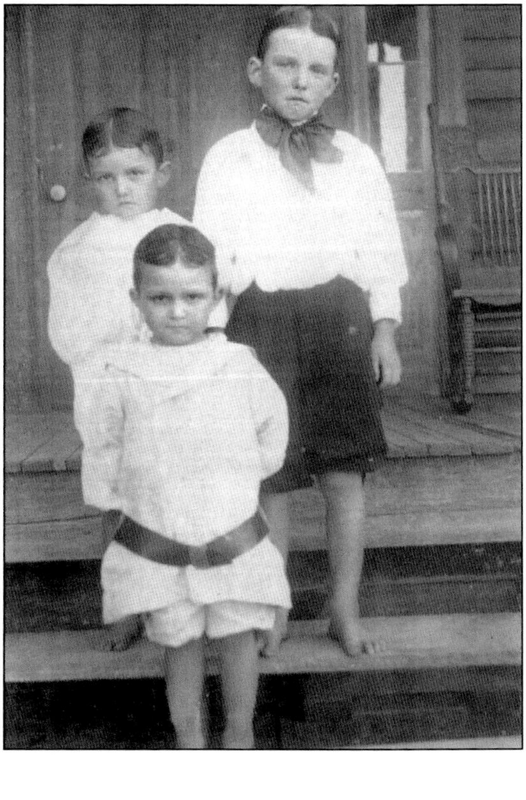

Anne Smith's daddy, Rudolph Hood, poses with his brother Zeno and sister Eulie in 1915.

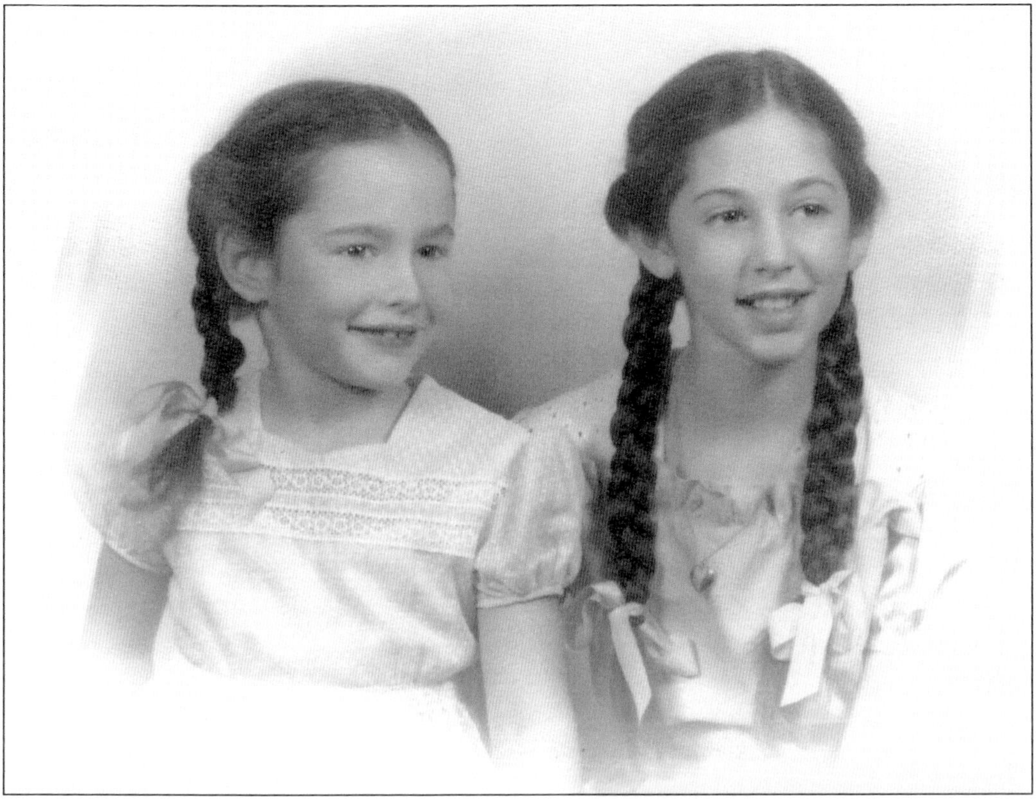

Peggy Ann Wood and her sister Julia Margaret Wood had their picture made in 1947.

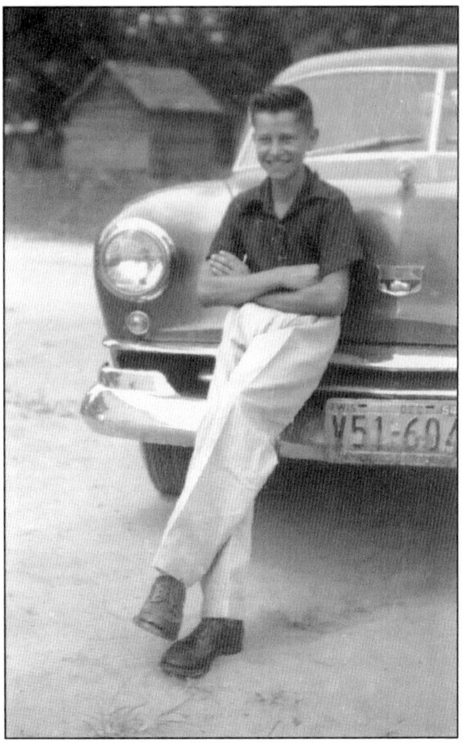

Bennie Hall was the son of Willis Benjamin Hall II; he is pictured in 1942.

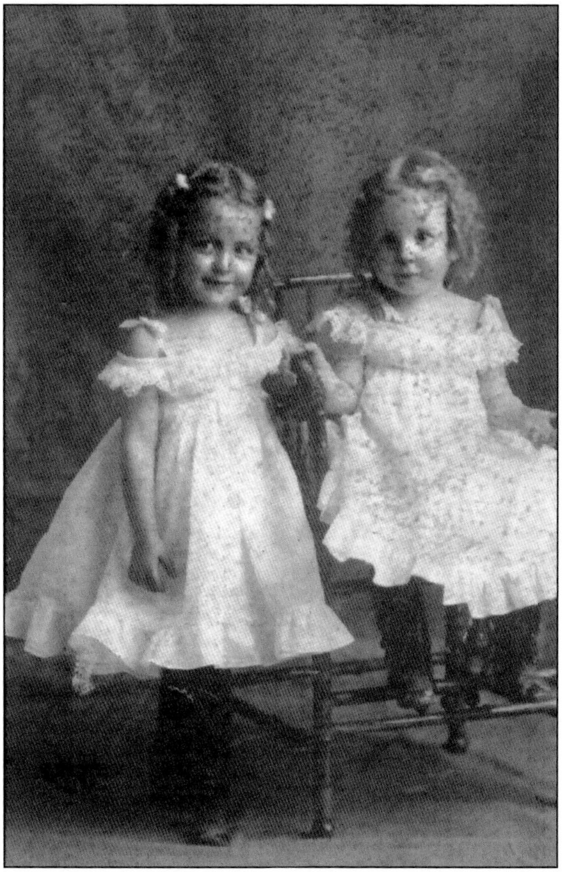

Geteva Rogers and Inallra Rogers wore ruffles in 1900.

Jessie Wood and his brother Frank C. Wood enjoyed being pulled in a cart by the billy goat. They are the children of Newman Wood.

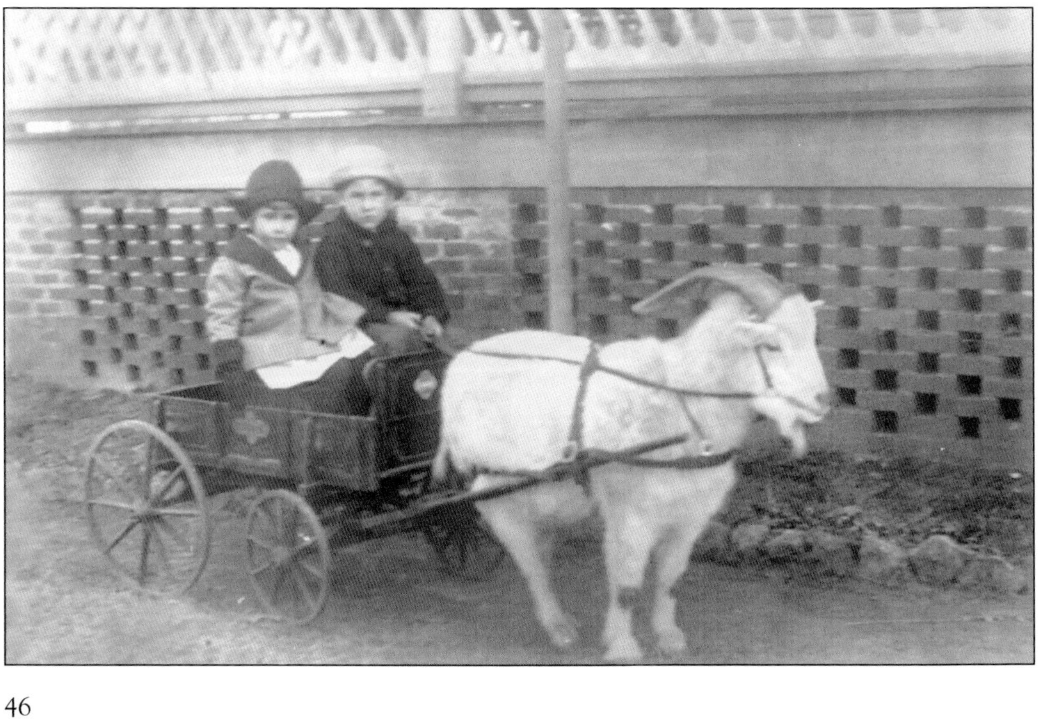

The Vickers girls, from left to right, are Dora Lillian, Annie Bessie, and Sallie Mae.

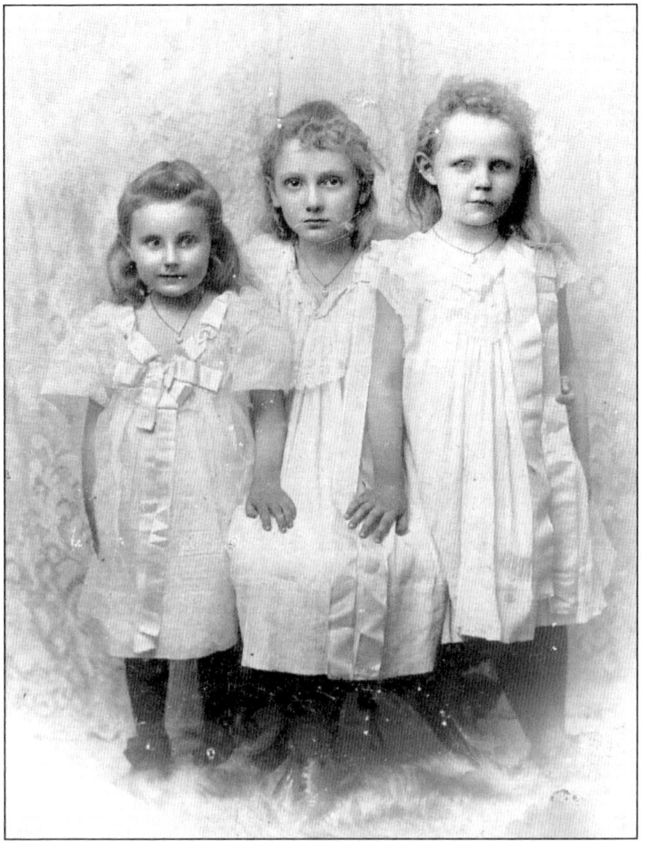

What fun William Thomas, left, and Chandler McMaster had playing with their goat cart, c. 1924. They are in front of the passenger depot in Tennille. The depot was razed about 1967.

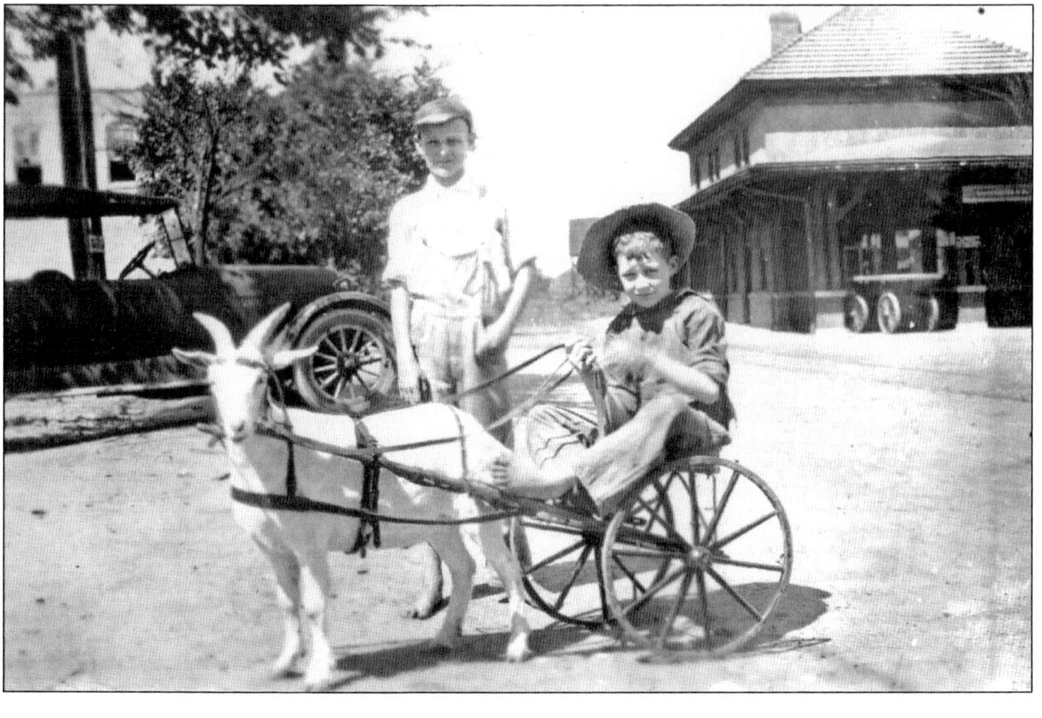

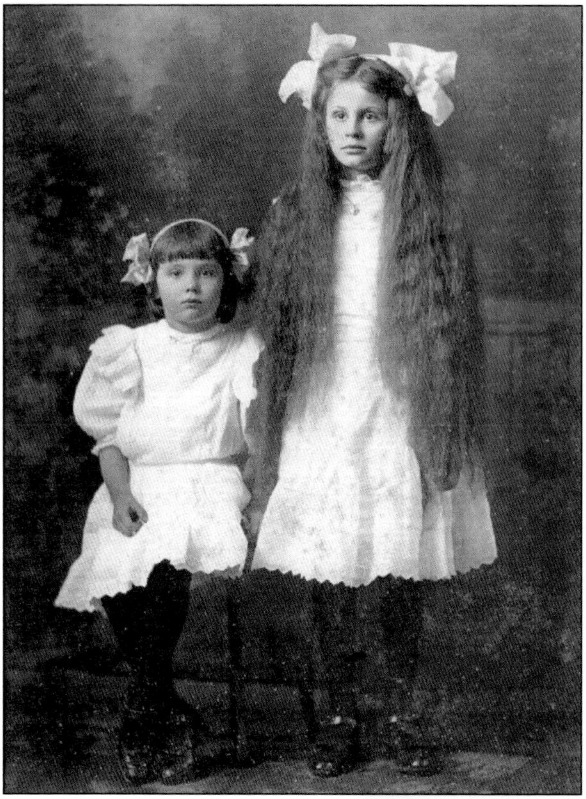

Ruth Carol and Mary June Burns were the daughters of Zella Mills Burns and John Burns. Mary was born in 1902, while Ruth came along in 1905. Ruth was believed to be the first woman lawyer in the area.

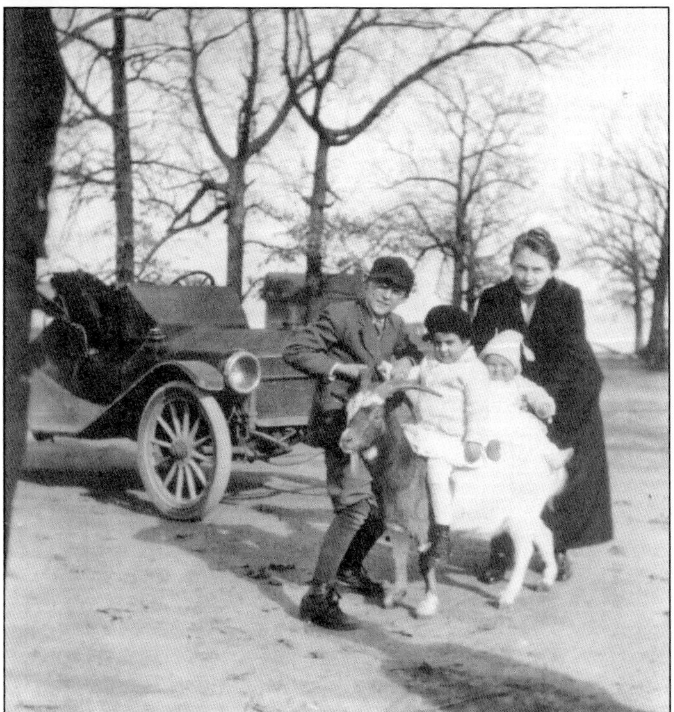

Spending the day on George Vickers's farm are Helen Gilbert, Louise Vickers, Adell Vickers, and George Vickers. They have traveled in a 1913 Model T.

Four

TIME FOR SCHOOL

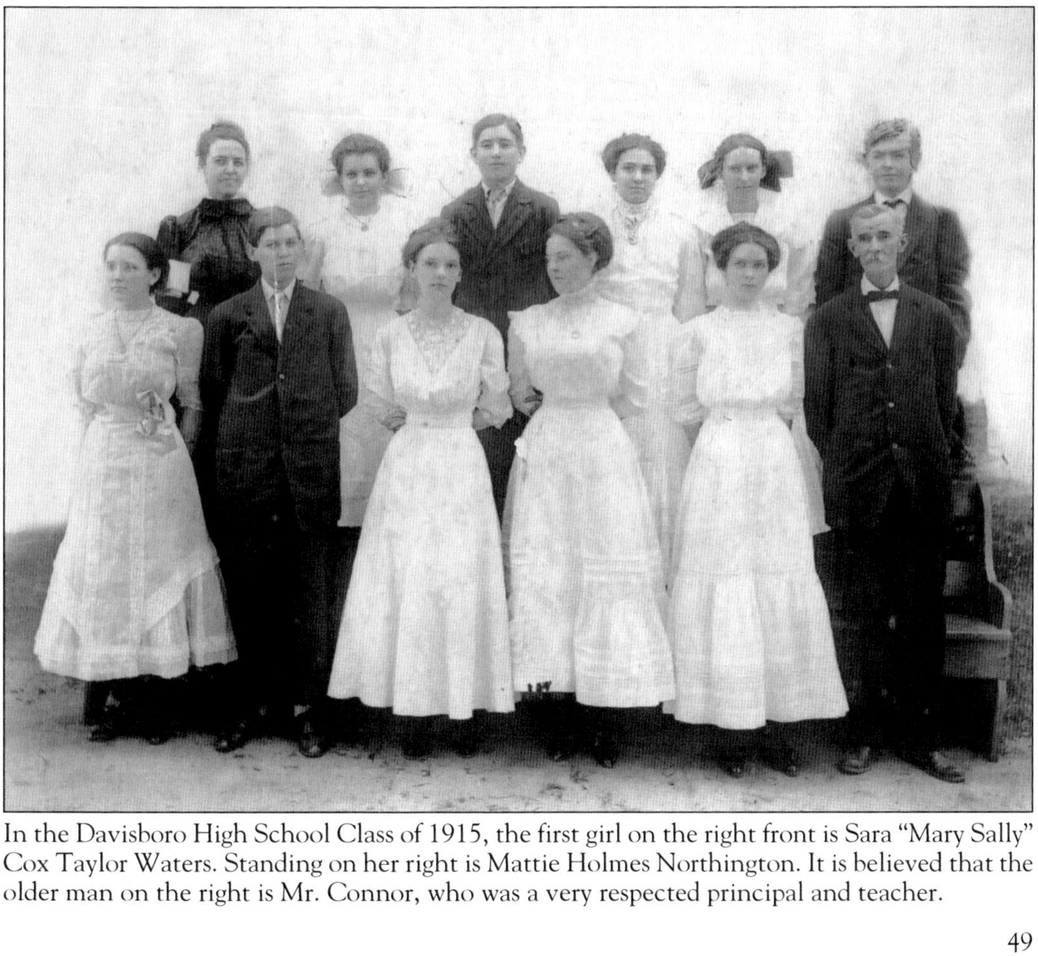

In the Davisboro High School Class of 1915, the first girl on the right front is Sara "Mary Sally" Cox Taylor Waters. Standing on her right is Mattie Holmes Northington. It is believed that the older man on the right is Mr. Connor, who was a very respected principal and teacher.

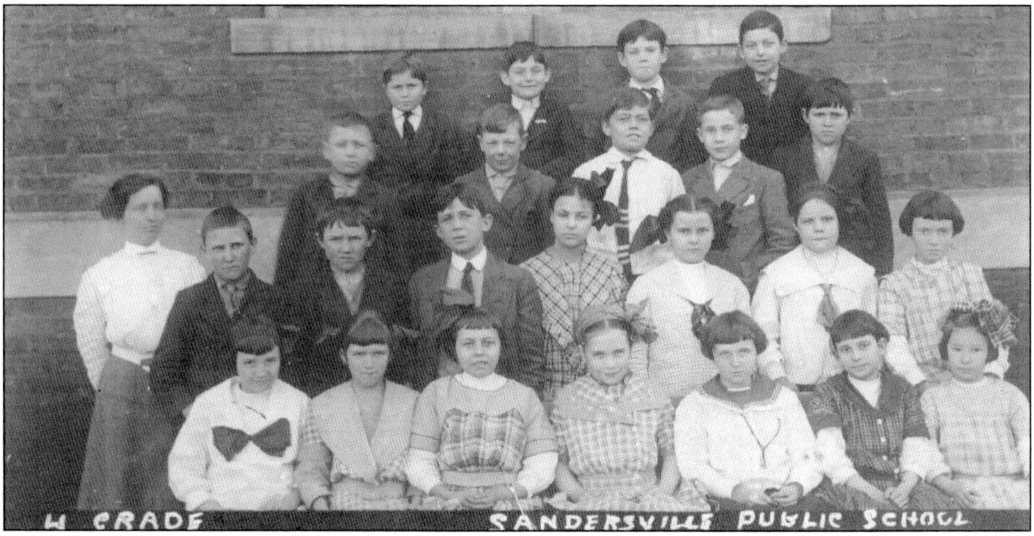

Miss Claude Wynne, left, was the teacher for this fourth grade class at Sandersville Public School in 1907. William M. Sheppard Sr. is the first boy on the second row and Sarah Rogers (Mrs. Ralph Roughton) is the fifth from left. Miss Claude taught at least two generations of children as she also taught William M. Sheppard Jr. and his sister Annie Mozelle Sheppard.

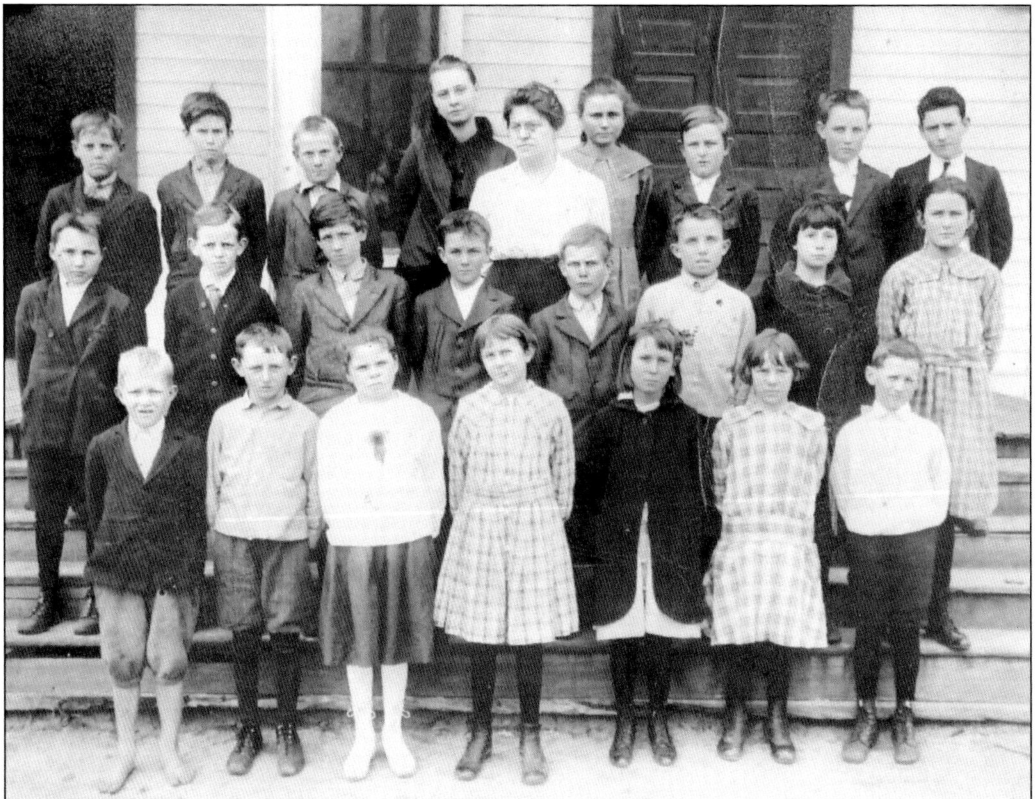

Mrs. Lilyian H. Joiner was the teacher of the fourth and fifth grades at Harrison Elementary School in 1917. (Georgia Archives.)

B.J. "Happy" Johnson, shown in a school photograph, attended Tennille Institute, c. 1928. Johnson is believed to be the first person from Washington County to be killed in action during World War II. (Georgia Archives.)

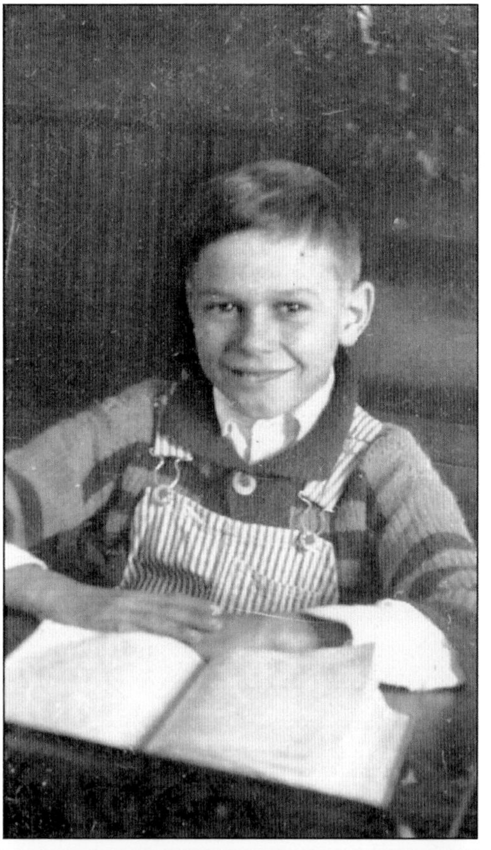

A county-wide 4-H demonstration was held in the home economics department at Sandersville High School, c.1920. (Georgia Archives.)

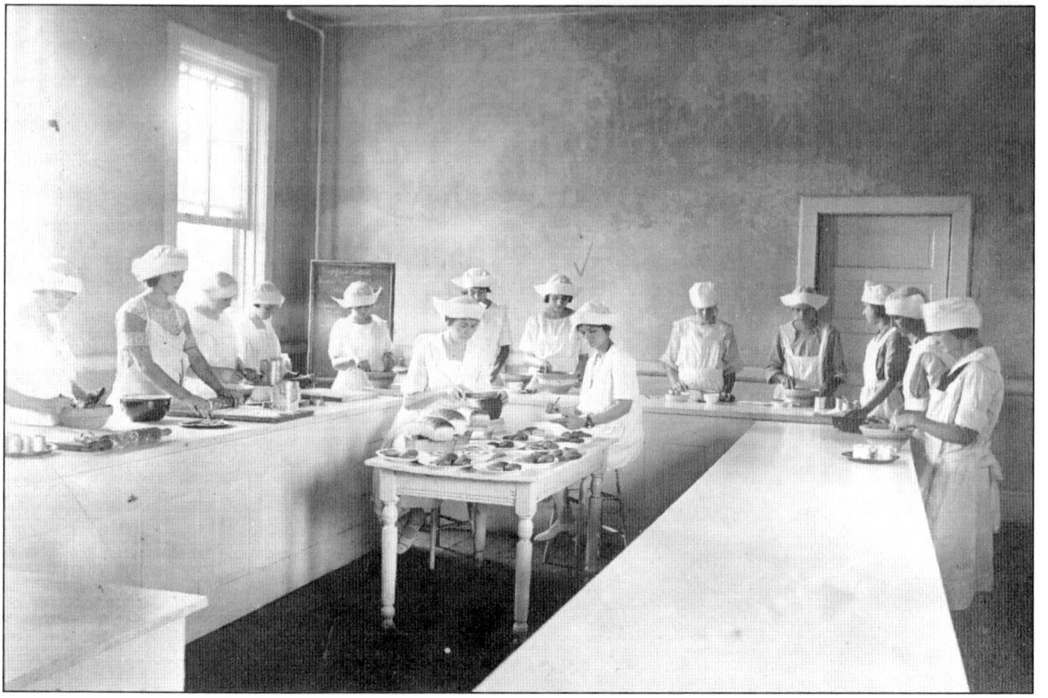

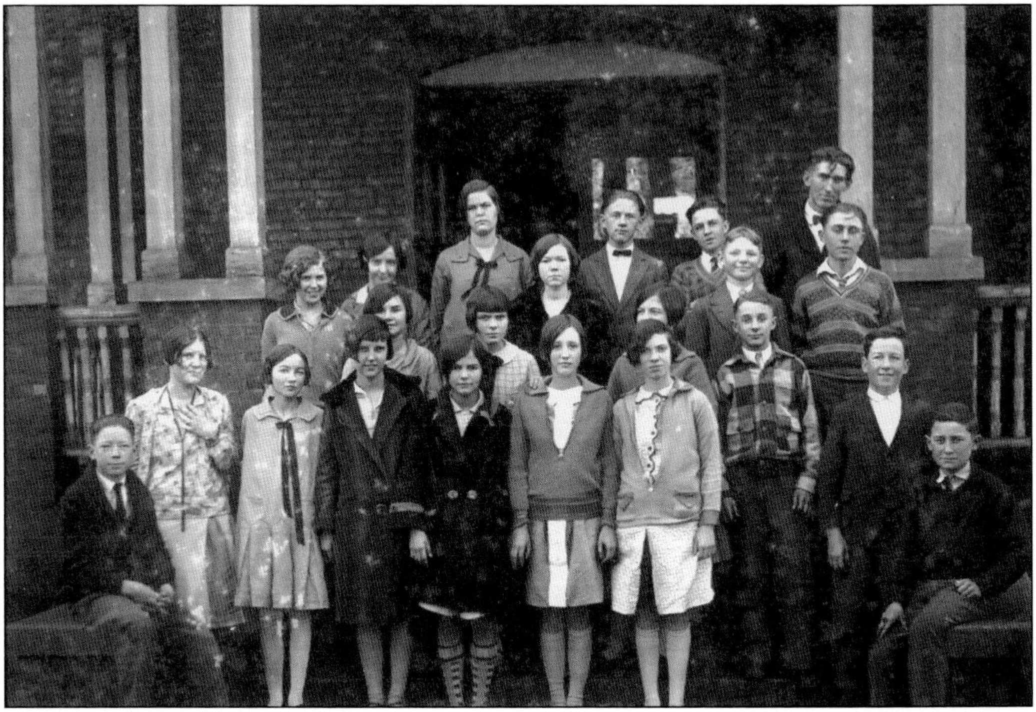

The eighth grade class at Sandersville High School posed for this picture in 1927. Harold Sheppard is a member of the class.

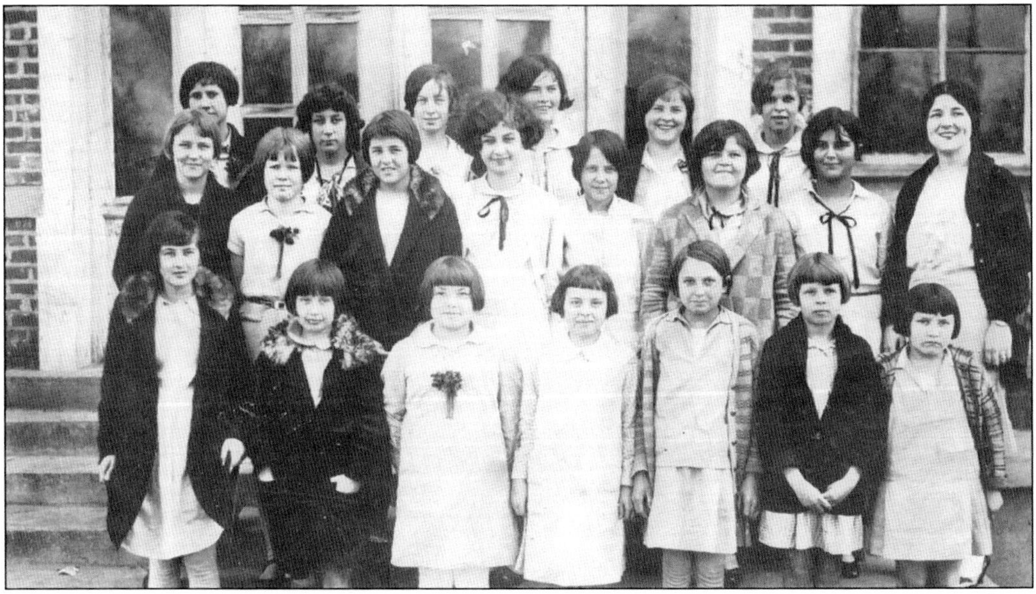

The Davisboro music class in 1928 included, from left to right, (front row) Elizabeth Collins, Mildred Aldred, Maud Florence Downs, Gladys Wilson, Marjorie Pate, Harriett Moye, and Dorothy Chalker; (middle row) Eugenia Downs, Julia Lewis, Christine Collins, Willie Smith, Sybil Wilson, Bessie Maud Horton, Elizabeth Hattaway, and Miss Hatcher (teacher); (back row) Gessela Holton, Bobbie Chalker, Louise Northington, Margaret Hattaway, Enid Lewis, and Valeria Moye.

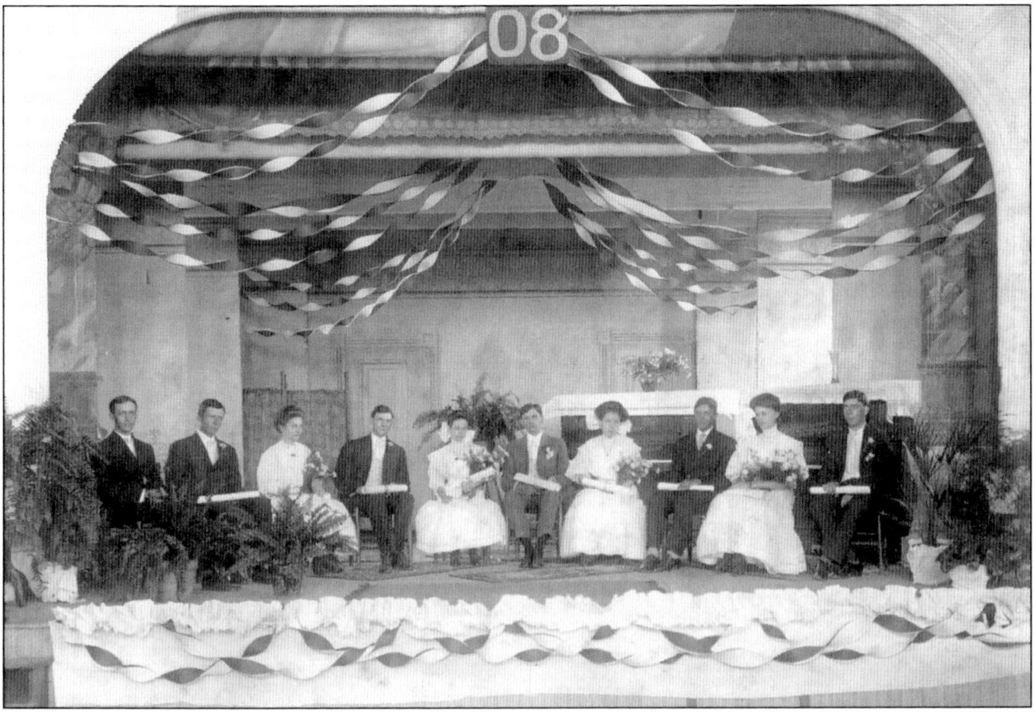

Tennille High School principal C.V. Asbury, left, awarded diplomas to the 1908 graduating class, which included Peret Northington, Mary Franklin Jackson Morron, Clem Brown, Lonise Brown, John Voss, Willie Ivet, Horace Sheppard, Mary Helen Adams Brown, and Harry Gilbert Sr.

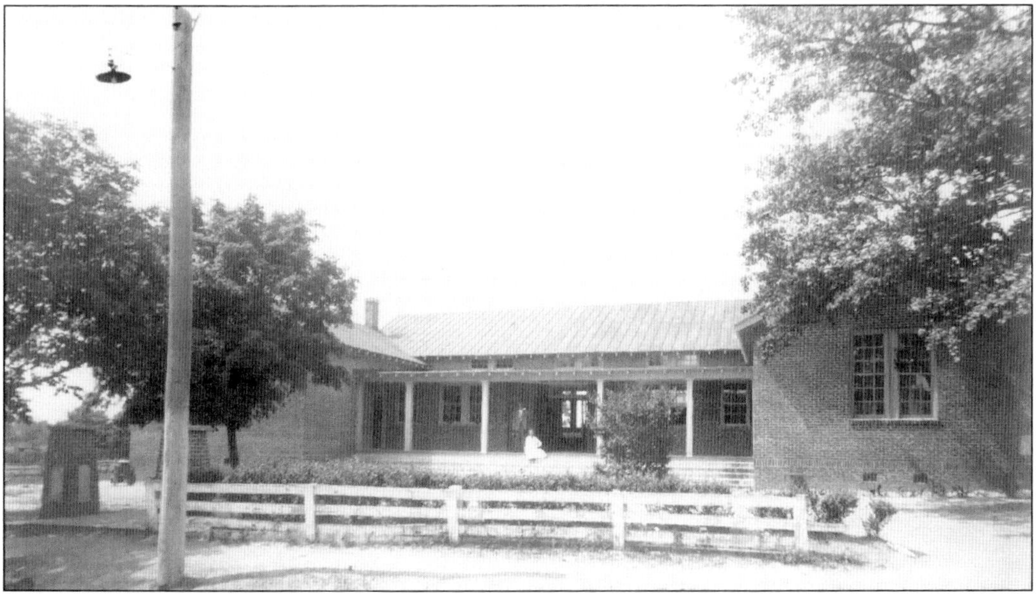

Prof. Thomas Jefferson Elder began the Sandersville Industrial School for African-American children in 1889, serving as principal and teacher. Later the school was named for him. He was able to obtain a Rosenwald grant to build this brick structure in 1928–1929. On the National Register of Historic Sites, it is now used as a community center.

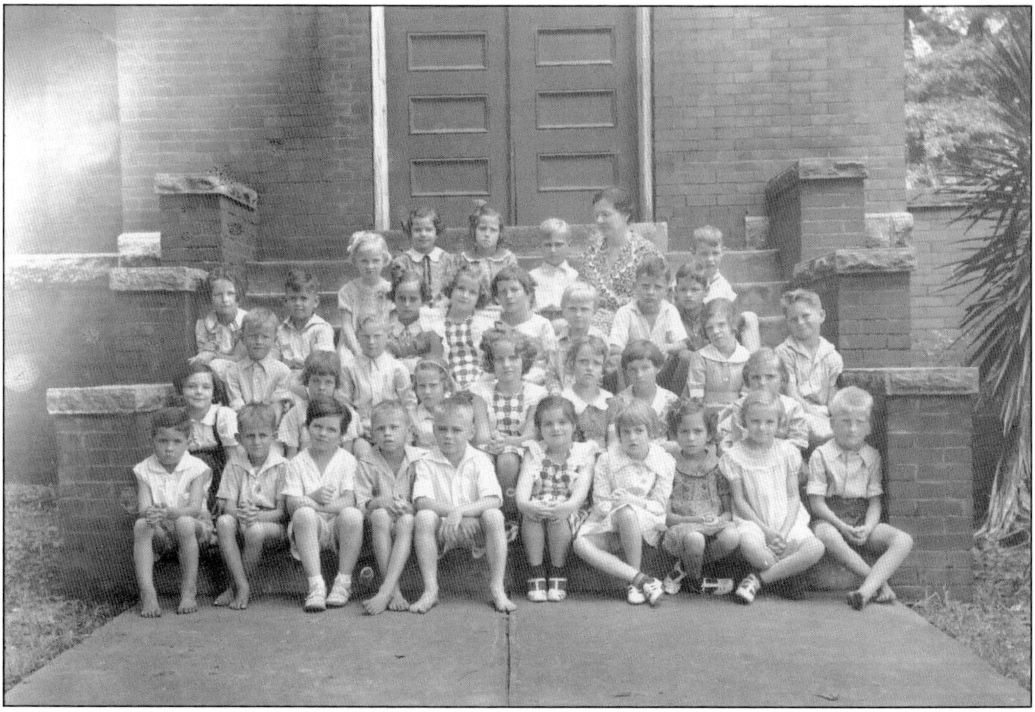

Miss Ellen Bradley was the teacher of this first grade class at the Sandersville Public School on East Church Street, *c.* 1936. Class members include Ben Tarbutton Jr., Mary Jane McElrath, and Ann Smith. Notice the bare feet on many of the children.

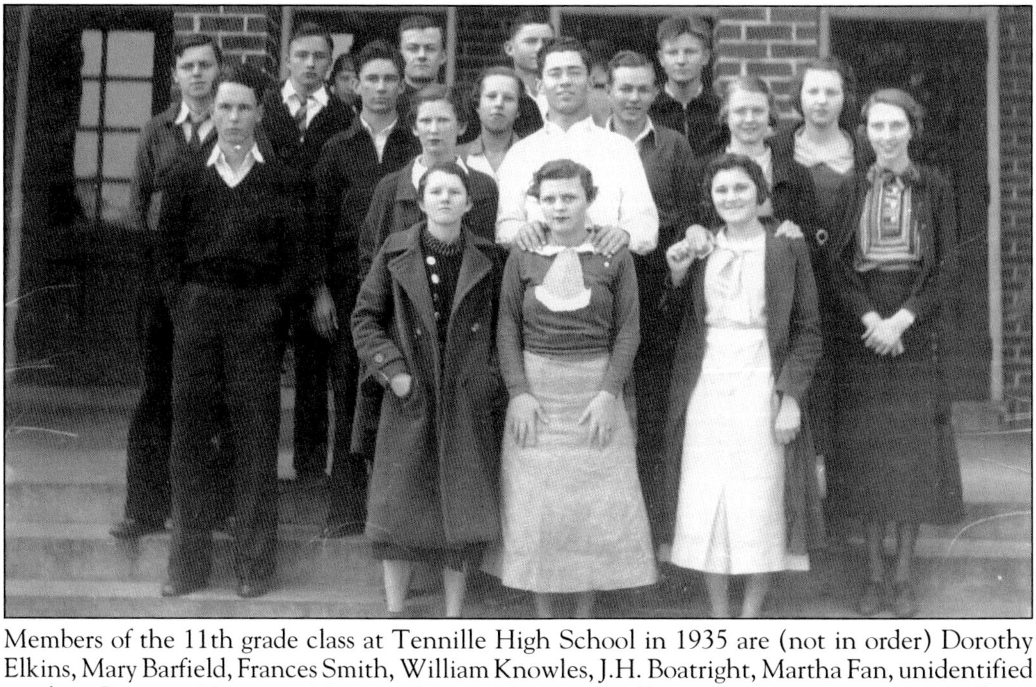

Members of the 11th grade class at Tennille High School in 1935 are (not in order) Dorothy Elkins, Mary Barfield, Frances Smith, William Knowles, J.H. Boatright, Martha Fan, unidentified teacher, Braxton Harrison, Margaret Miner, Benjam Waller, Miney Stanley, Harry Gilbert, Billy Gunnels, Frank McDade, Dewitt Mandeville, Tom Layton, and Other Horton.

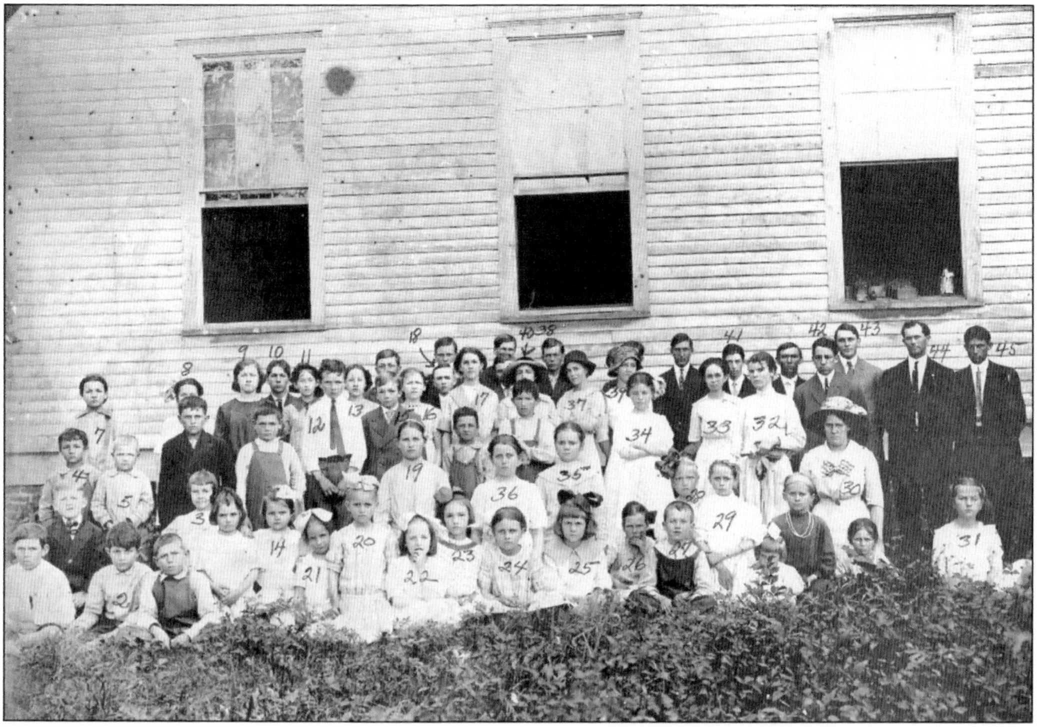

Students at the Warthen School gathered for a picture in 1912. (Georgia Archives.)

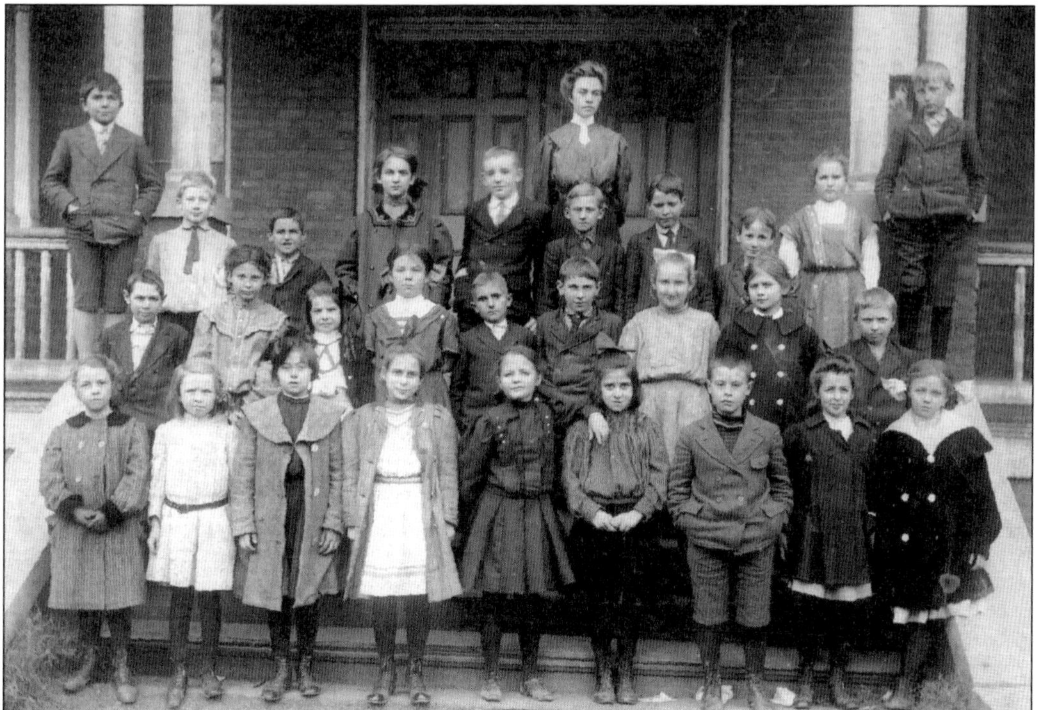

Ida Shelnutt (Wylly) is the second from the right in the front row of this sixth grade class at Sandersville Public. School. Fannie Lou Irwin is the teacher.

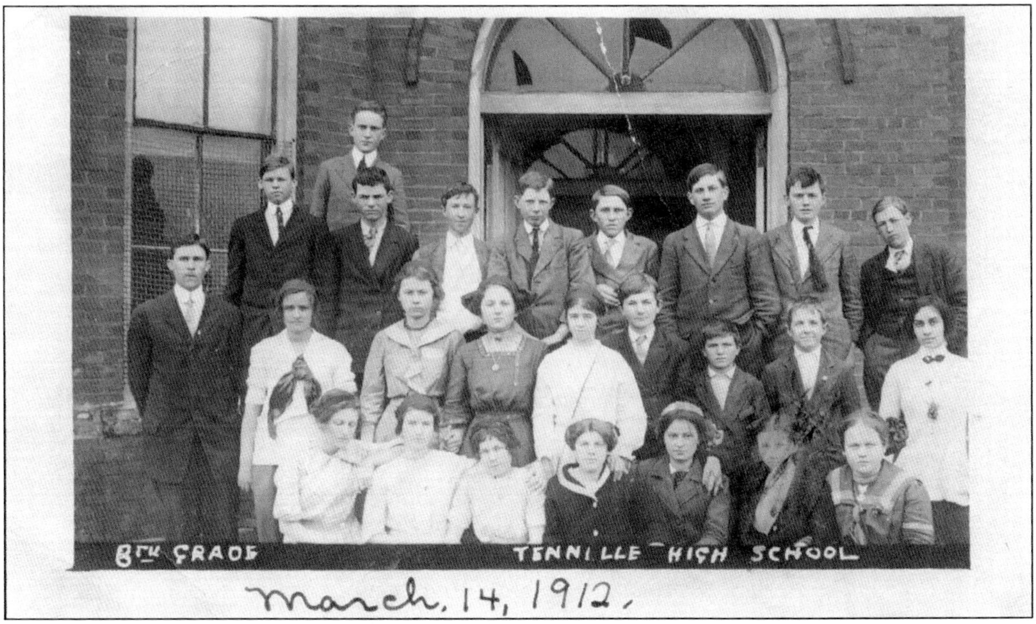

At Tennille High School the eighth grade class posed for a picture on March 14, 1912.

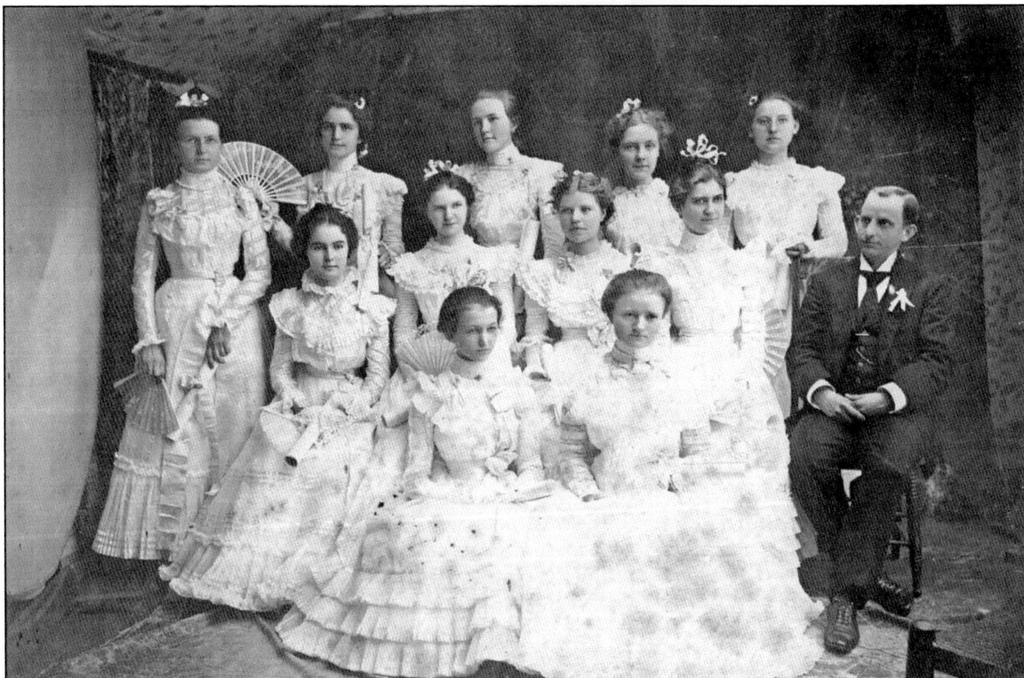

Believed to be a 1901 graduating class, members, from left to right, are (front row) Frankie Walden, who married T. Oliver; and Hattie Garbutt, who married M.L. Gross; (middle row) Mary Tarbutton, who married Robert F. Freeman; two unidentified people; Mattie Mae Wall, who married Thos. Selma Turner; and Principal Cincinnatus Whitehurst; (back row) Mancie Evans; Mary Cooley, who married Edward T. Averett; Annie Mary Wood, who first married James Hartwell Holmes and later Judge Rawlings; and Marie Hale (Nellie).

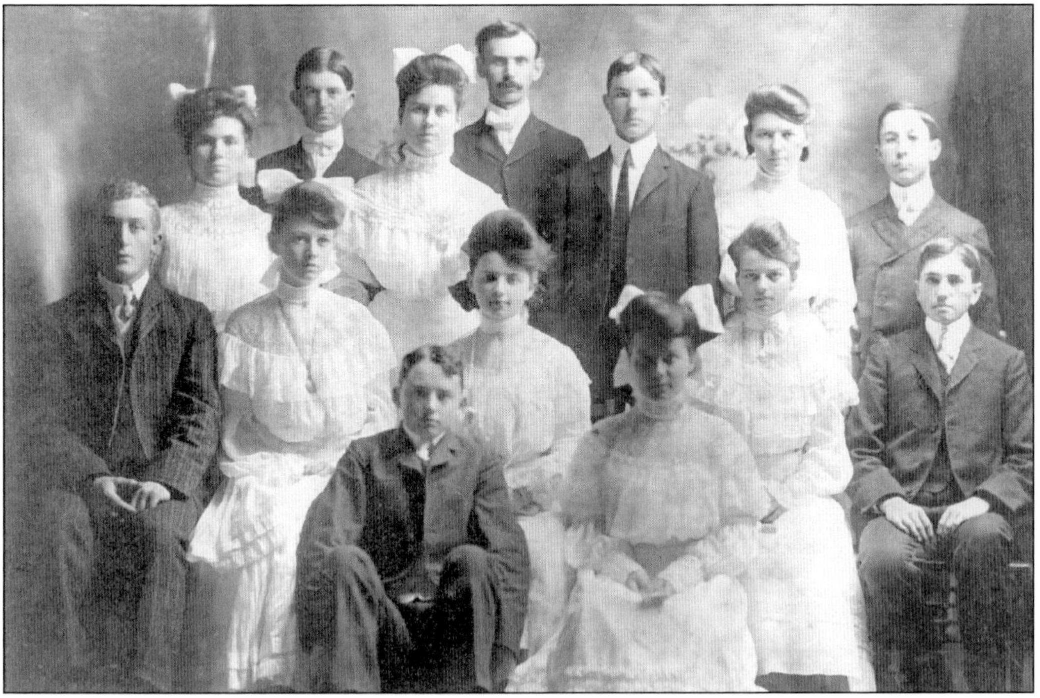

The 1903–1904 graduating class from the Tennille Institute was an attractive group of students. (Georgia Archives.)

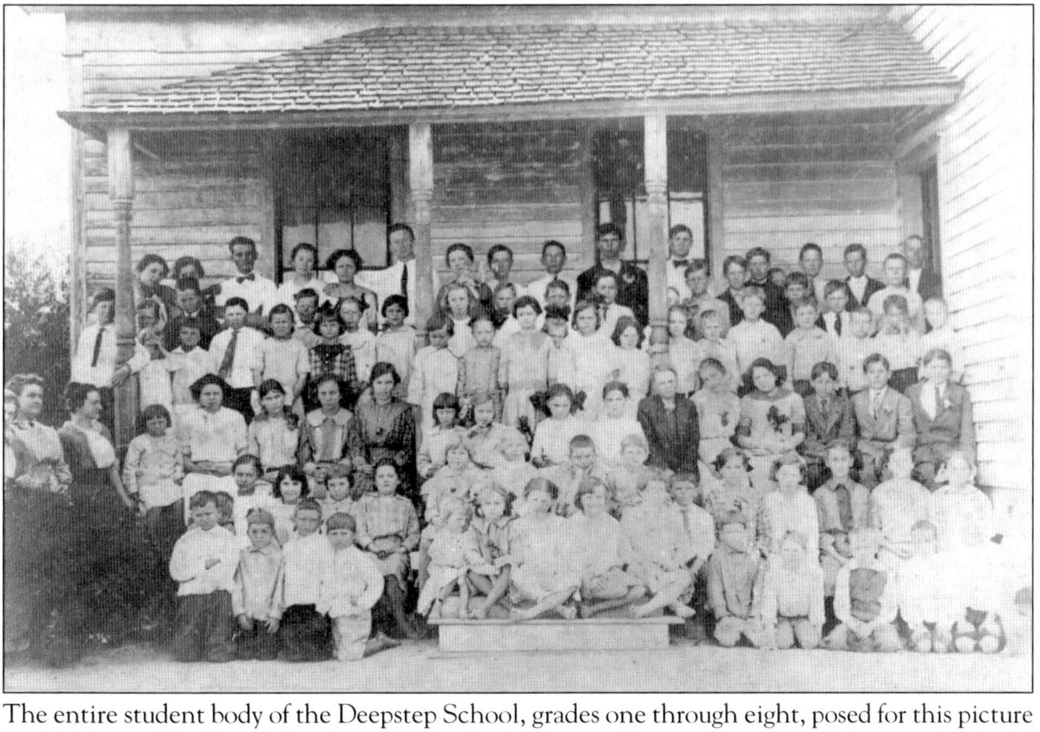

The entire student body of the Deepstep School, grades one through eight, posed for this picture in 1914. At the lower left are teachers, from left to right, Louise Doolittle, Cora Price, and Annie Doolittle. (Georgia Archives.)

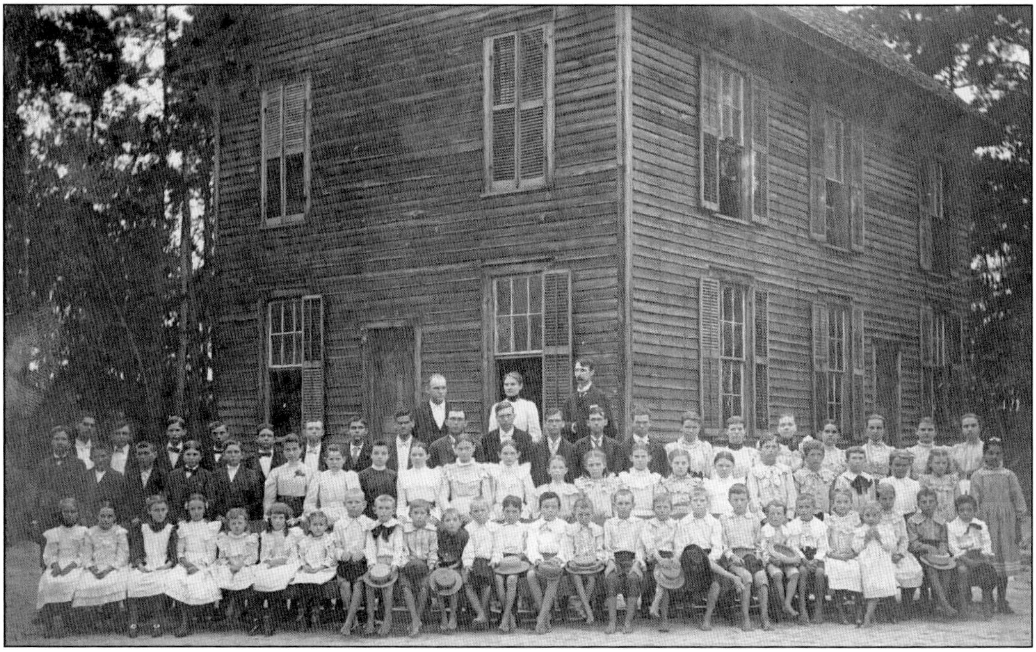

Shiloh School, located off Linton Road in the Union Church area, operated from about 1885 to about 1925. It was located in Thena, one of the area's "lost" communities. At one time, Thena had a post office, a cotton gin, and a store. Notice that most of the girls are wearing stockings and shoes, while the boys are barefoot but holding hats.

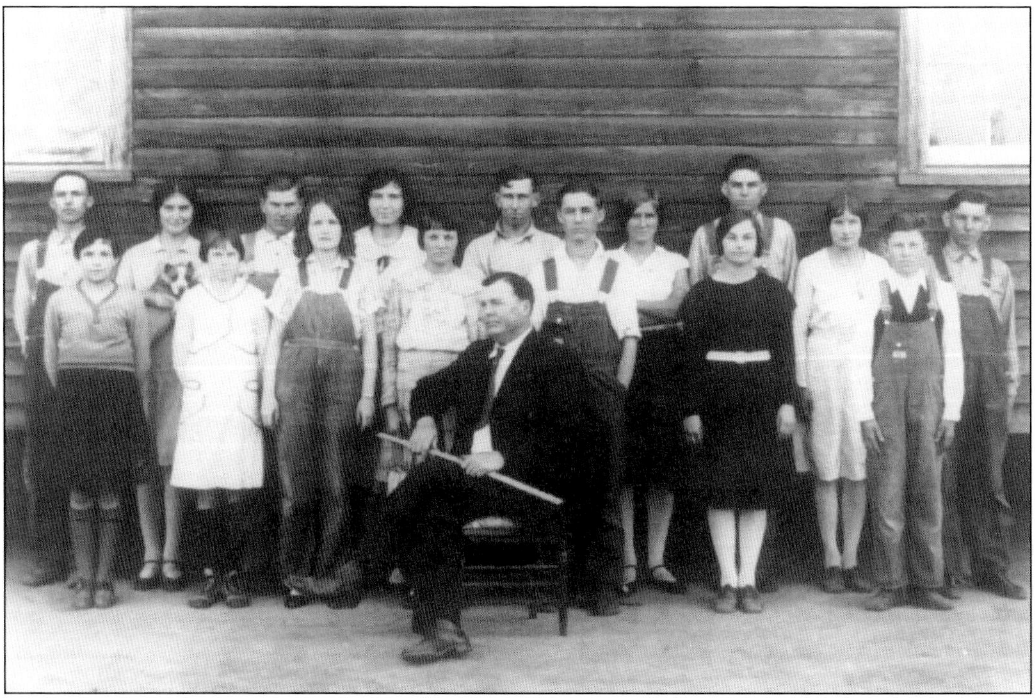

Wonder if this unidentified teacher really needed to use that yardstick on his students?

Five

Portraits of Times Gone By

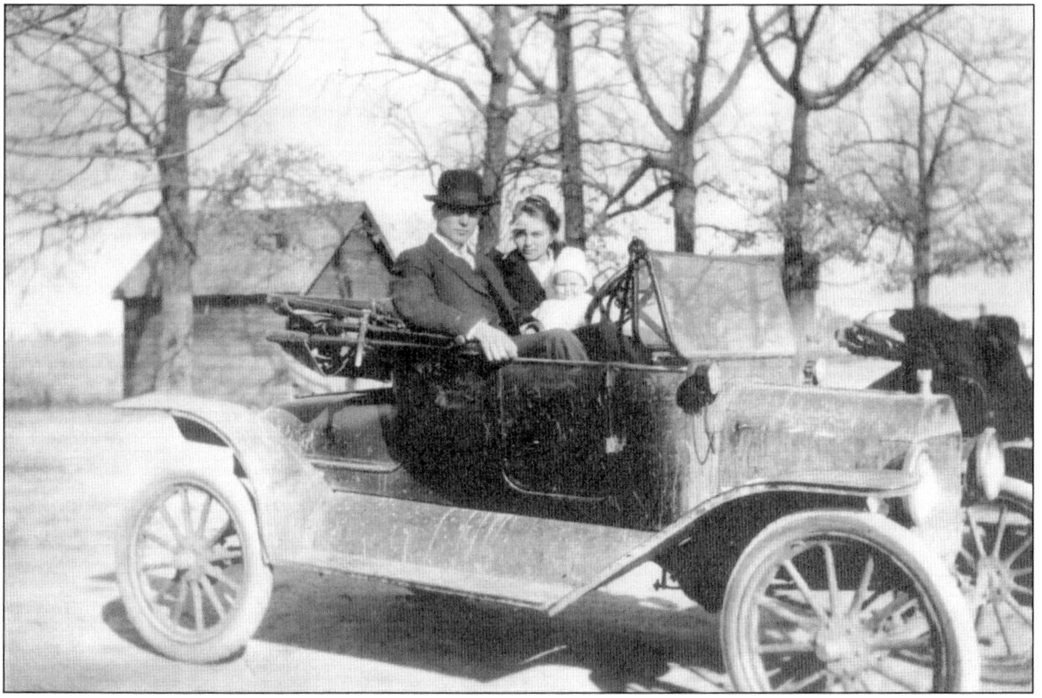

Out for a spin in 1913 are George and Louise Vickers and baby Adelle.

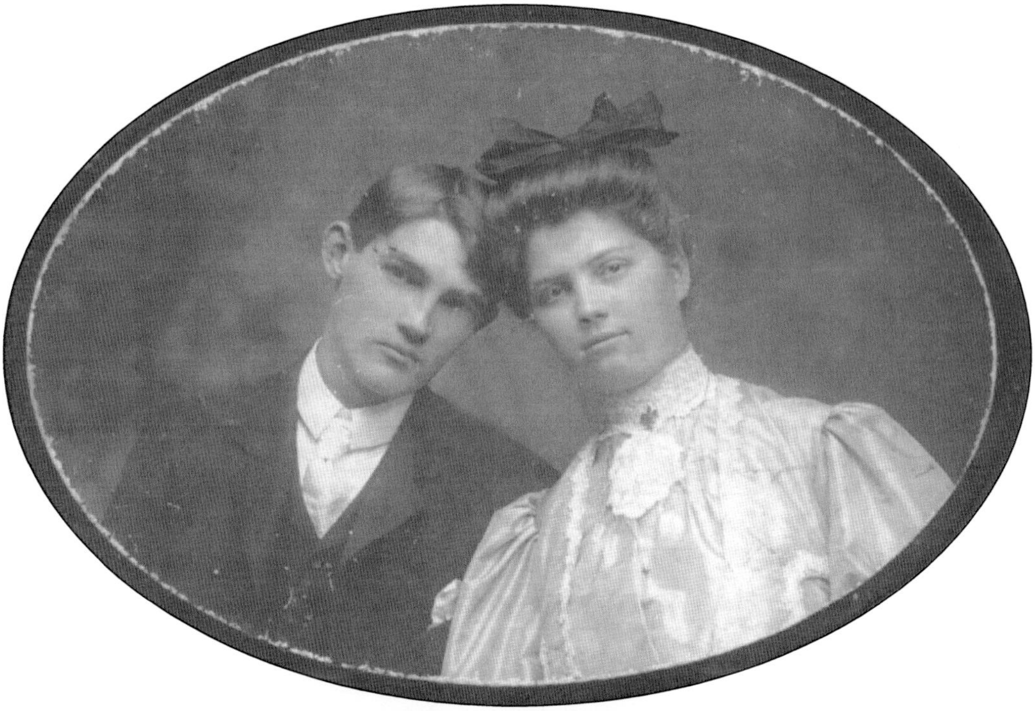

Tom and Inez Sheppard Pittman are shown in 1903.

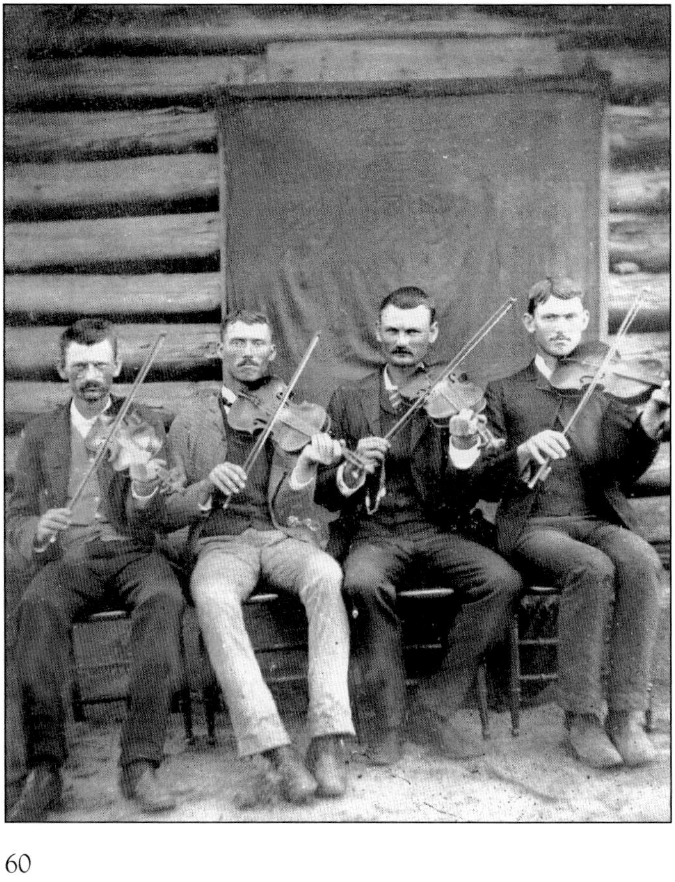

Four men are shown playing the fiddle in this old tin-type.

Jessie Womble died in the flu epidemic of 1919.

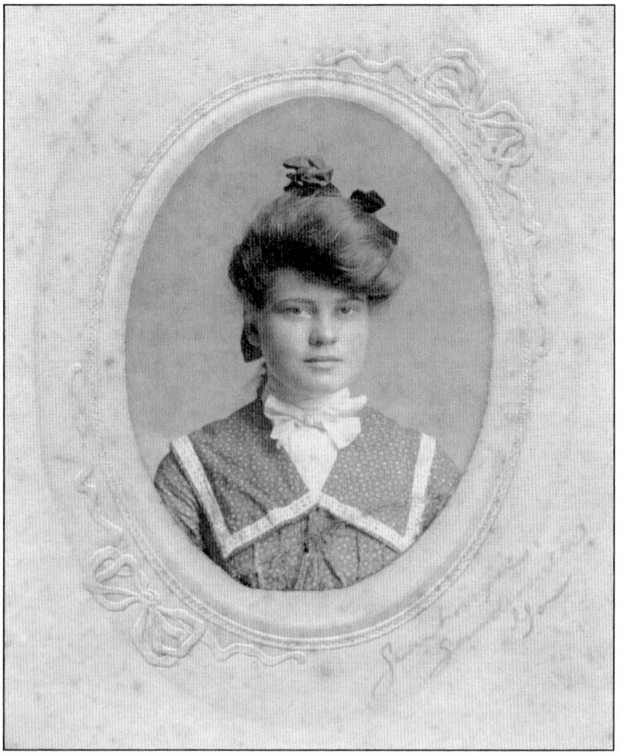

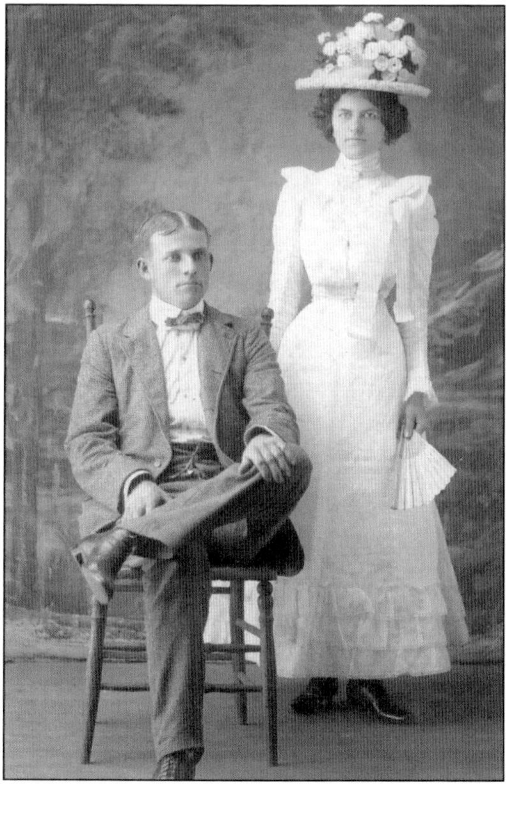

Could this be a c. 1910 wedding photo for this unidentified couple?

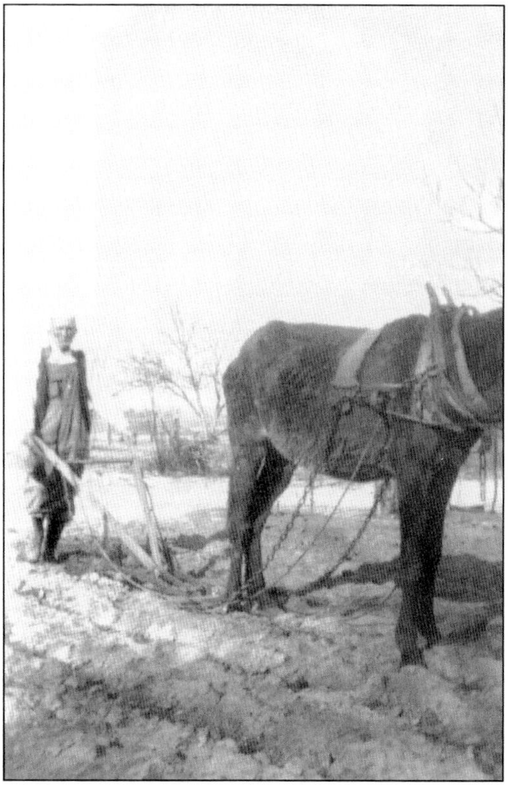

William "Uncle Boonie" Doolittle plows in the 1940s.

(*below left*) Pierce Everett, left, is shown c. 1936 with Jessie T. Webster, who may have been playing cowboys when he paused for the photographer. Note the cap pistol and hatchet he is wearing. (*below right*) Stephen Augustus Smith, shown c. 1902, lived from 1852 to 1921.

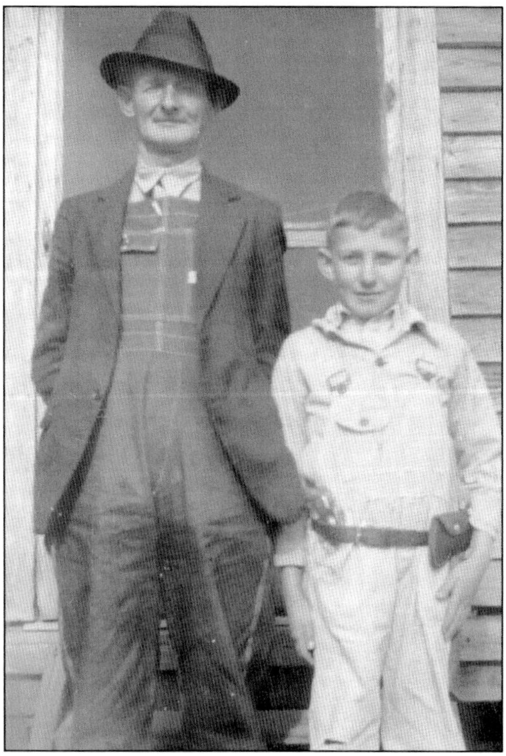

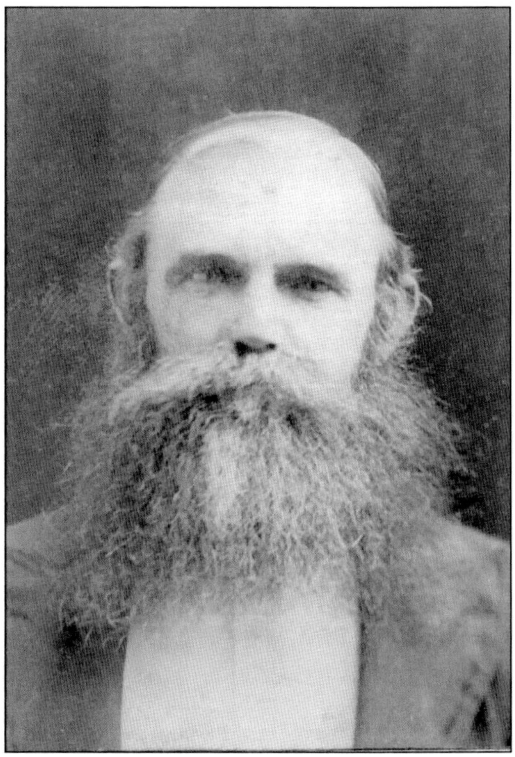

A mail carrier out of the Davisboro Post Office, Elizabeth Irene McAfee Kitchens was married to William "Bill" Rawlings Kitchens. She drove a buggy to make her deliveries and was killed while on her route in May 1922. She is shown here *c.* 1910.

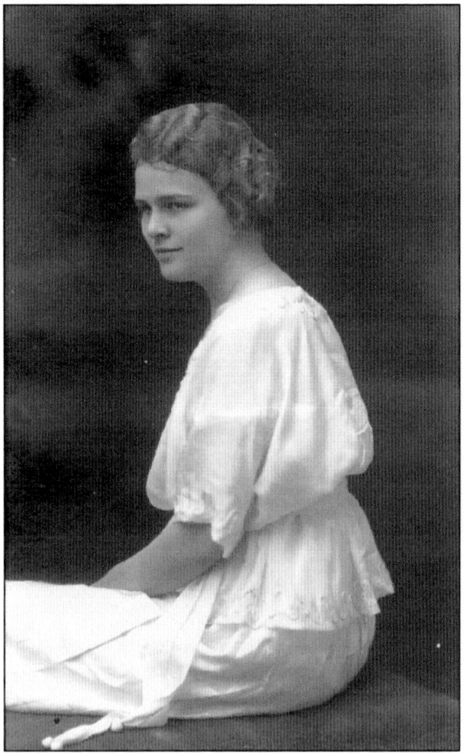

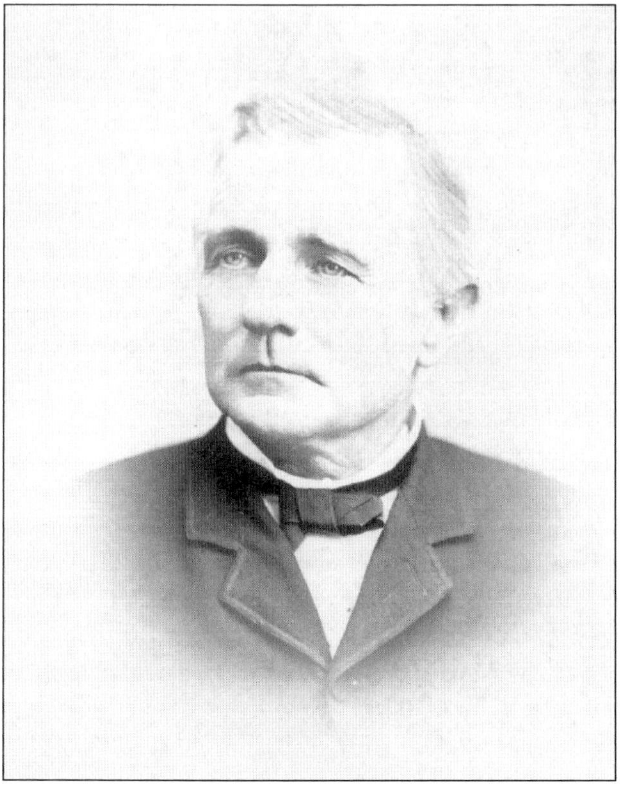

Geo. D. Warthen was a young man when this photograph was taken. Born in 1847, he died in 1927. He is most noted for establishing a bank in his name, which continues to operate today.

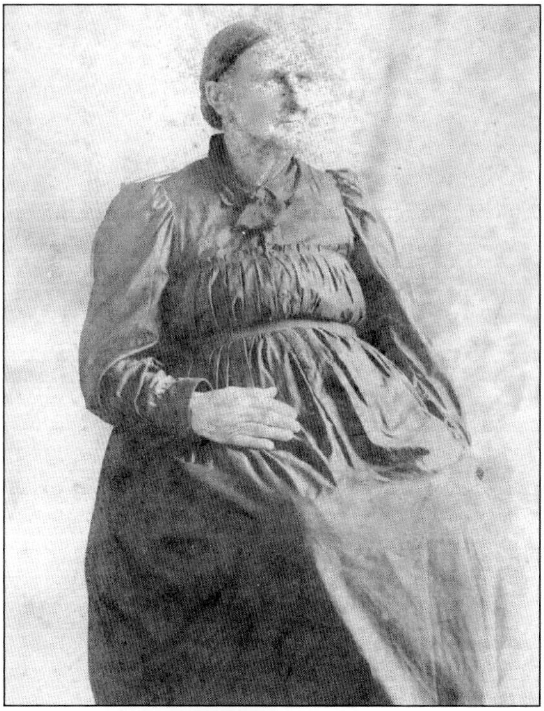

Nancy Pierce, shown in 1899, had eight children.

Mrs. Lula Newman admires the beautiful camellias grown in Sandersville, *c.* 1940.

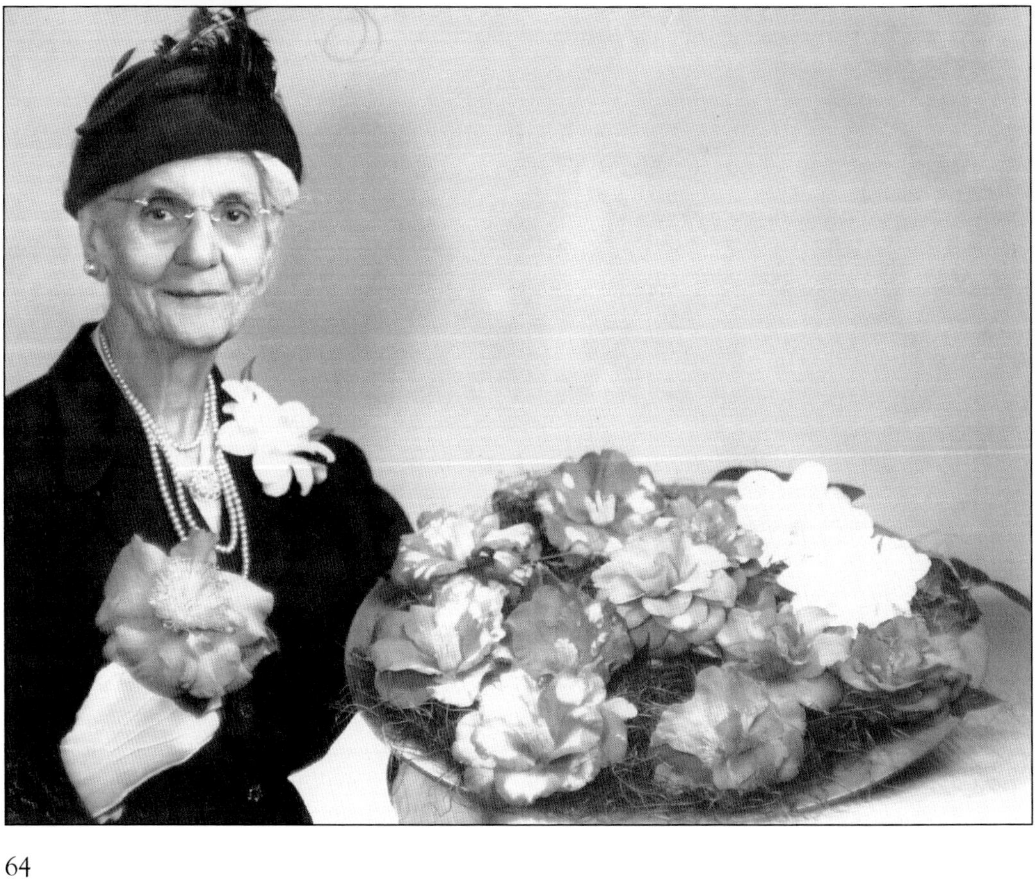

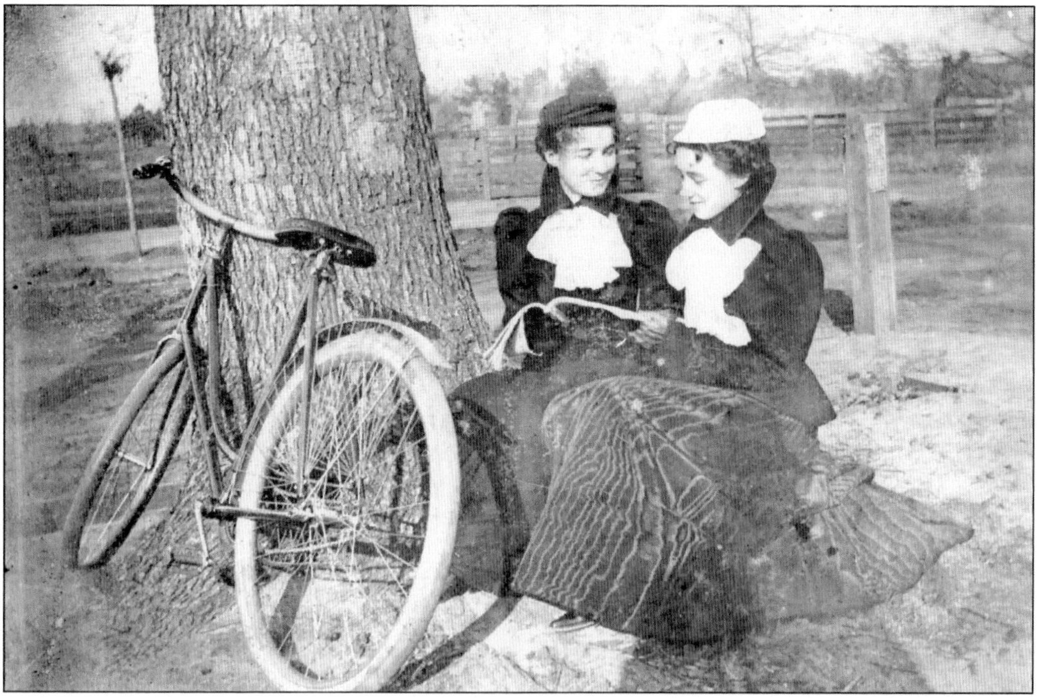

Bell Brown, left, and Olivia Harris are dressed for a bicycle ride in Sandersville in 1895. (Georgia Archives.)

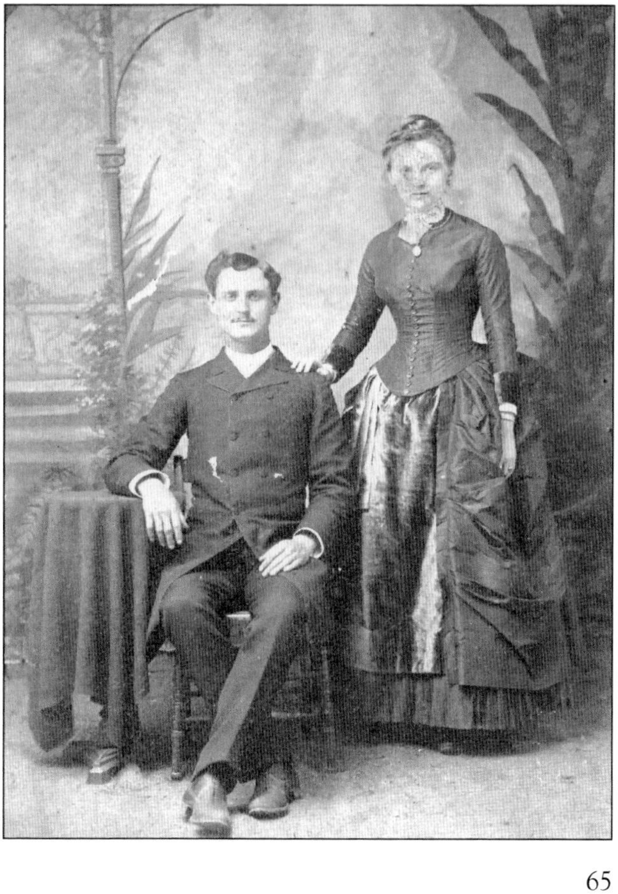

Dr. and Mrs. Thomas E. Vickers were photographed on April 7, 1886. In addition to caring for the community's health problems, he also taught school. (Georgia Archives.)

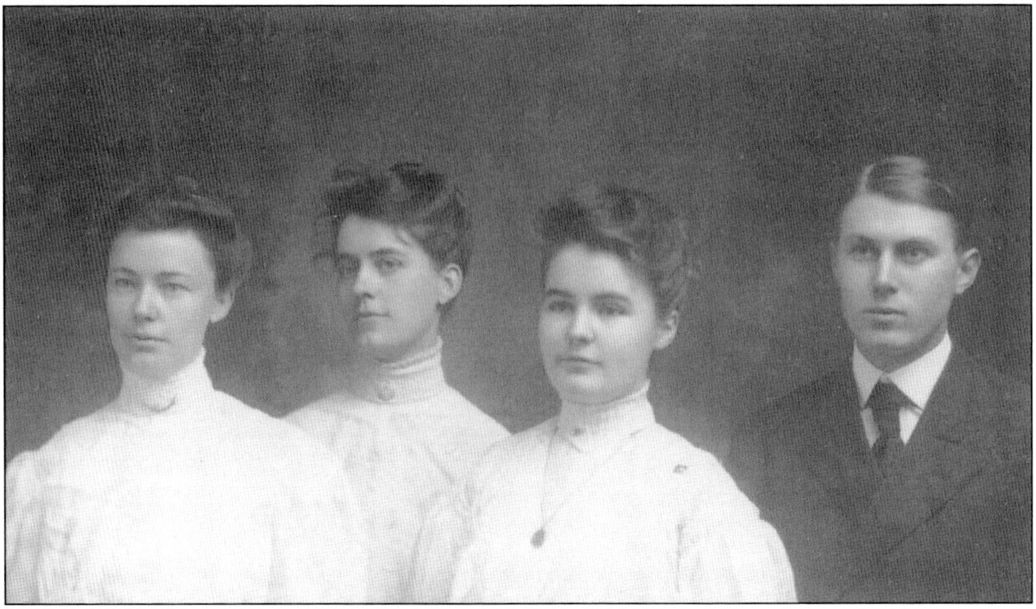

The Tarbutton family, c. 1910, consisted of sisters Mattie, Sadye, and Mary and brother Ben Tarbutton Sr.

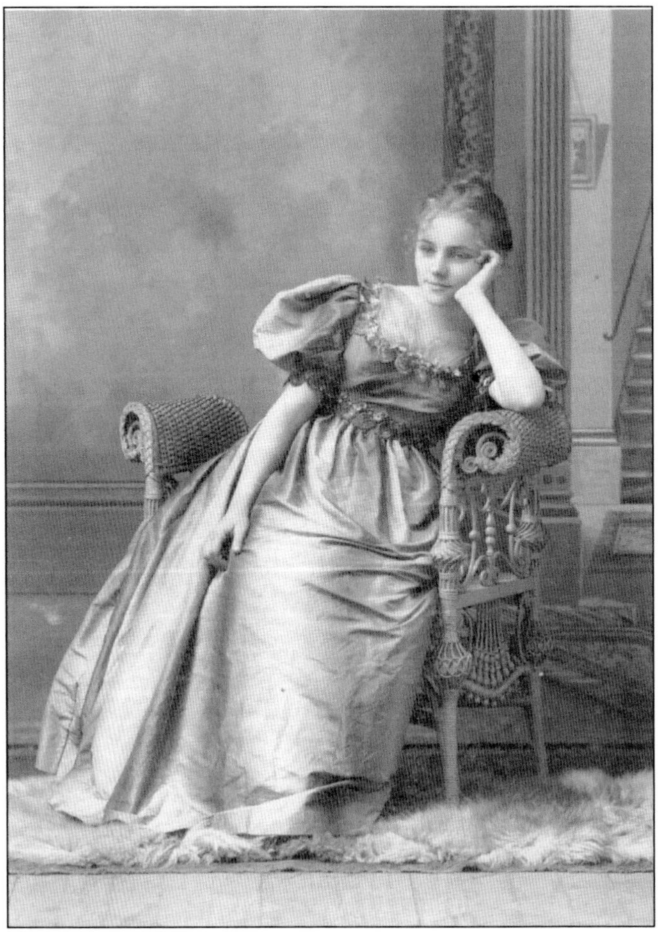

Mrs. Eddie Lee Warthen is pictured in 1898.

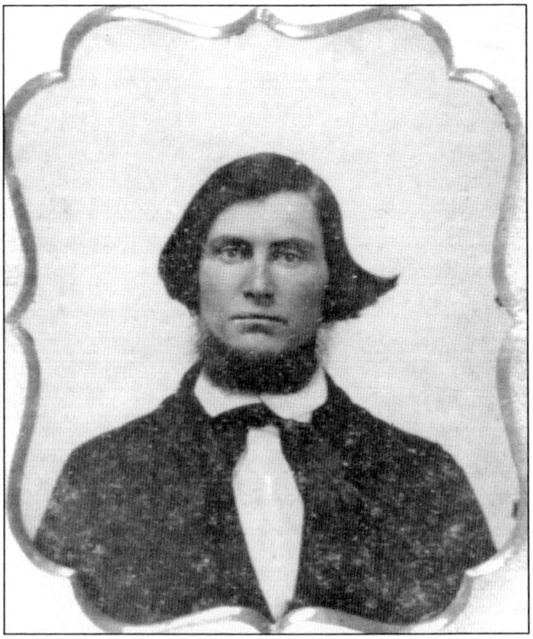

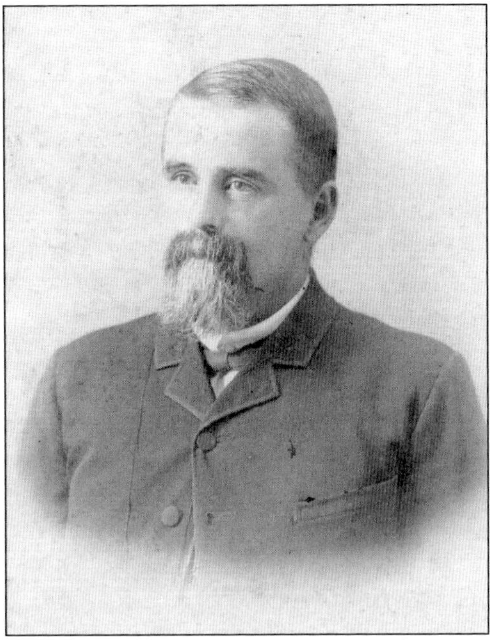

(above left) John Irwin Giles is depicted in 1862. *(above right)* Mr. O.H.P. Beall was a charter signer on the application for the Davisboro Farmers Bank, was one of the first investors of the Davisboro Cotton Oil and Guano Company, and in 1887, was a constituting member of the Davisboro Baptist Church.

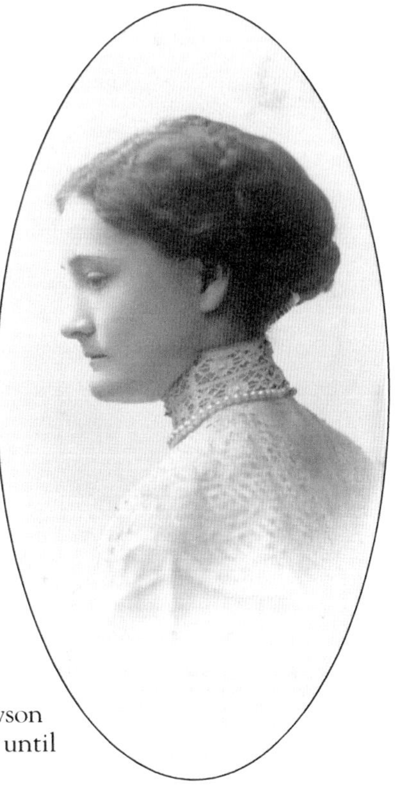

Marie Odum Hudson of Vidalia was the wife of Orran Lawson Hudson, owner of the Sandersville Coca-Cola Company, until his death in 1960.

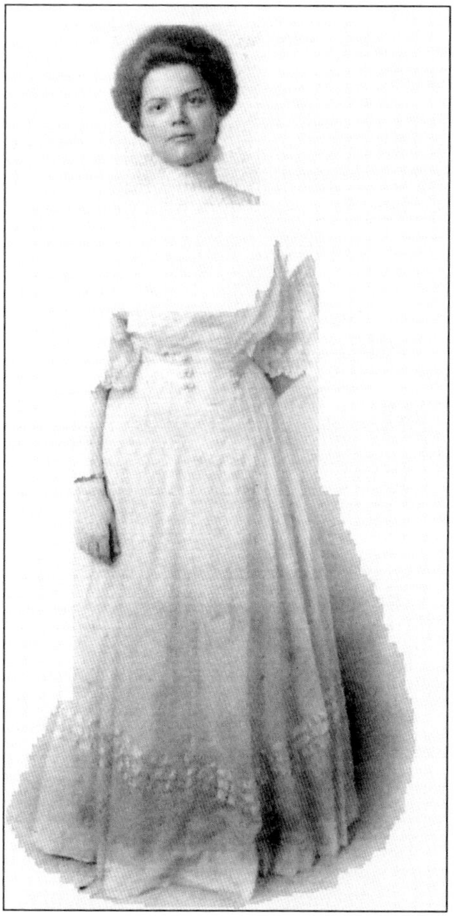

The daughter of Mattie G. Wood Smith and John English Smith Jr., Ella Smith Cooley married C. Brevard Cooley in December 1907.

Asa Duggan Lord and Mary "Mollie" Rodney Lord are pictured c.1898.

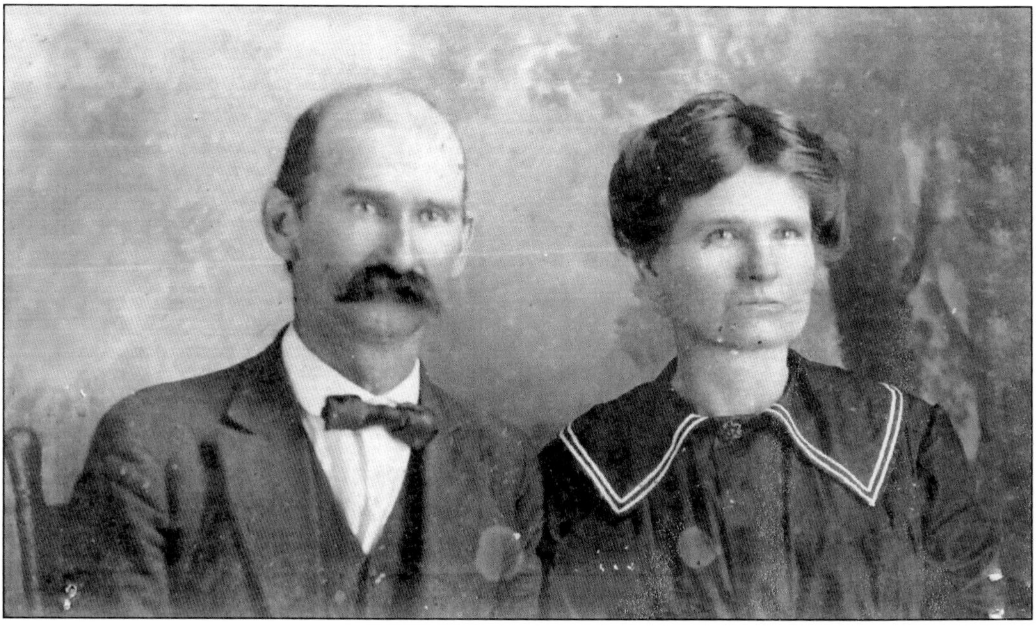

Ivey Walker Duggan was an educator in Washington and Hancock Counties and later was business manager at Shorter College in Rome, Georgia. He is shown here with his second wife, Sallie Cone Duggan.

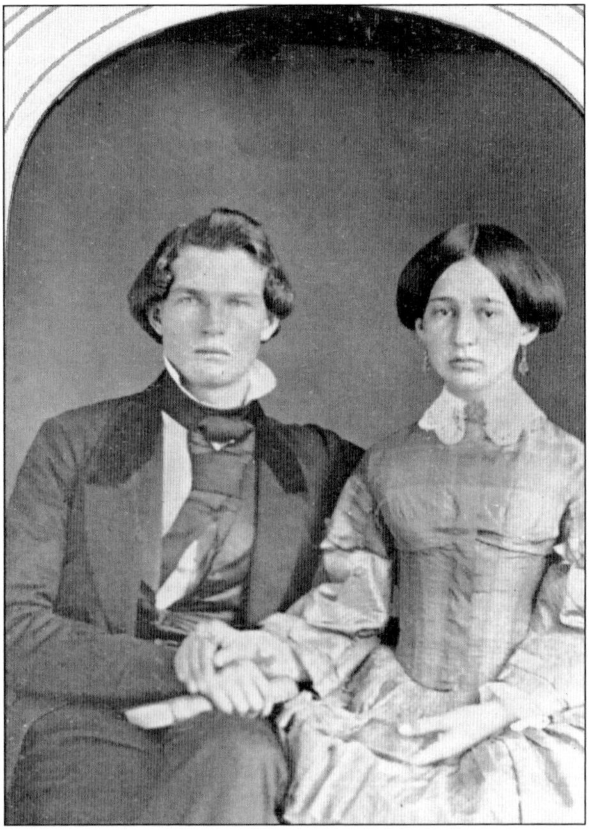

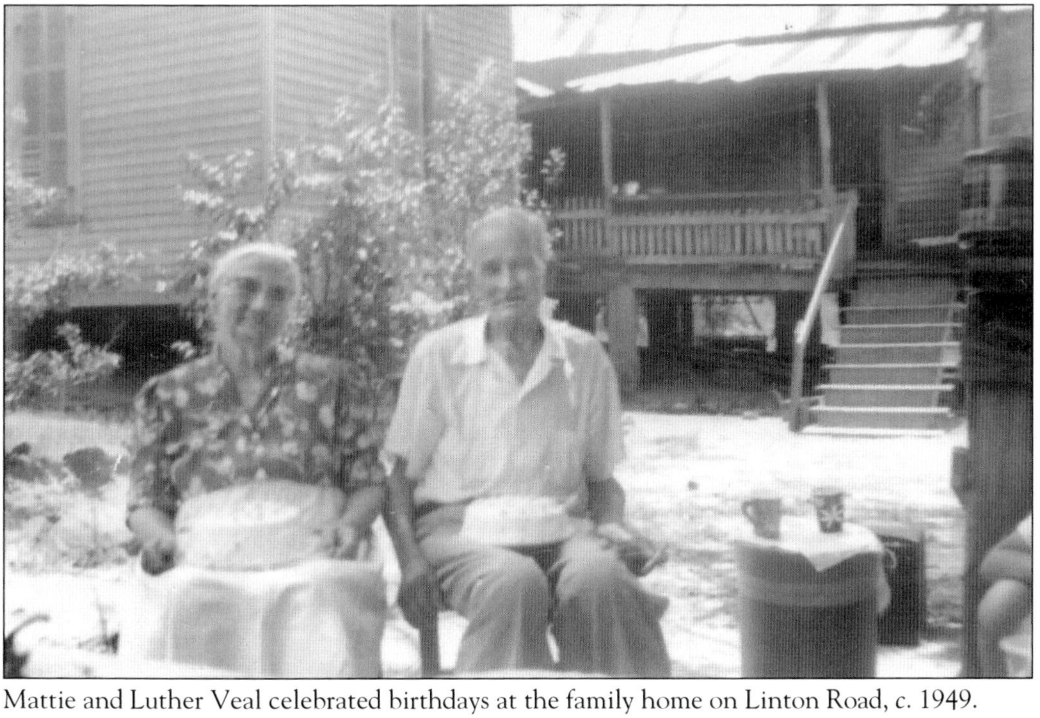

Mattie and Luther Veal celebrated birthdays at the family home on Linton Road, c. 1949.

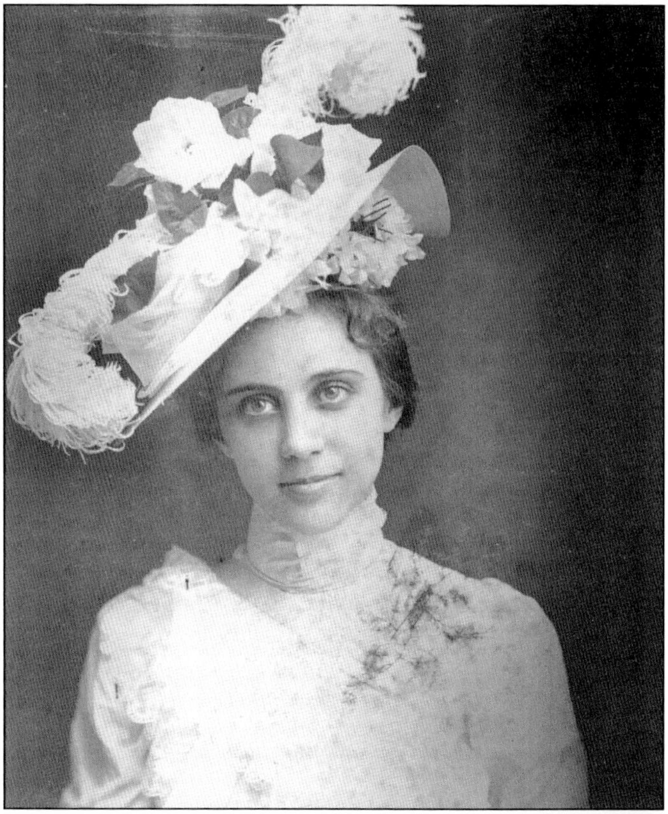

This is a fashionable Sandersville woman in the 1900s. (Georgia Archives.)

The first automobile in Tennille is believed to be this one owned by Dr. D.E. McMaster in the early 1900s. Sitting on the seat is young D.E. McMaster, and Mrs. Pauline McMaster stands next to him. (Georgia Archives.)

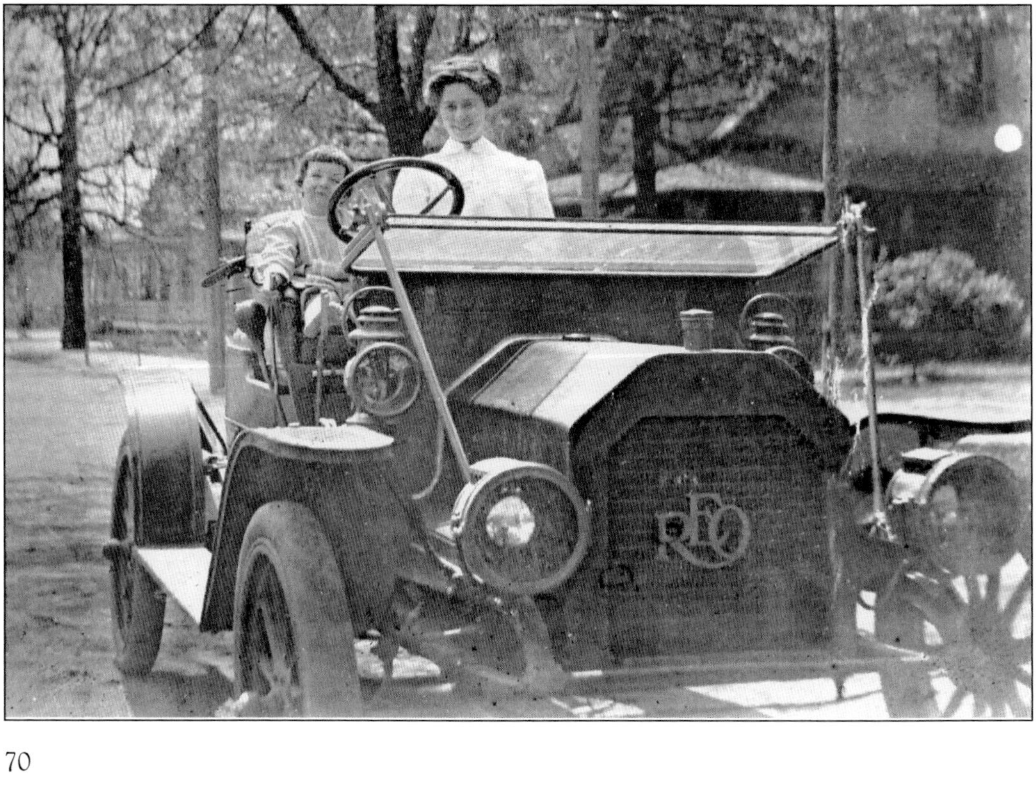

Margaret Lamb, c. 1825, is the great-great-great-grandmother of Odessie Boyd.

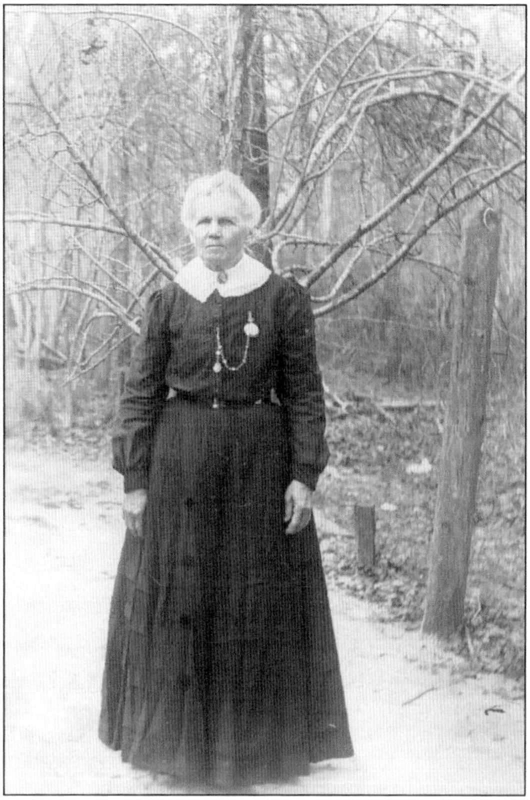

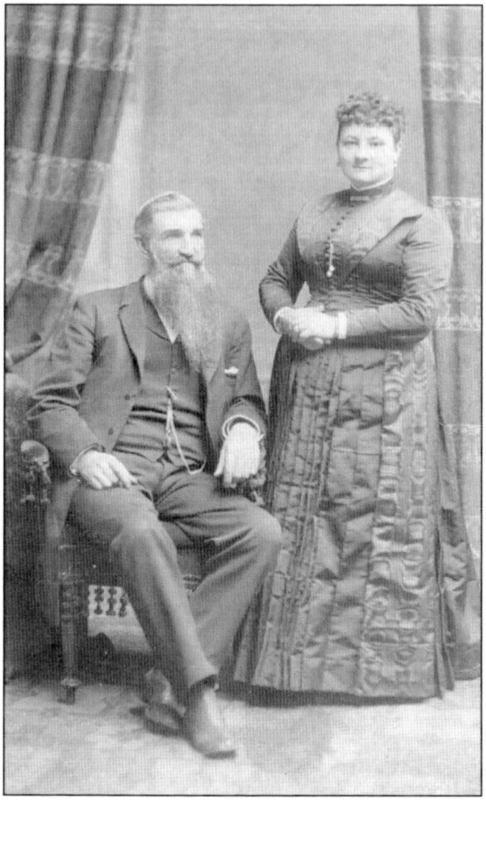

Capt. William Benjamin Francis and his wife, Leslie Inman Francis, are pictured here. Mr. Francis inherited the Francis Plantation near Davisboro in 1843 at the age of one. He served one term in the Georgia Legislature as a representative from Washington County, from 1888 to 1889.

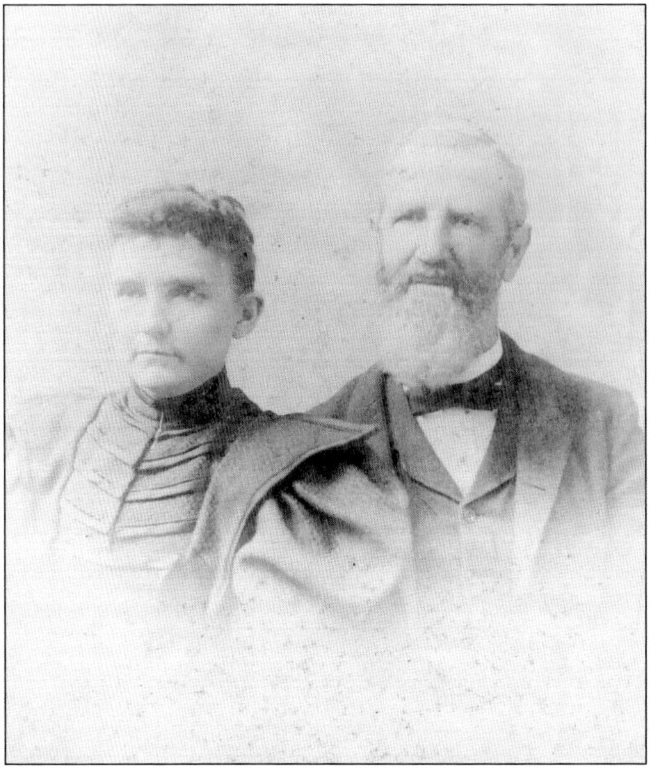

Dr. A.F. Cheatham was a physician in Davisboro in the 1880s. He and his wife were charter members of Davisboro Methodist Church in 1884. He was the great grandson of Georgia governor David Emanuel.

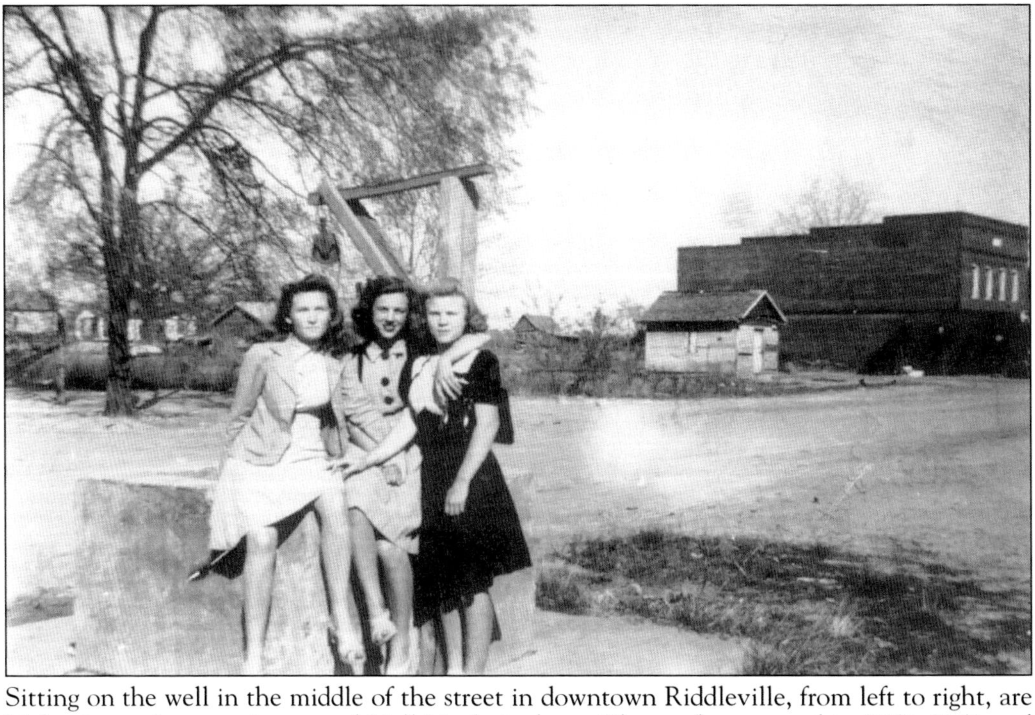

Sitting on the well in the middle of the street in downtown Riddleville, from left to right, are Mabry Jones, Jeanette Josey, and Nell Hooks Jackson. The road was paved in 1951–1952 and the well was covered up.

This family posed for the photographer in front of their log cabin home, *c.* 1875, resulting in this tin-type.

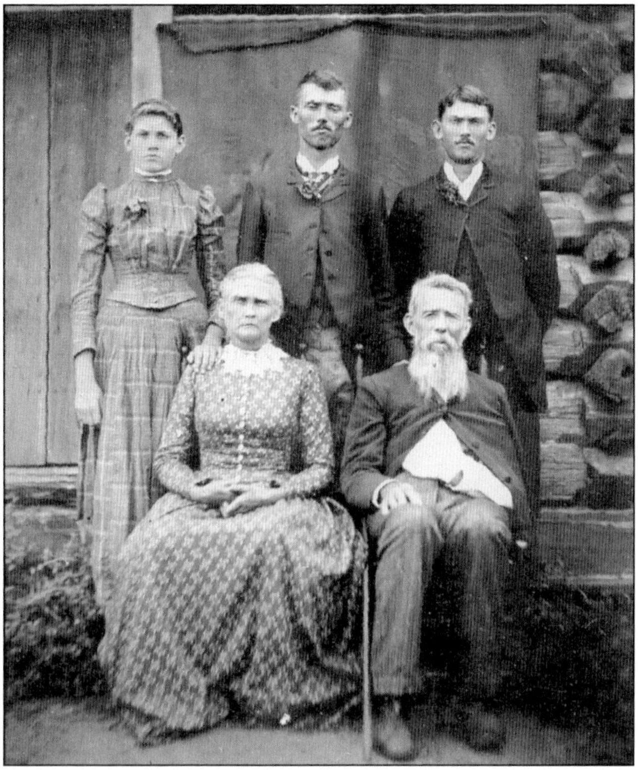

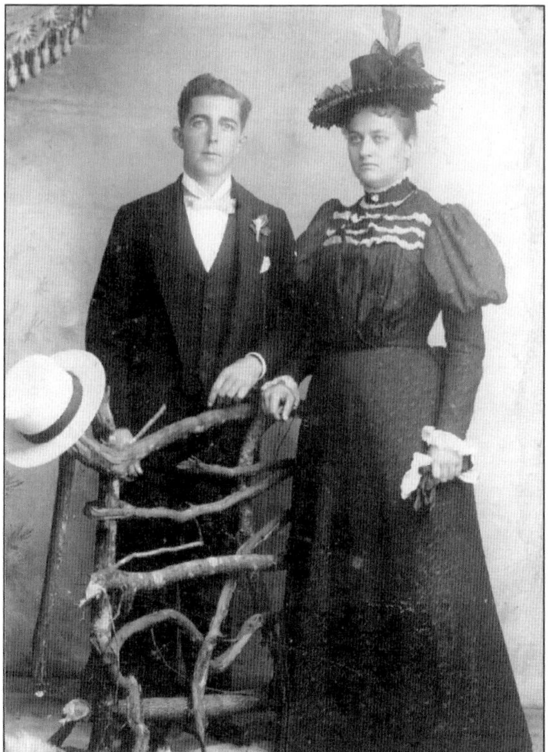

It was about 1898 when Mr. and Mrs. J.J. Palmer posed for the photographer.

Cynthia B. Cox Taylor was a fashionable teenager *c.* 1905.

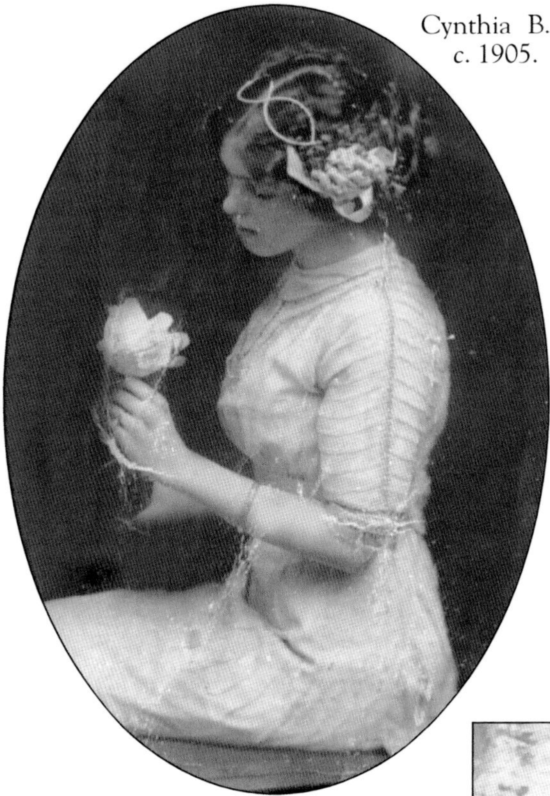

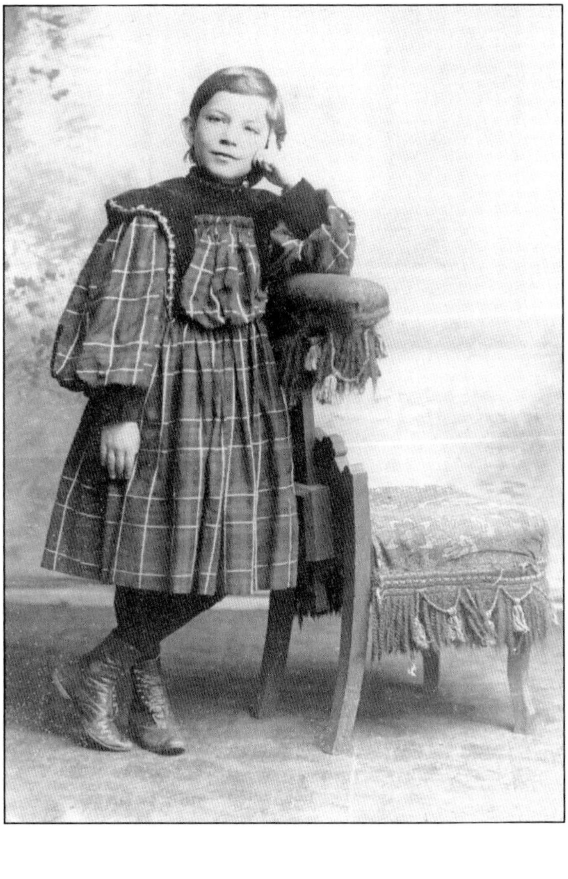

Fannie Lou Irwin later married cousin Findley Irwin.

Six

Business Times in Town and Country

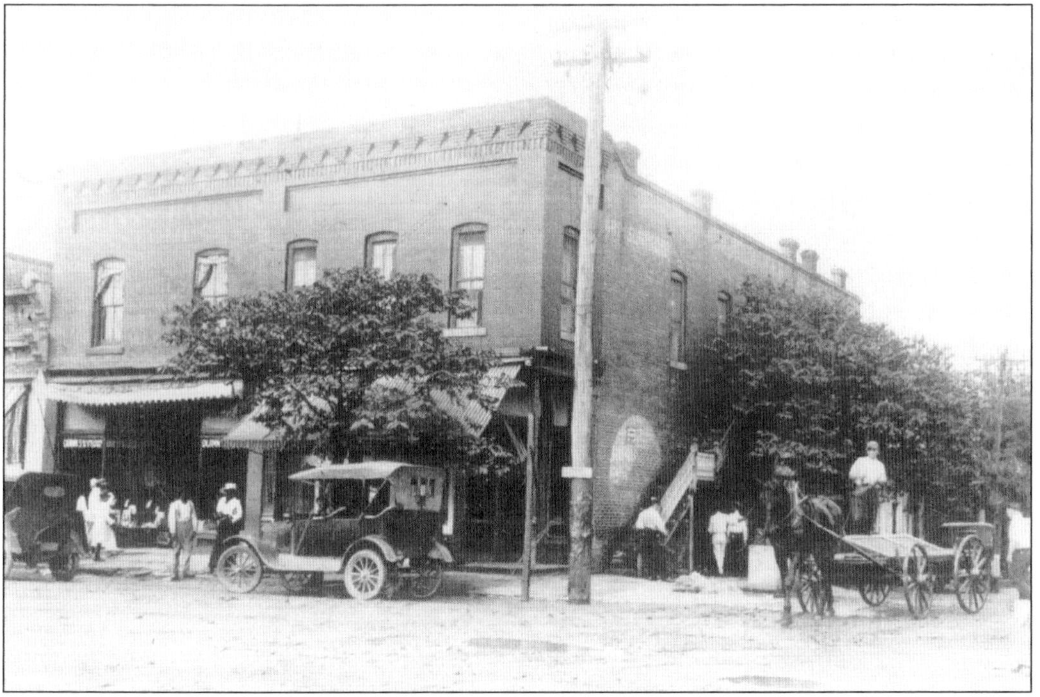

Patients of Dr. N.J. Newsom climbed the stairs to the right of West Drug Store to reach his second floor office, *c.* 1910. West Drug continues to occupy this site on the corner of North Harris and East Haynes Streets.

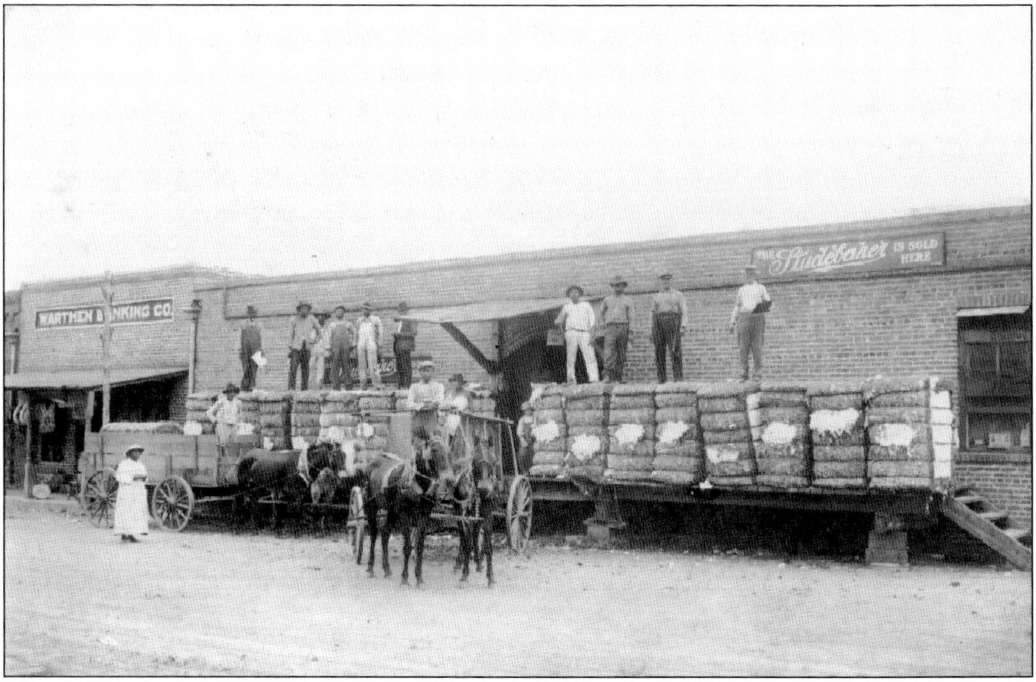

This c. 1910 photo was taken at the Cotton Warehouse in Warthen. It burned in the 1930s, but the Warthen Banking Company building to the left is still in existence. One of the men in the wagons is thought to be Mr. Corley Duggan.

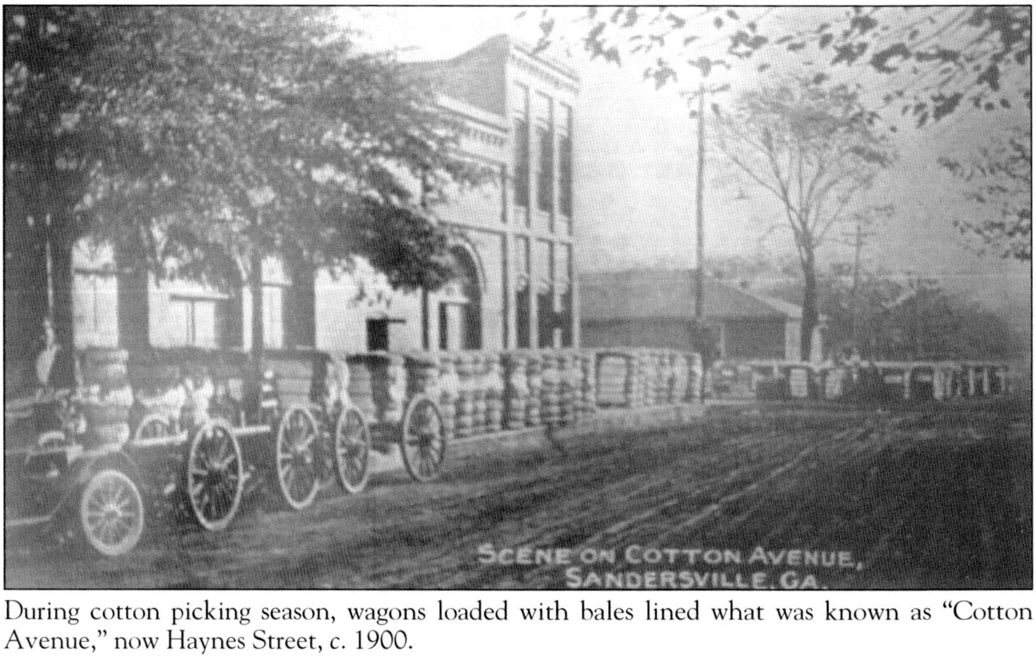

During cotton picking season, wagons loaded with bales lined what was known as "Cotton Avenue," now Haynes Street, c. 1900.

The Cohen Company Dry Goods Store was on the south side of the courthouse square. In this c. 1900 photo, the woman in the dark skirt is Gabrella Janet Roughton, daughter of Capt. George Washington Roughton.

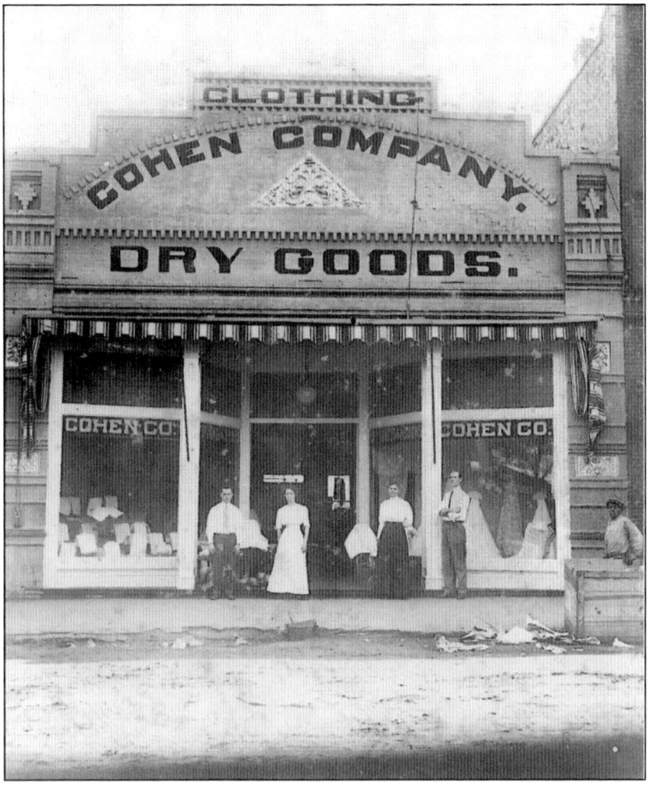

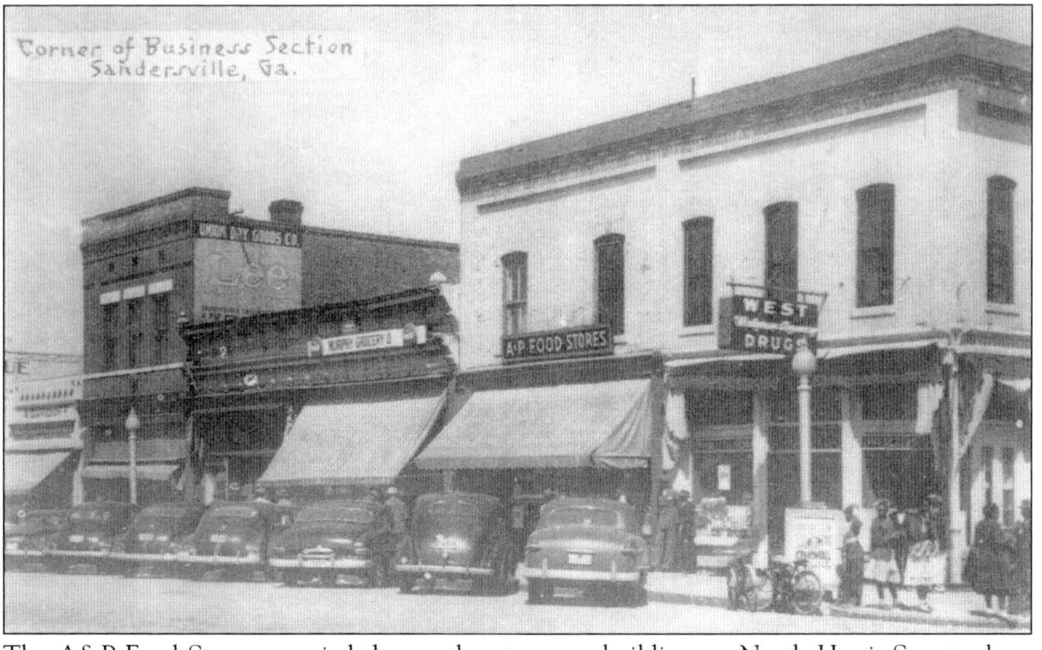

The A&P Food Store occupied the northeast corner building on North Harris Street, along with West Drug Store, c. 1940. Around 1948, A&P moved, and McMaster's Hardware moved into the space. When McMaster's left, West expanded into the whole building. The Union Dry Goods building was removed in 1976 and a small downtown park created in the space.

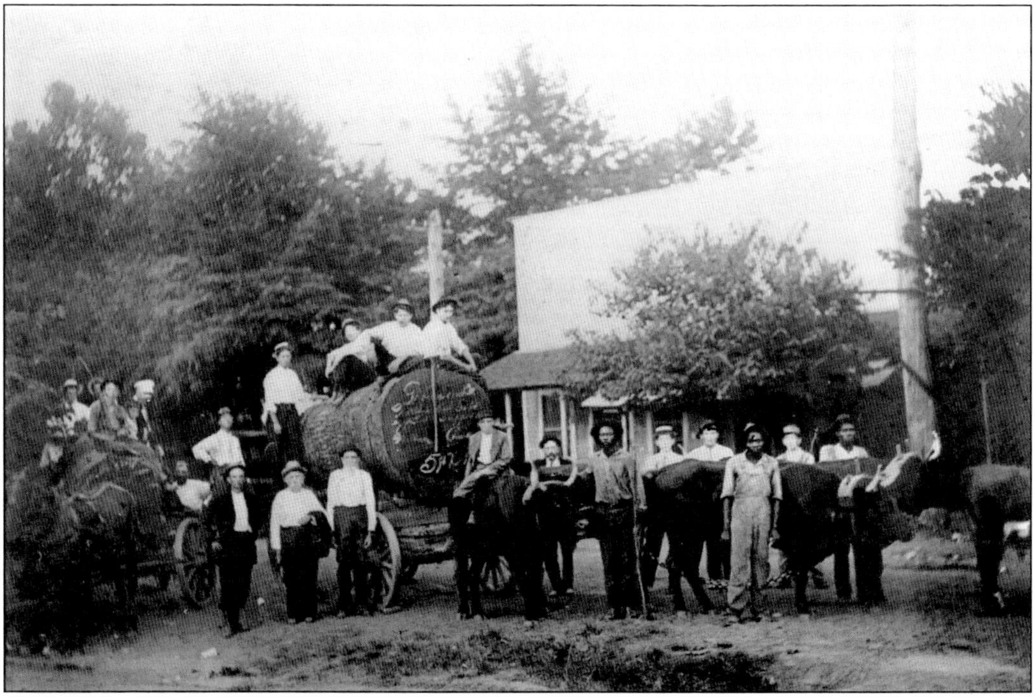

Just one tremendous oak log filled this timber wagon in 1905. There were eight oxen pulling the wagon.

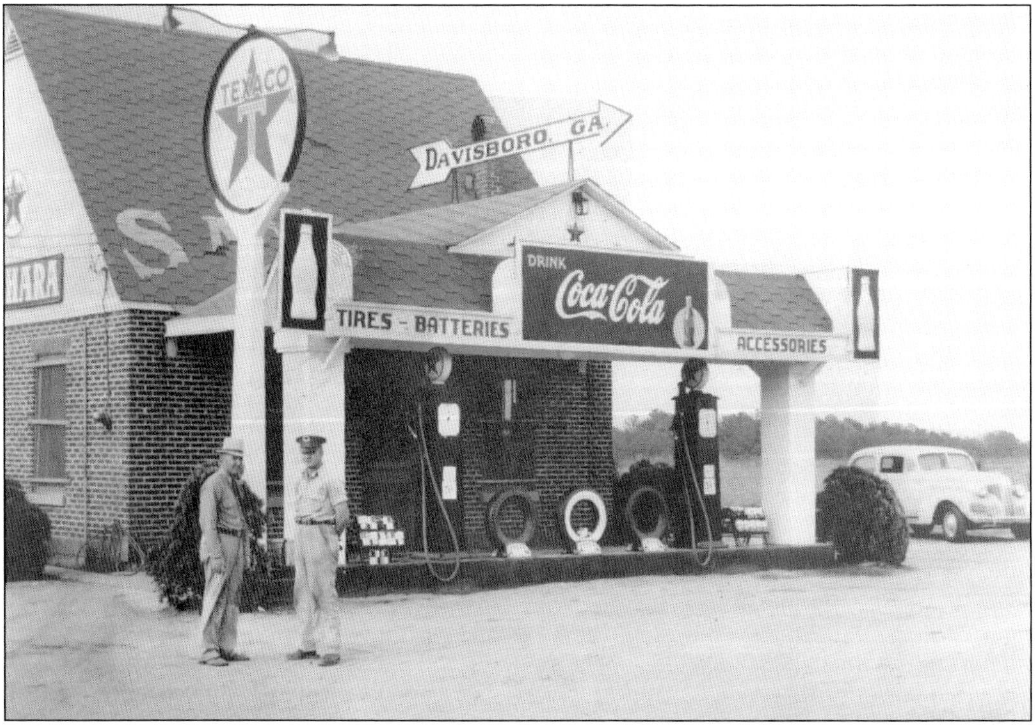

Bobby Lee Brown and Cordy Frances stand in front of the Sahara Station on Highway 24 in Davisboro, c. 1940.

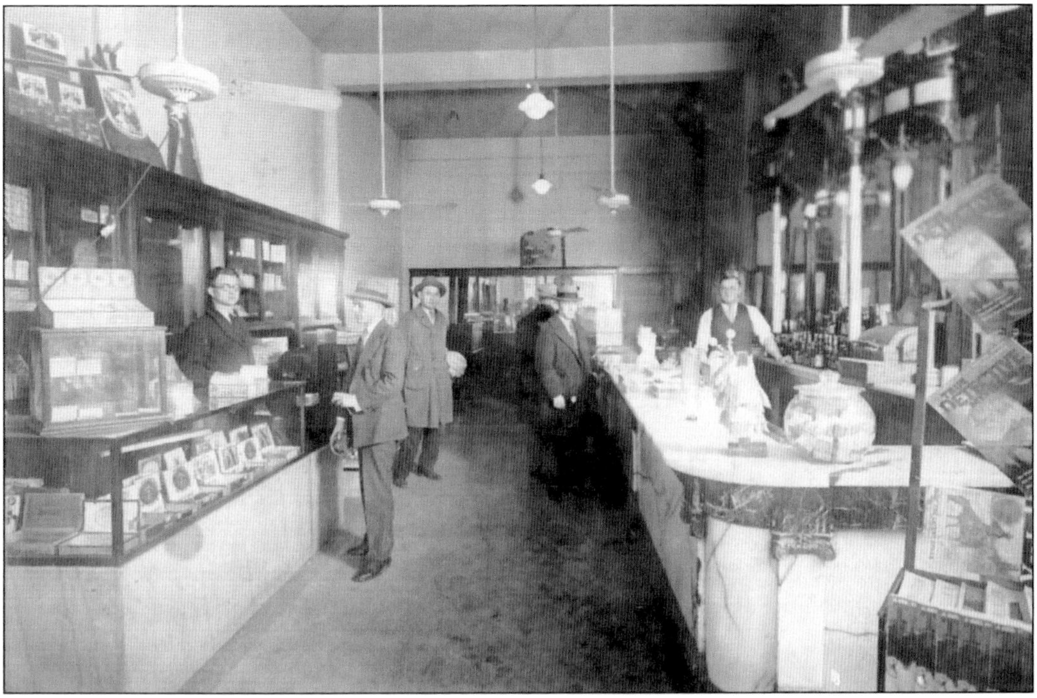

Cigars were sold from one counter and ice cream sodas from the other side of a local drug store.

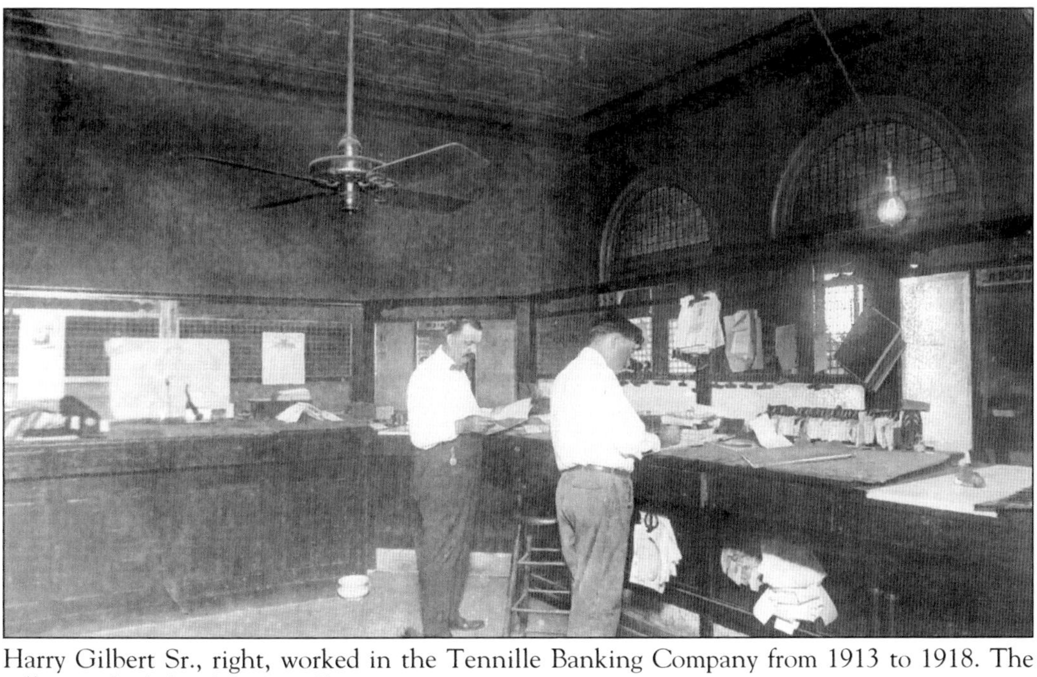

Harry Gilbert Sr., right, worked in the Tennille Banking Company from 1913 to 1918. The teller on the left is Mr. Arnell.

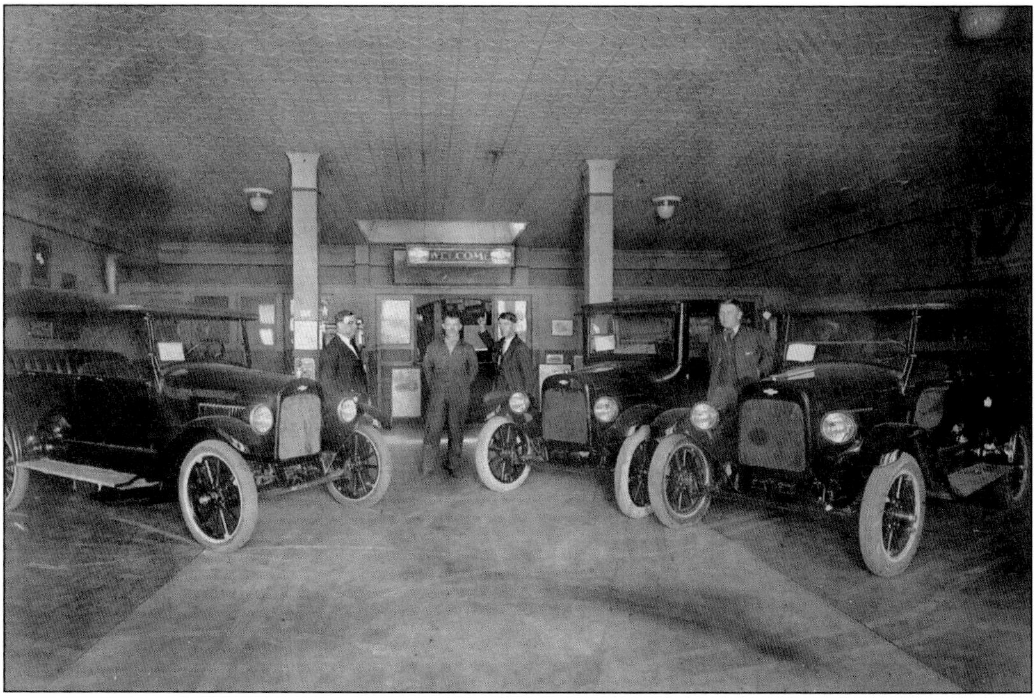

Alex C. Gilmore, Edgar Rawlings, George T. Powers, and Collins Jones sold cars at the Gilmore Auto Company.

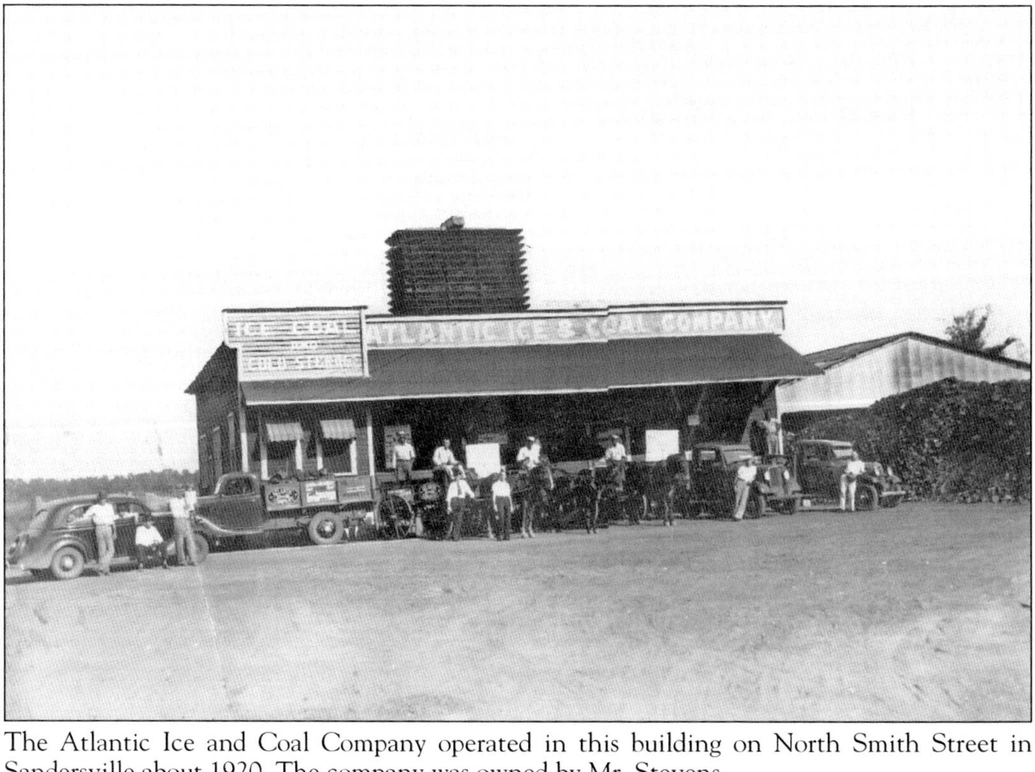

The Atlantic Ice and Coal Company operated in this building on North Smith Street in Sandersville about 1920. The company was owned by Mr. Stevens.

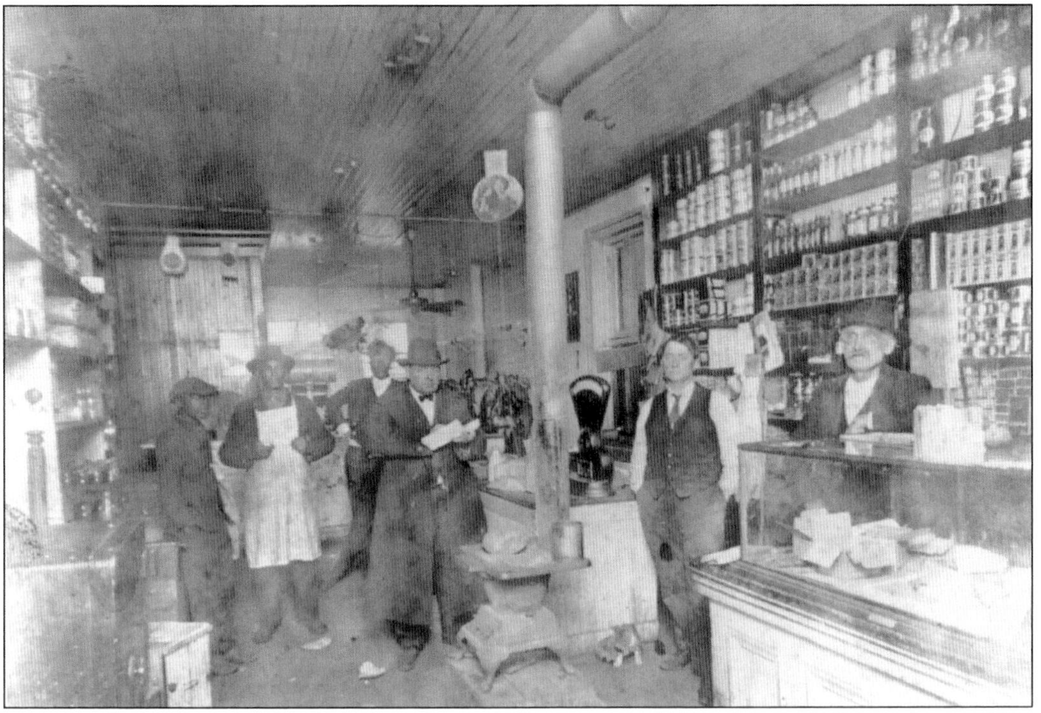

Working at Pittman's Store in 1920 were Bennie Pittman (second from right) and Granddad John Poole (right) as identified by Sol Pittman. Bennie was his father and John was his mother's father.

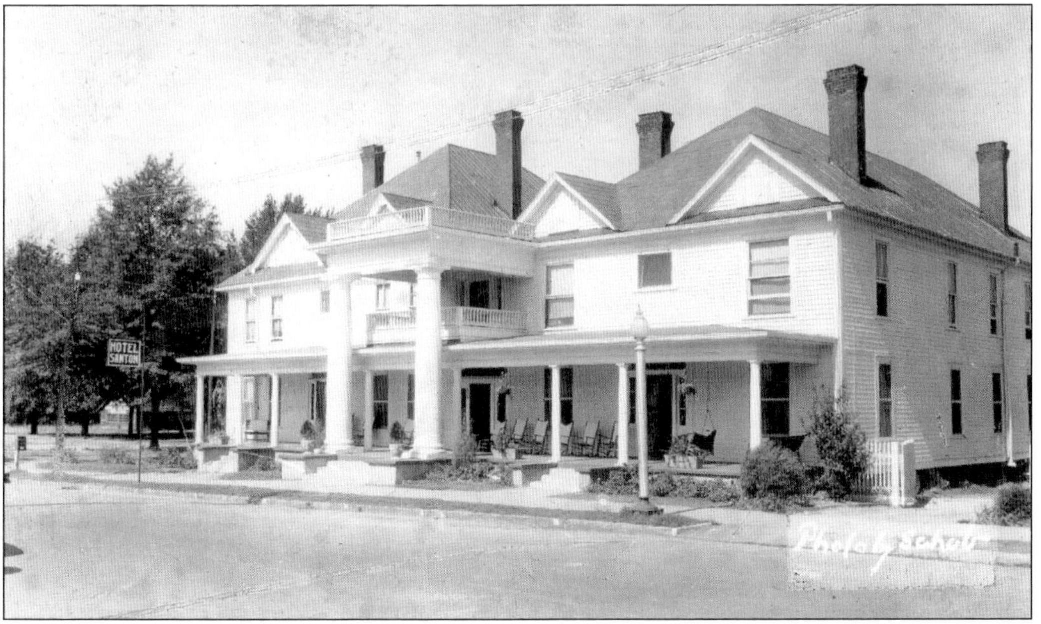

After remodeling in the 1930s or 1940s, the Victorian porches were removed from the Santon Hotel and replaced with this more classical entrance. By 1952, the building, located on the corner of South Harris and West Church Streets, had closed and been torn down for Miller's, the county's first supermarket. Now the site holds Citizens Bank.

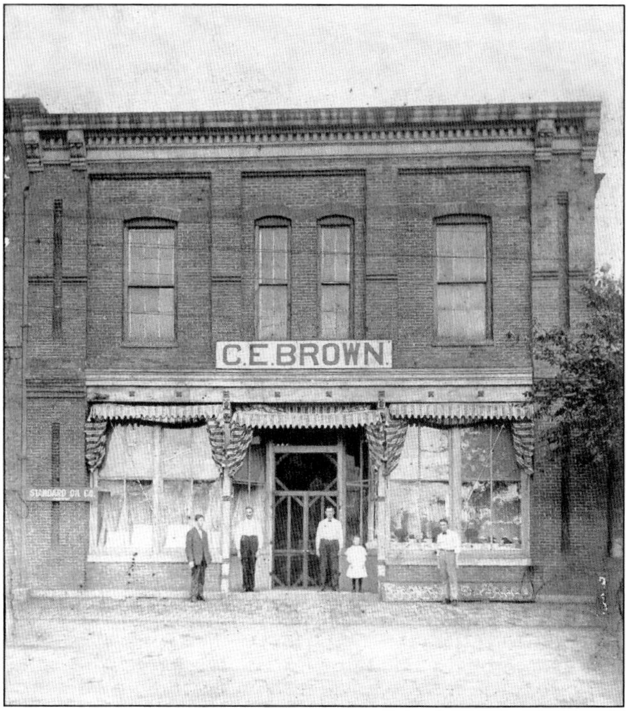

The C.E. Brown General Merchandise Store on the square in Tennille was a source of supplies for customers. This 1902 photo shows Newt Hall standing second from left. (Georgia Archives.)

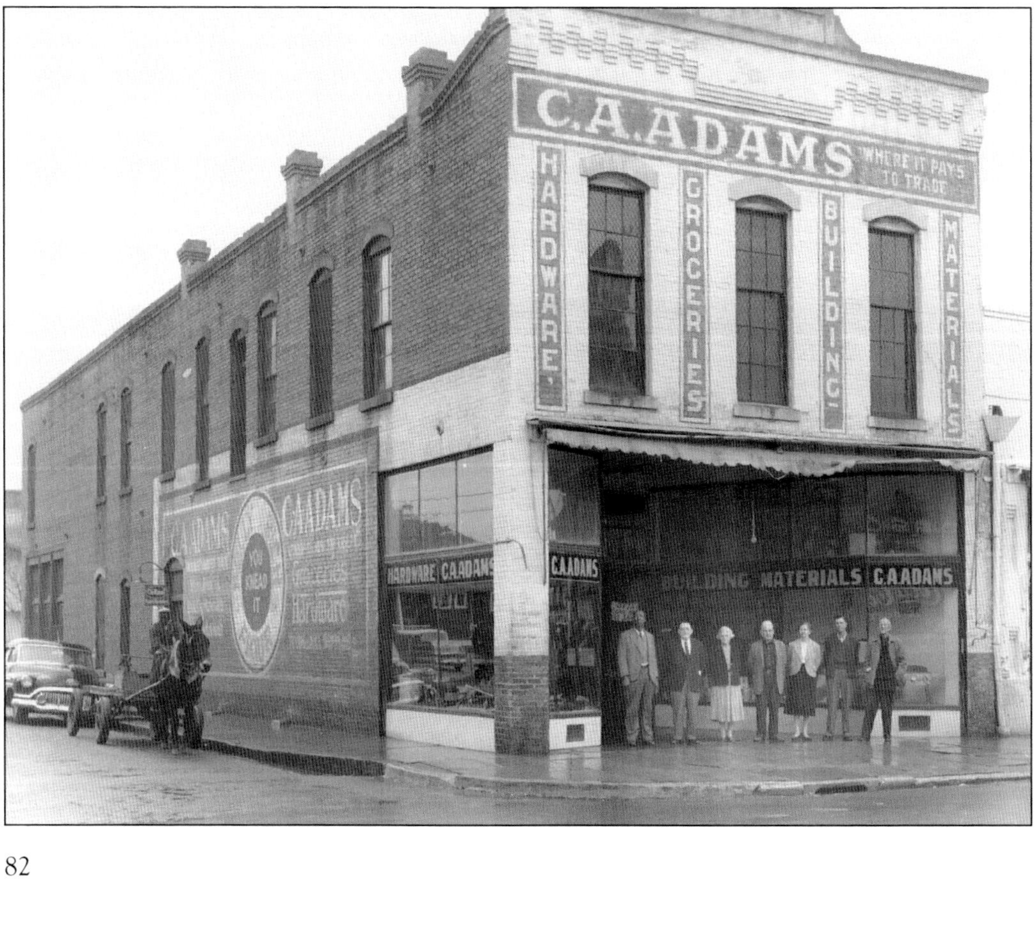

In the 1950s, C.A. Adams operated a general merchandise and hardware store on the corner of North Harris and Gilmore Streets. From left to right are James Curry Jr., C.A. Adams Jr., Lillie Mae Smith Irwin, Buford Grimes and his wife Eunice Sheppard Grimes, Rafus Garner, and William Gainer Summerlin.

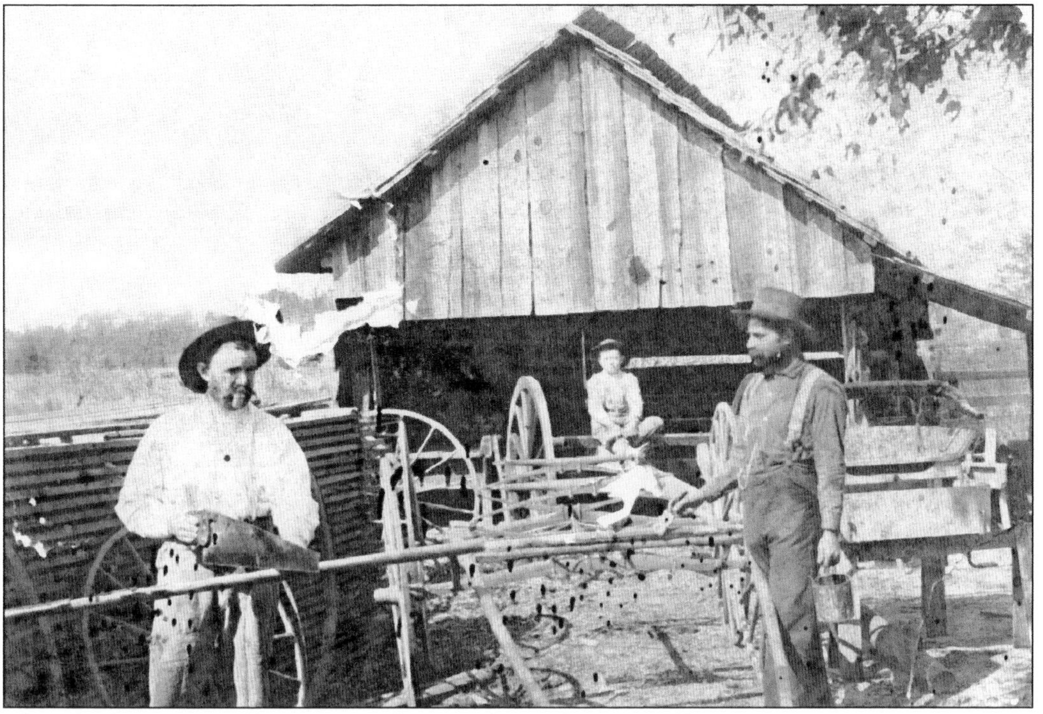

The Charles H. Womble Carriage Shop was located in Tennille in 1900.

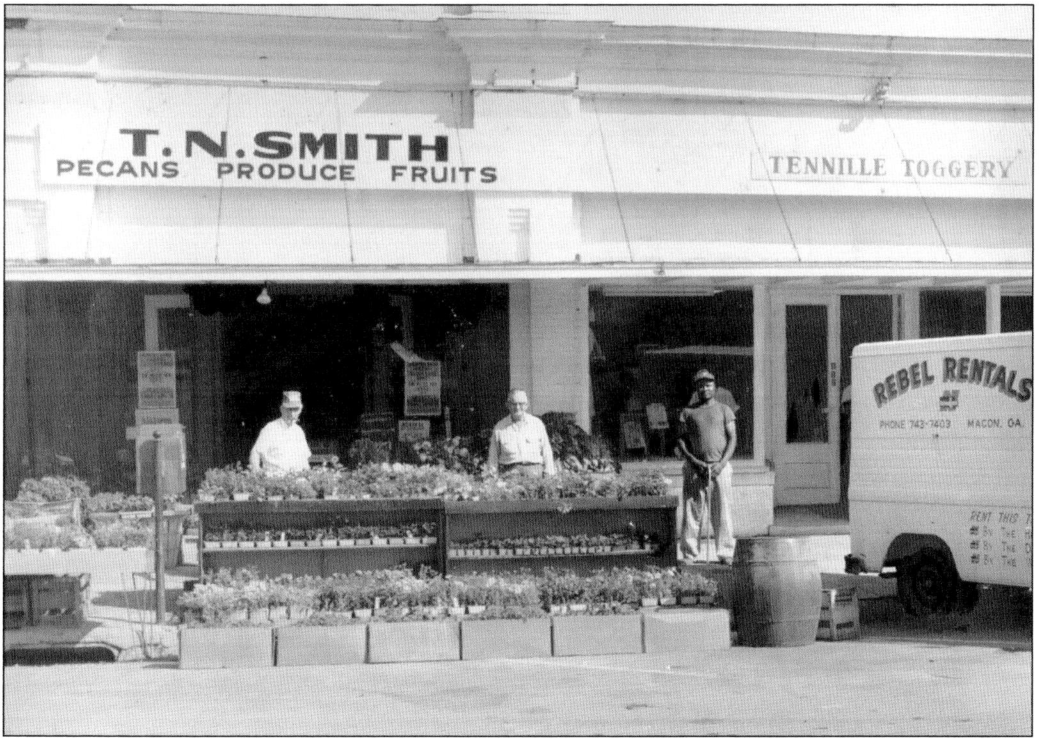

On the Tennille square, the T.N. Smith store sold produce and gardening plants. (Georgia Archives.)

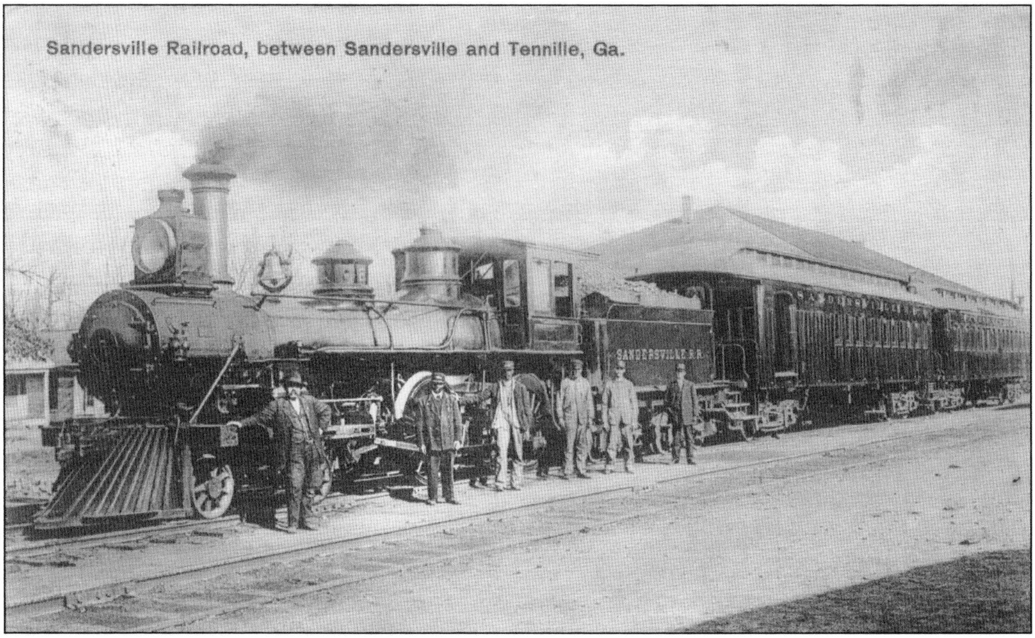

This postcard, dated August 1911, shows the Sandersville Railroad train, which ran between Sandersville and Tennille.

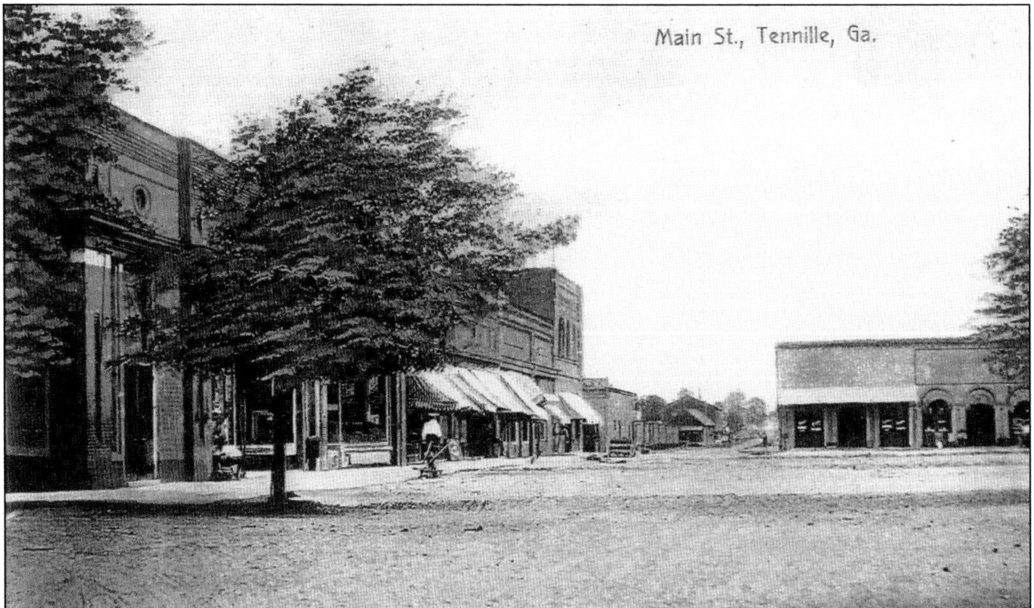

In this view of Main Street in downtown Tennille, c. 1906, the building on the right housed Tennille Banking Company and a grocery.

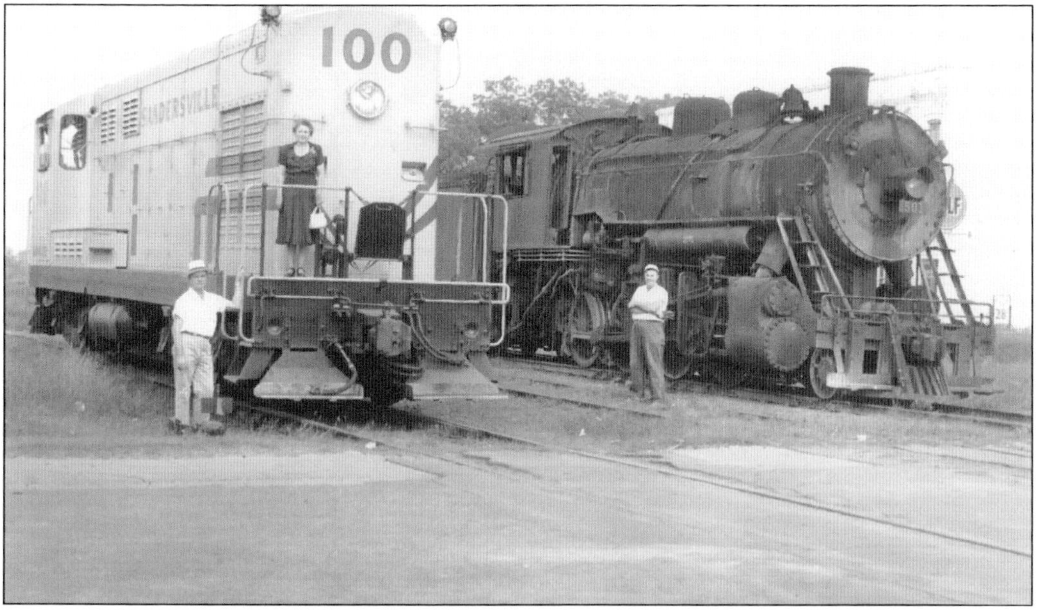

In September 1953, Sandersville Railroad welcomed the first diesel locomotive, shown on the left. Posing with the engine, from left to right, are Herbert Blackburn, general manager; Rosa M. Tarbutton; and Clay Brett, conductor. A steam locomotive is on the right.

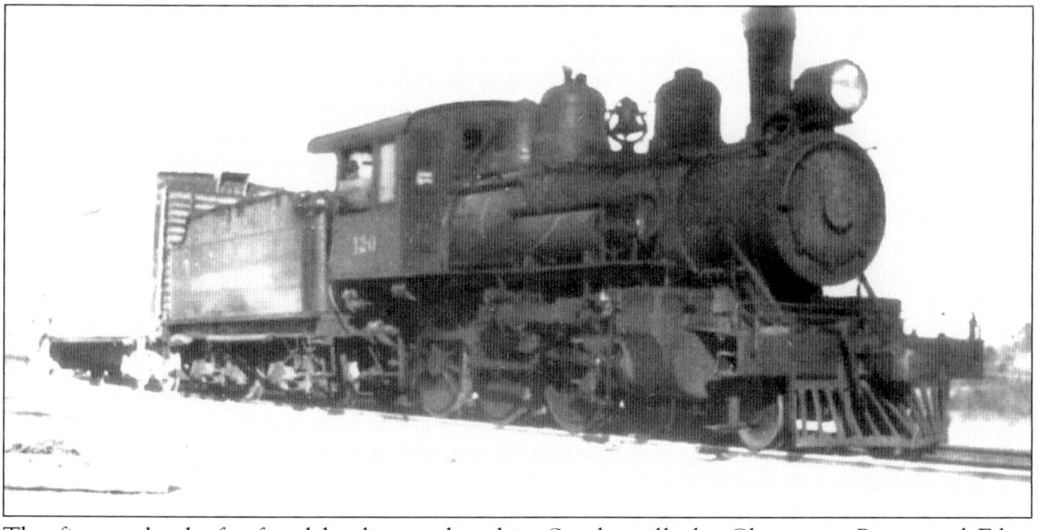

The first carload of refined kaolin produced in Sandersville by Champion Paper and Fiber Company left on this train in December 1938.

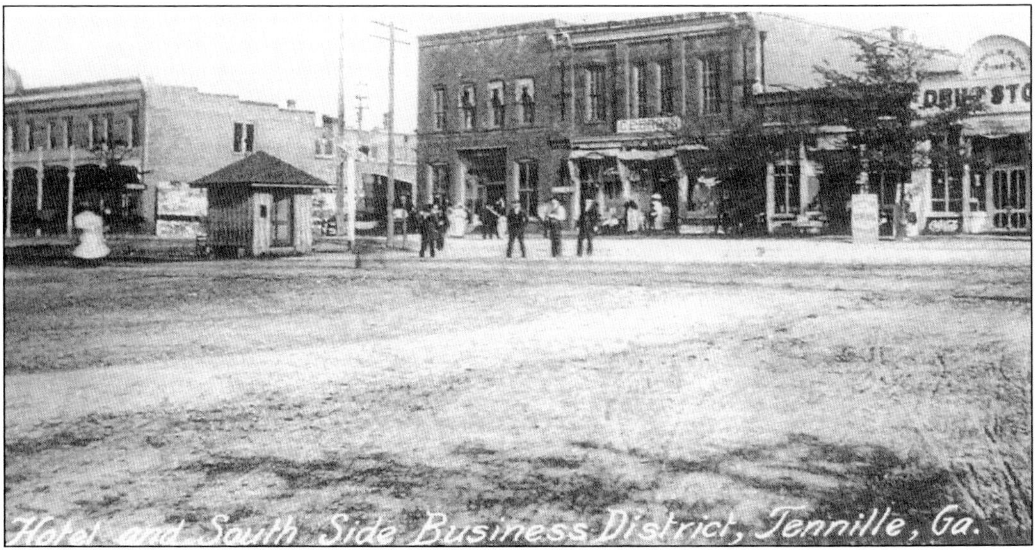

Visible are the Pritchard Hotel, left, and the south side of the Tennille Business District. Some of the buildings are still in use today.

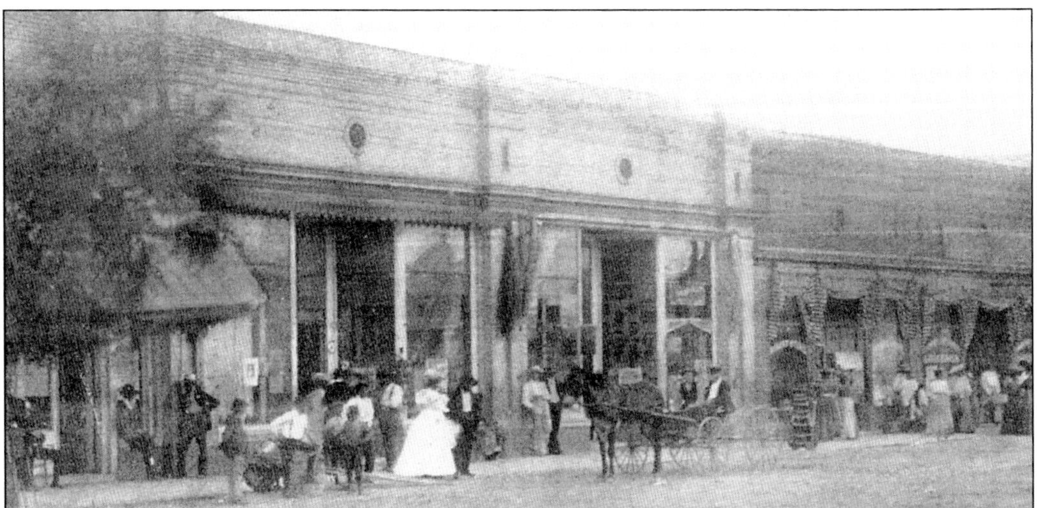

Little structural change has happened since this 1906 photo of downtown Tennille except the fashions, the methods of conveyance, and the paved streets.

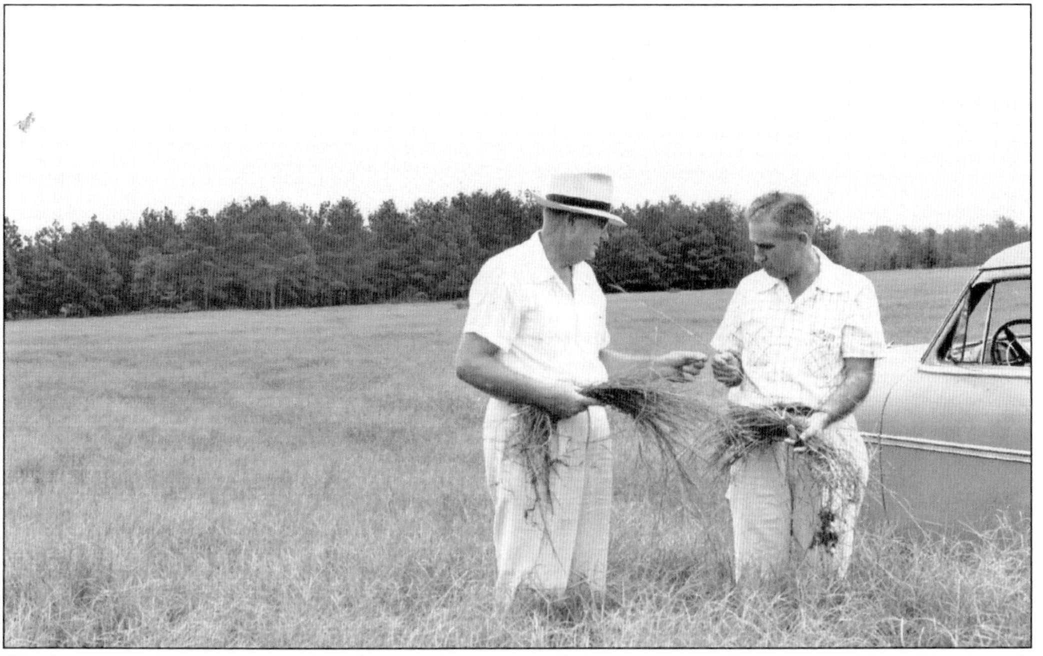

Washington County agent Sanders G. Mercer and district agriculture agent E.C. Westbrook examine Coastal Bermuda grass on J.C. Archer's farm in 1953.

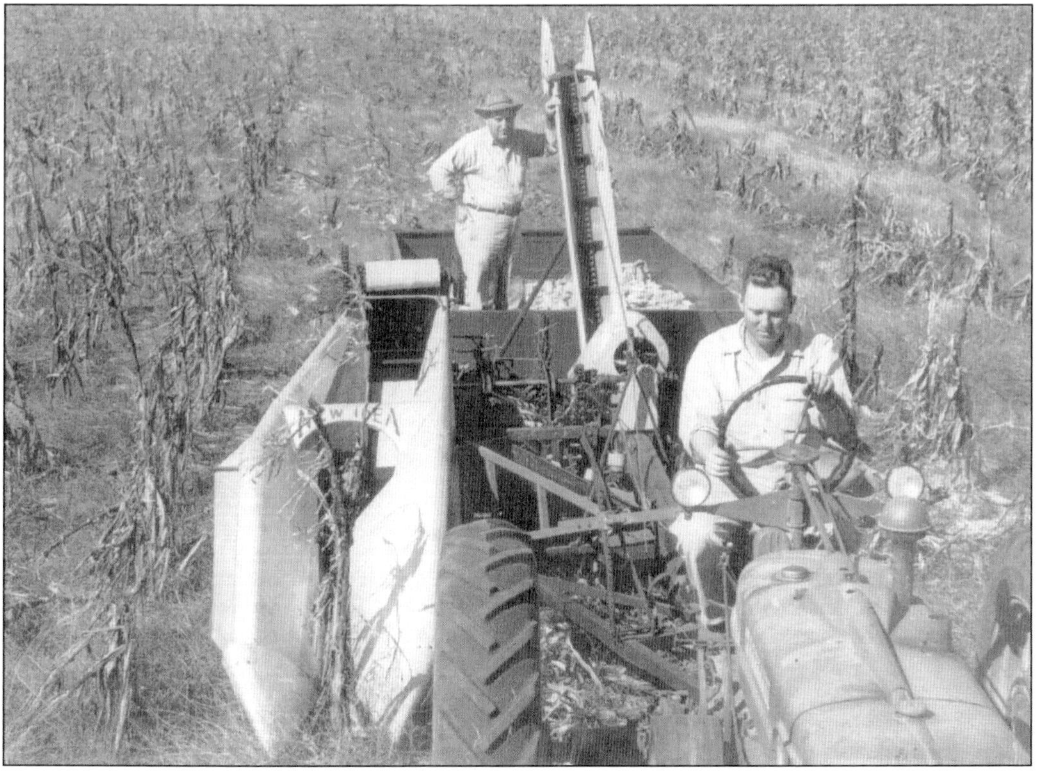

J.W. Hitchcock drives the tractor while H.I. Elton guides the ears of corn into the wagon, c. 1950.

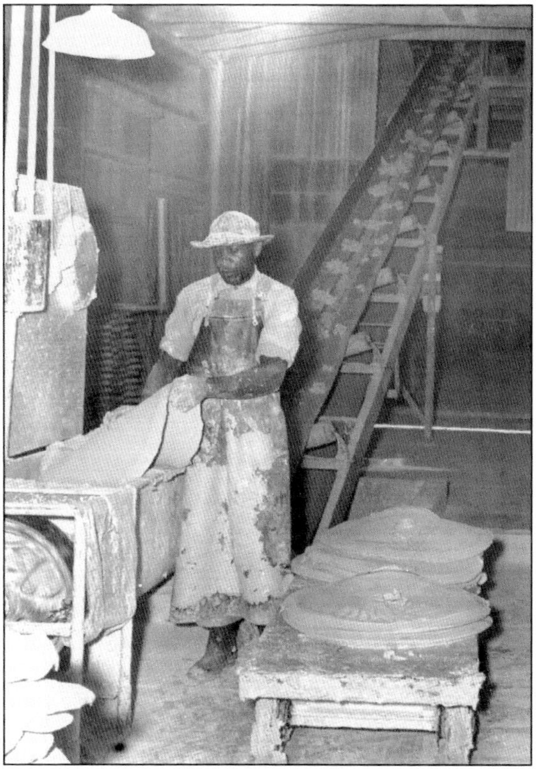

Slurry kaolin was pressed into cakes, which were then fed into a rotary dryer and pulverized for bagging and shipping to the customer, as shown here, *c.* 1950.

When Hubert Tanner had to go to the hospital just as his lupine was ready to cut, his neighbors brought in four combines, enough trucks, and help, saving his crop. Neighbors included Jimmy Smith, Sweetpea Rhodes, Claude Brower, Makey Brower, Allen Veal, L.W. Smith Jr., Ray Anderson, William Vaughn, Gene Davis, Joe Rheney, J.M. Kent, and T.N. Smith.

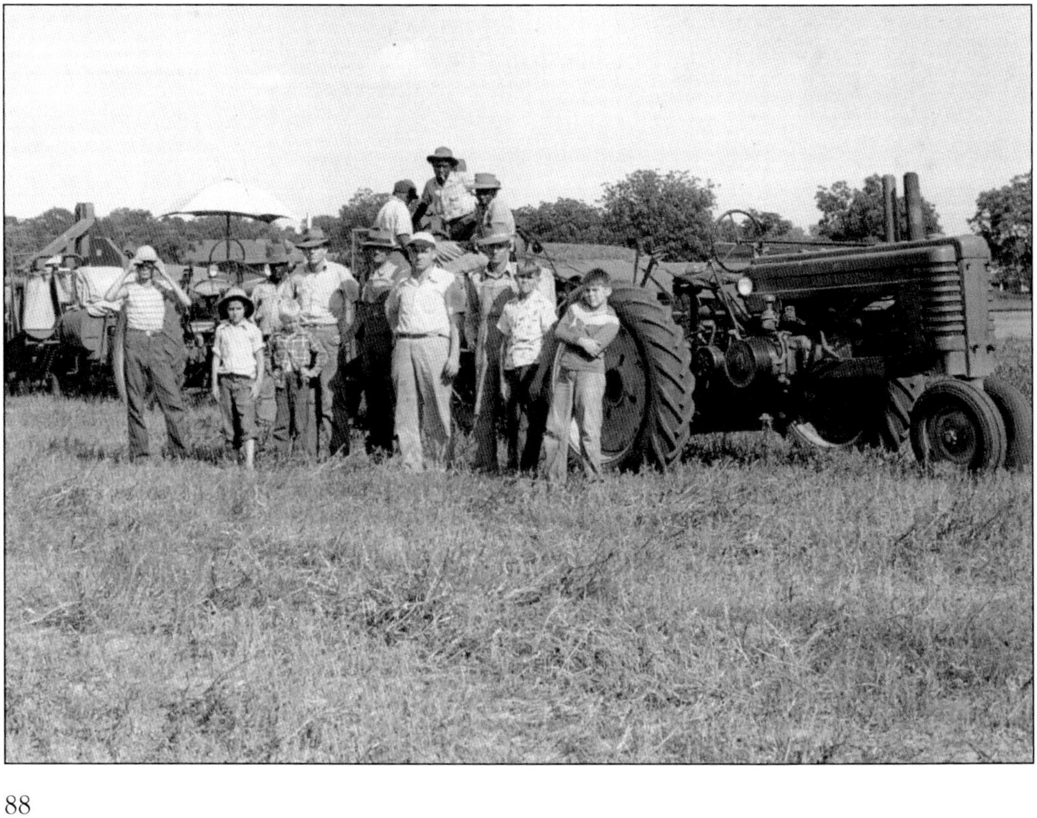

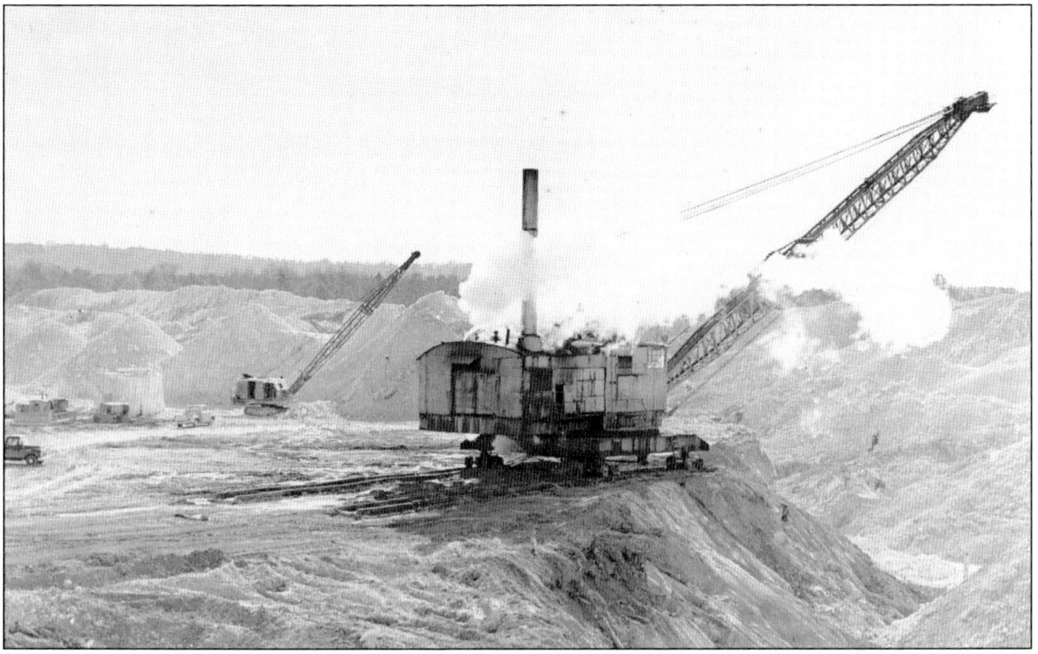

The steam dragline removed the top soil (overburden) from the deposits of clay at a Thiele Kaolin Company mine. The dragline was first powered by coal, which was later changed to oil. This unit was bought second-hand in the 1950s. Kaolin became a major industry in the area in the 1930s. (Georgia Archives.)

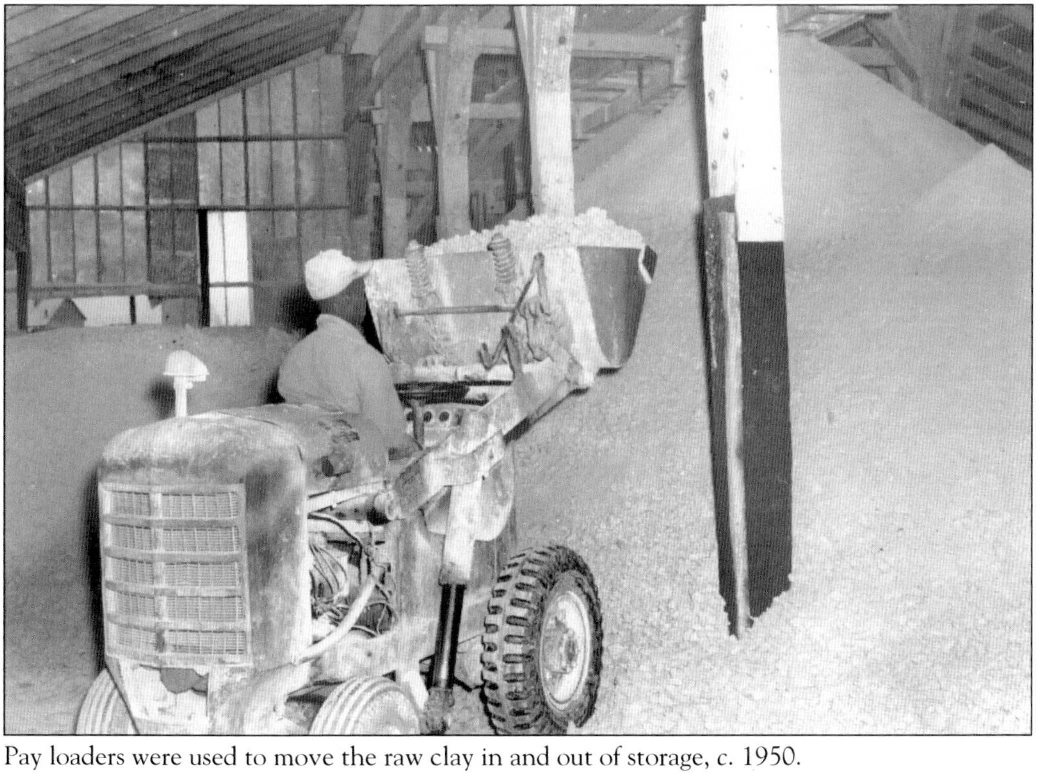

Pay loaders were used to move the raw clay in and out of storage, c. 1950.

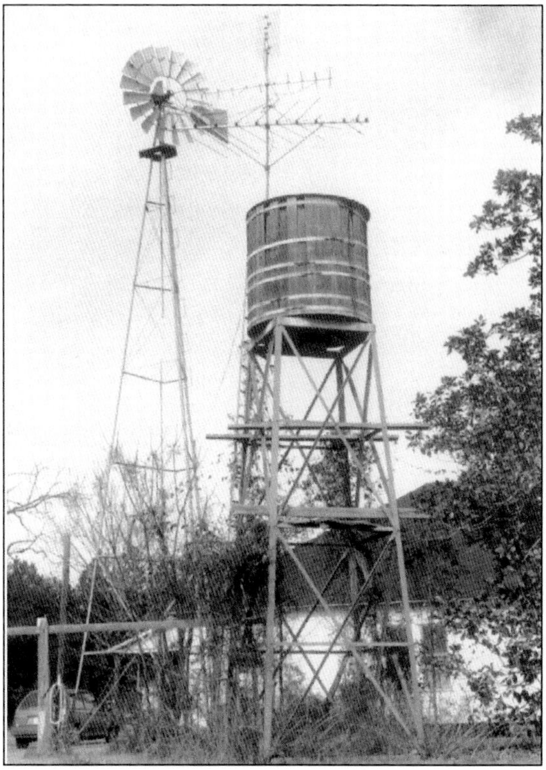

The windmill pumped the water from the well up into the storage tank, where it was stored until needed by the farmer and his household. This tank and windmill were on Fred Chamber's farm in Deepstep.

In the fall, when the sugar cane was ready, it was gathered and then fed into a grinder, powered by a mule walking in a circle. The cane juice was collected in a vessel and cooked into cane syrup. This image was taken *c.* 1940.

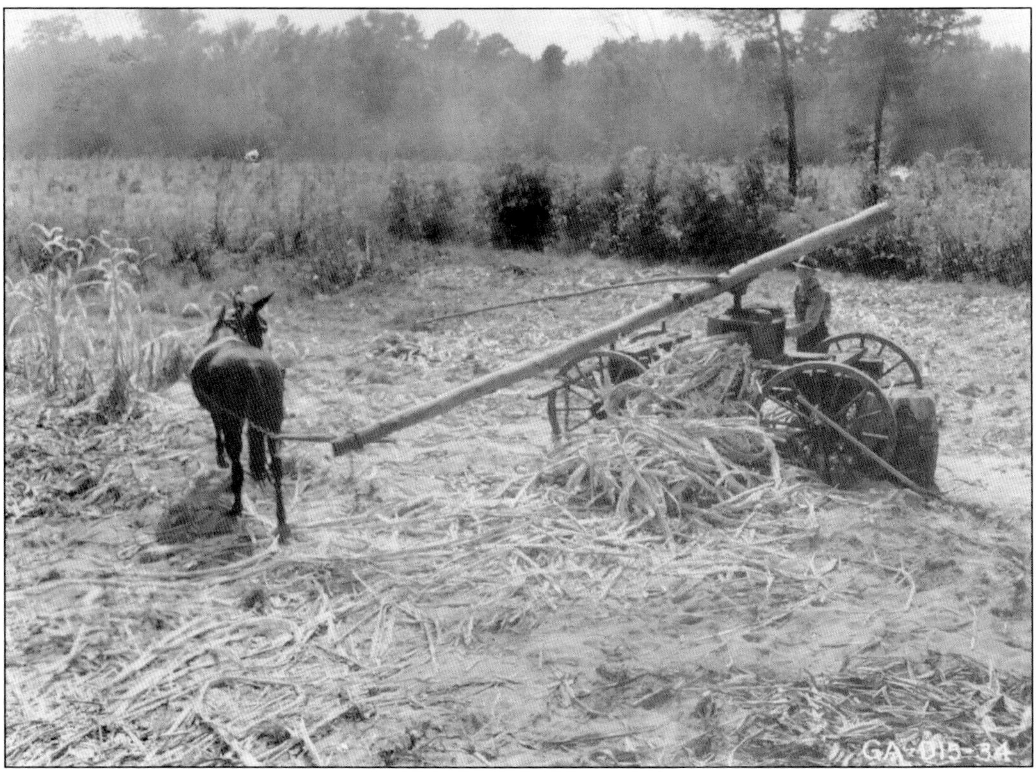

Carlus H. Cooper delivered ice in this 1929 truck.

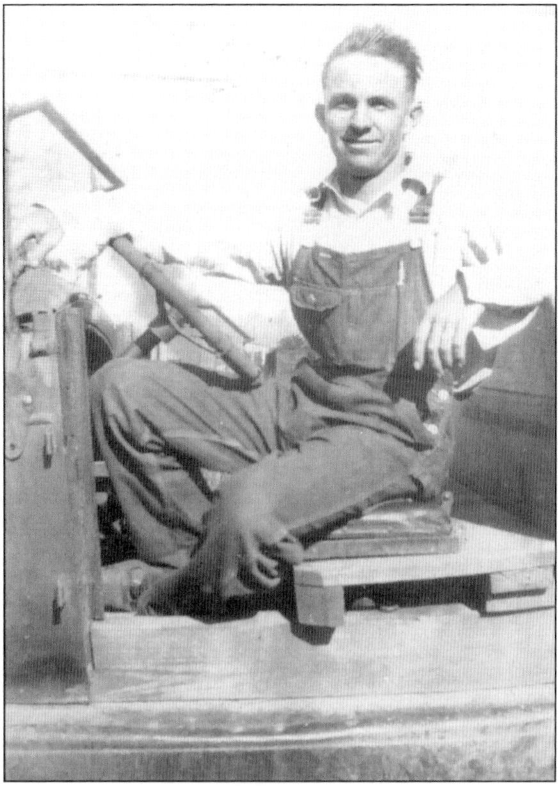

In 1938, Cleve Bivings Miller Sr. opened S&T Flour and Feed Company at 120 South Harris Street next to the Pastime Theatre. Later, it became Miller's Feed and Seed, operated by brothers Cleve B. Miller Jr. and Edward Pless Miller, who opened the first supermarket when they moved into a modern brick building on the corner of South Harris and Church Streets. The store closed and the building was razed in the 1990s.

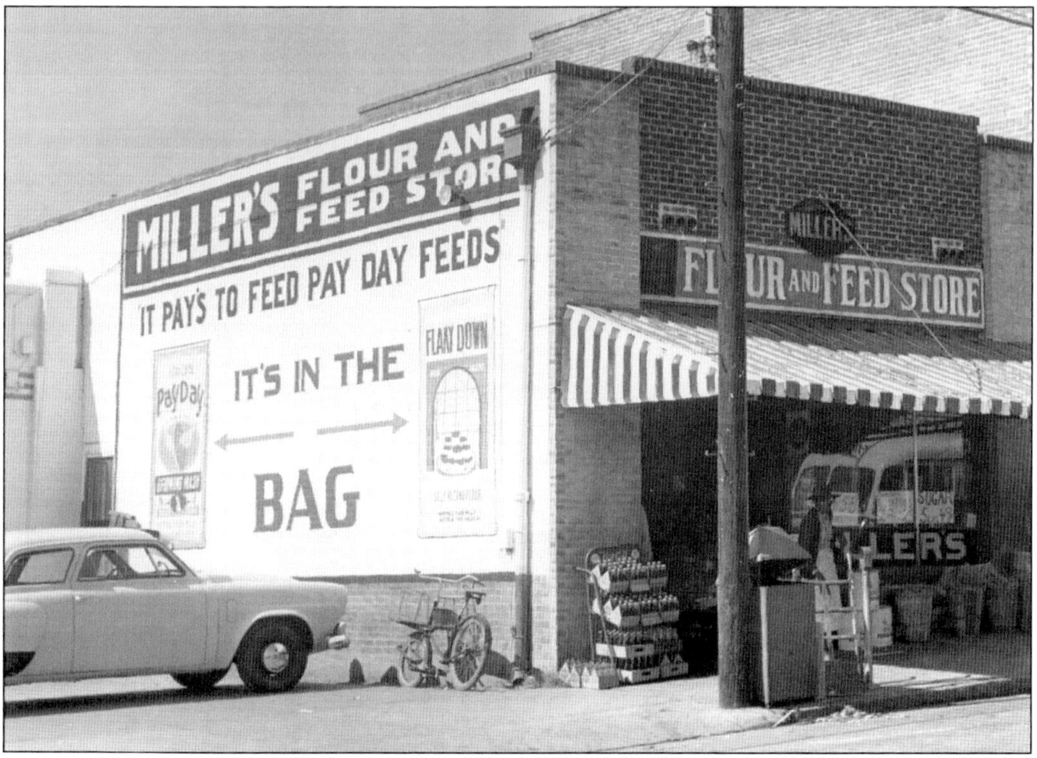

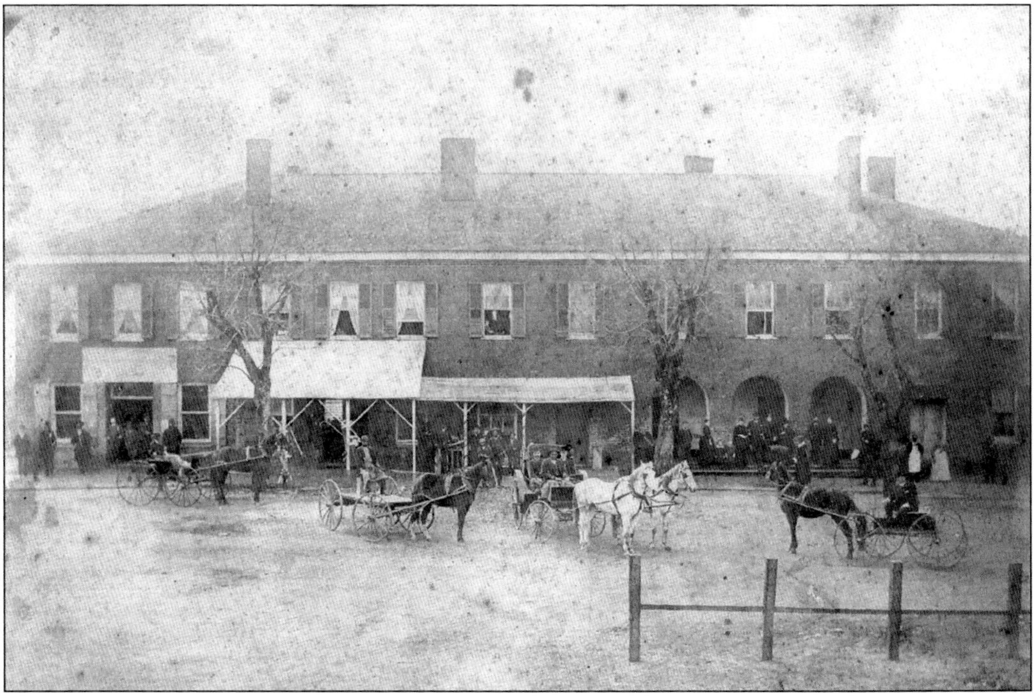

This 1889 photo of downtown Sandersville shows the Sandersville Hotel built in 1856 on the southwest corner of South Harris and Haynes Streets. Hotel rooms were on the second floor and stores filled the first floor area. The three archways to the right led into the hotel lobby and the dining hall.

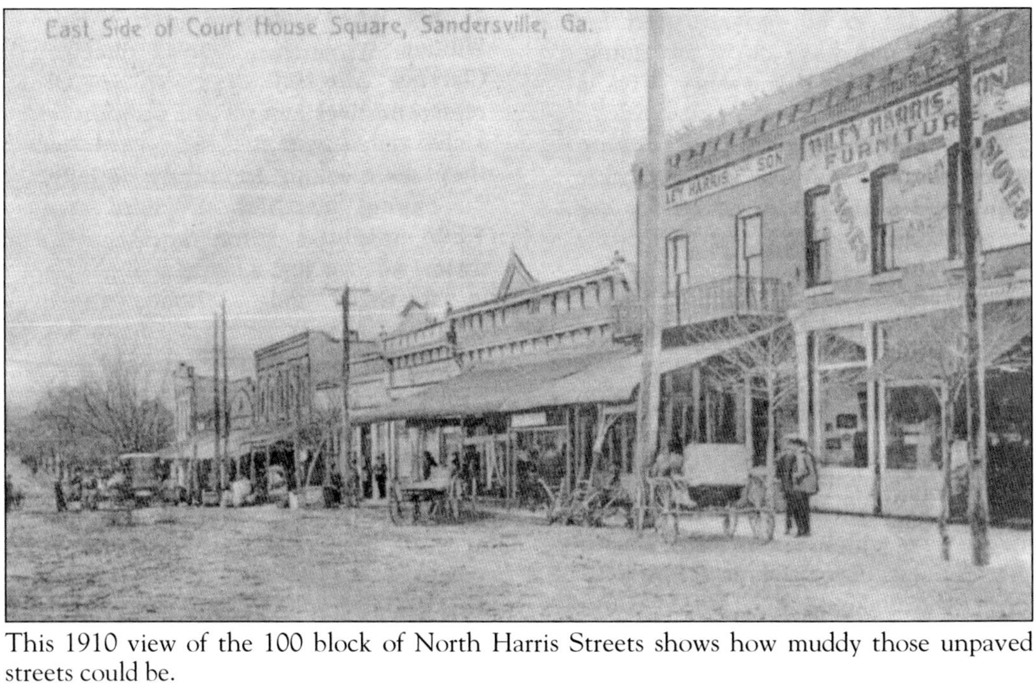

This 1910 view of the 100 block of North Harris Streets shows how muddy those unpaved streets could be.

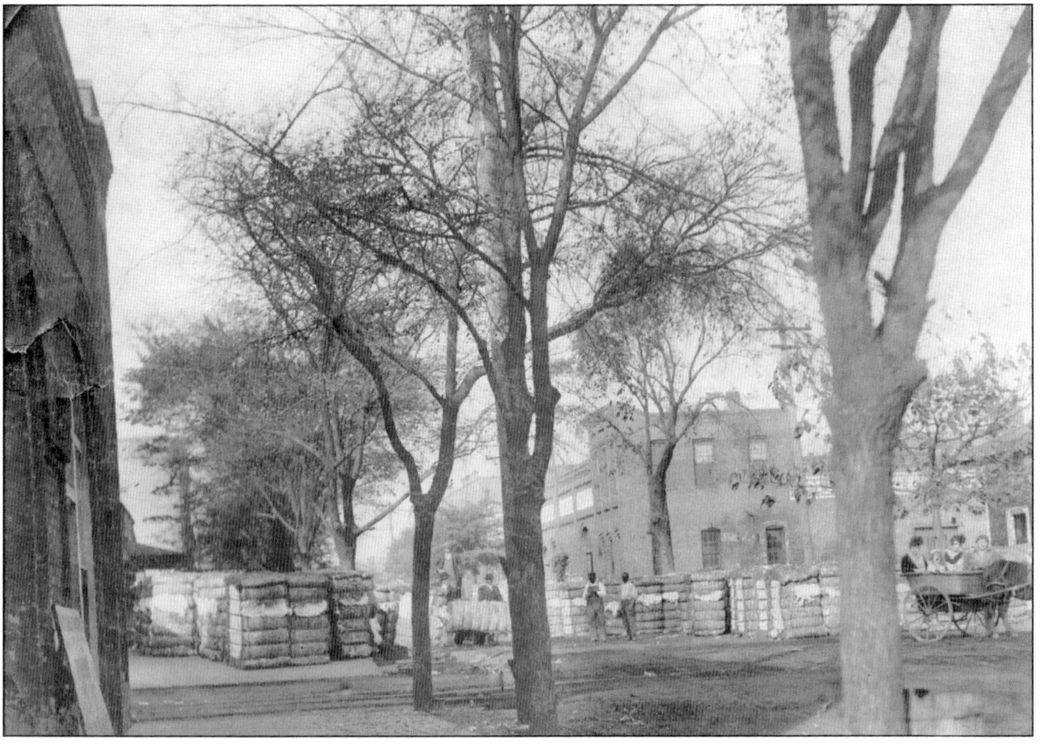

The Planters Warehouse on East Haynes Street was operated by the Gilmore Brothers. Nell Hurst, who married Charlie Carter, is riding in the pony cart in this 1890 picture.

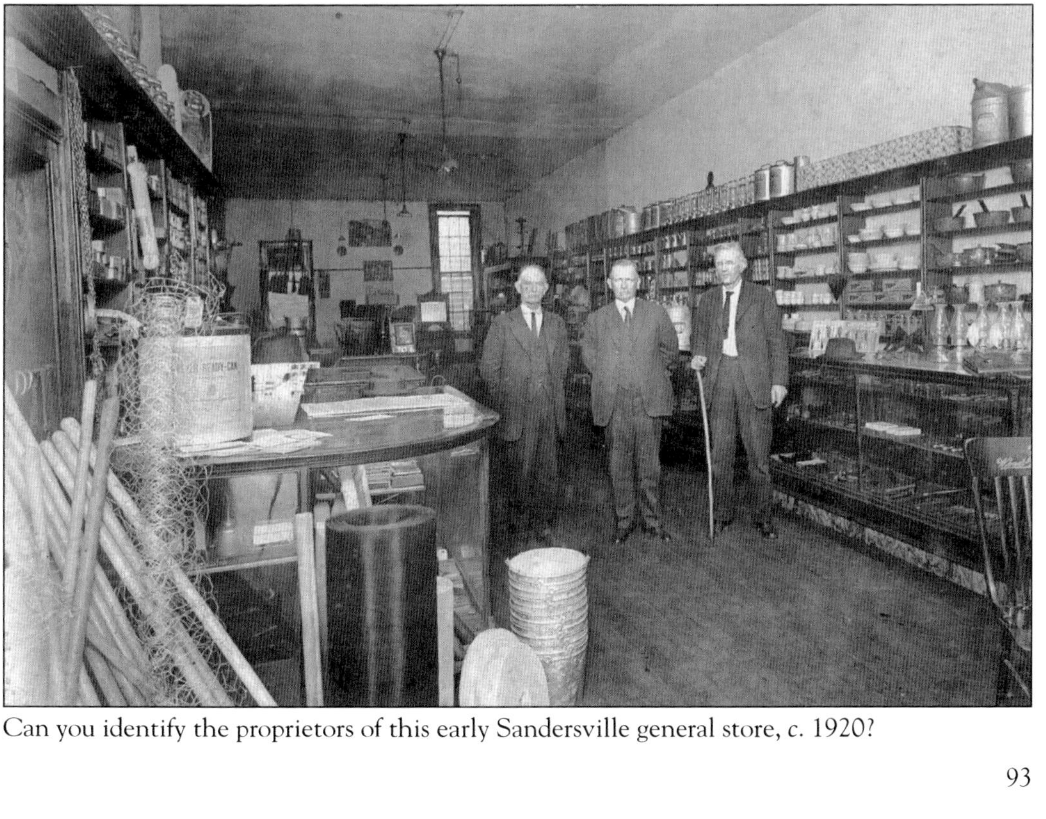

Can you identify the proprietors of this early Sandersville general store, c. 1920?

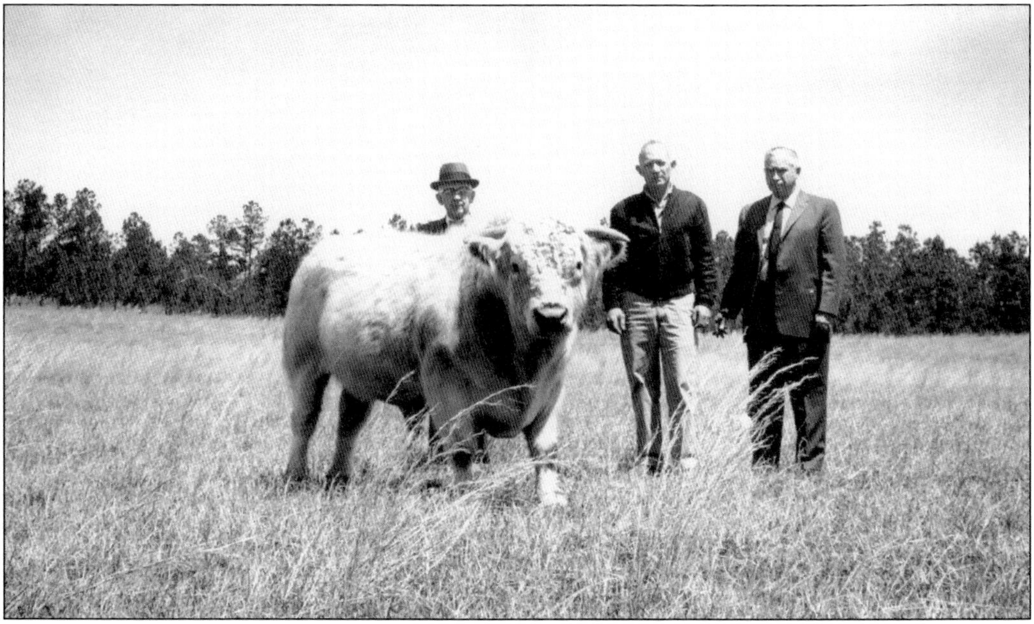

This outstanding Shorthorn Bull won awards in the 1950s for the following, from left to right: C.F. Irwin Sr., C.F. Irwin Jr., and S.G. Mercer.

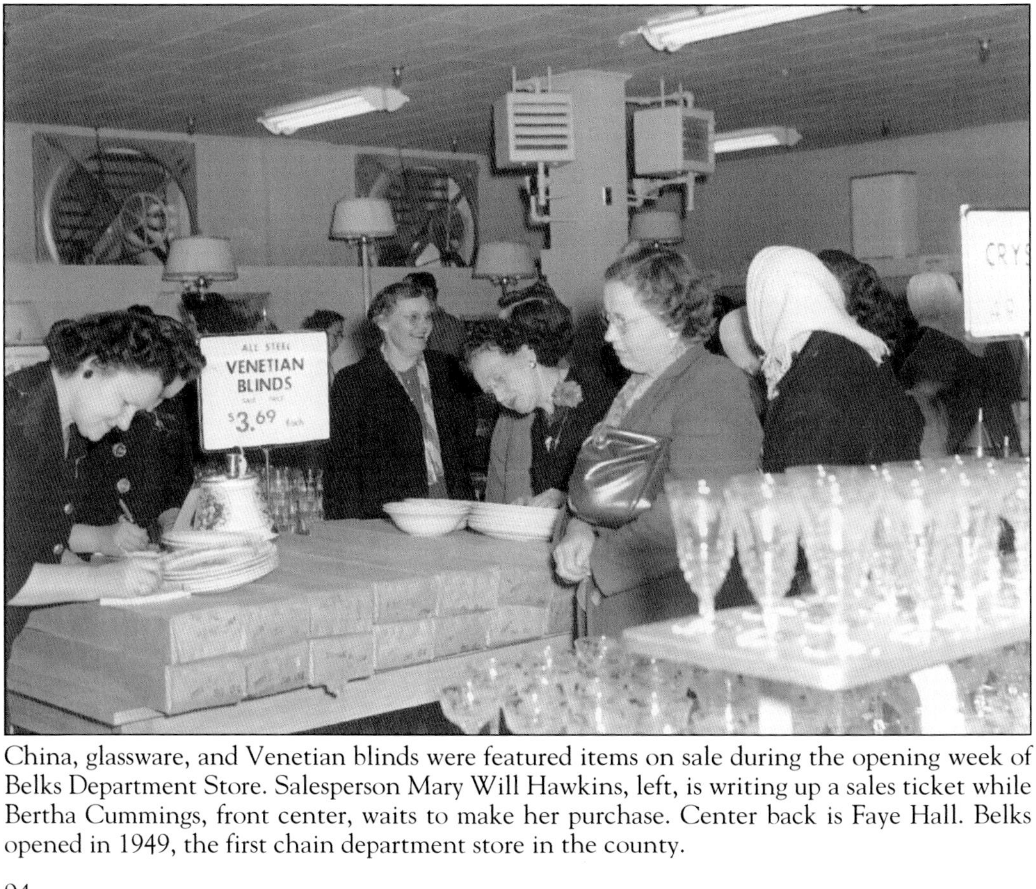

China, glassware, and Venetian blinds were featured items on sale during the opening week of Belks Department Store. Salesperson Mary Will Hawkins, left, is writing up a sales ticket while Bertha Cummings, front center, waits to make her purchase. Center back is Faye Hall. Belks opened in 1949, the first chain department store in the county.

Seven

They Served in Their Time

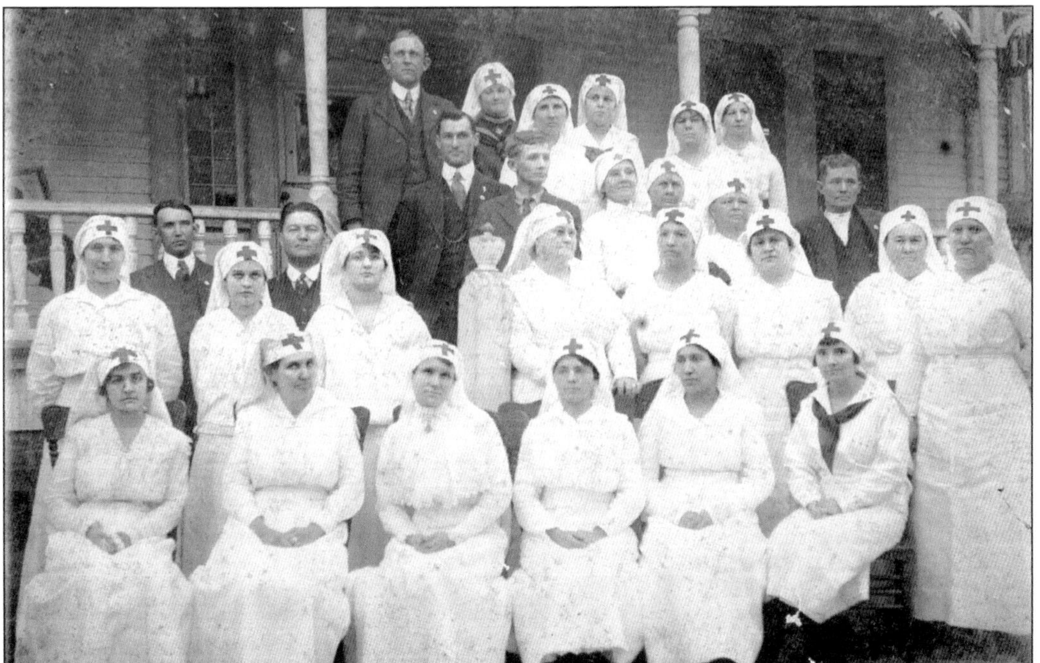

During World War I, members of the Harrison Community Chapter of the Red Cross knitted sweaters for the soldiers. (Georgia Archives.)

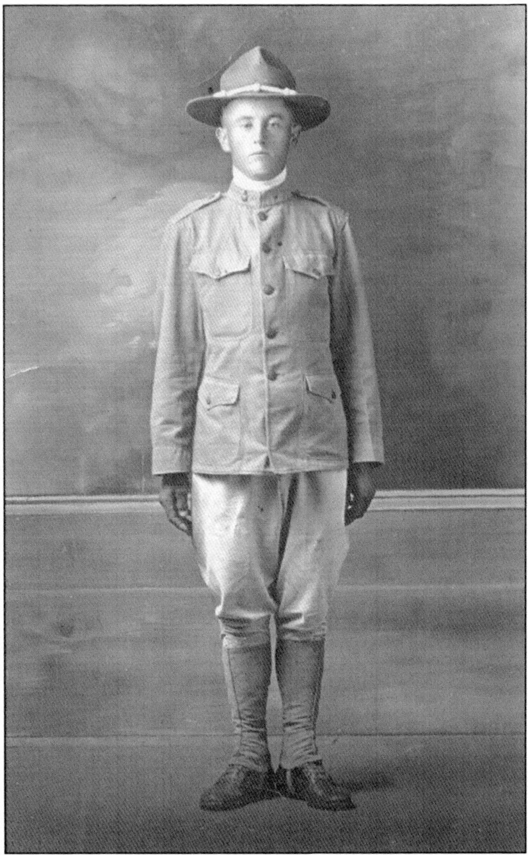

First Lt. Sidney Brown served in the Engineers Division of the U.S. Army during World War I.

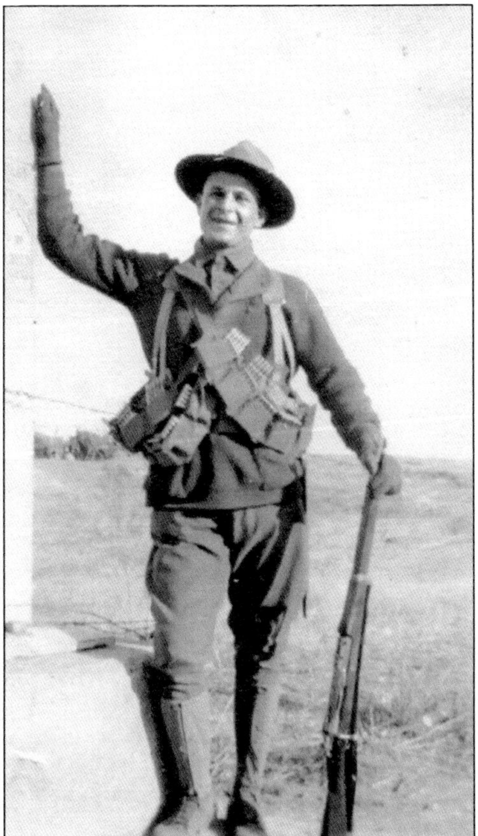

Carl E. Moye served in the Headquarters Company 118th Field Artillery during World War I. He is pictured at Camp Carlton in El Paso, Texas.

Louis Cohen clearly adored his granddaughter Henrietta Cohen in this April 1905 image. He was a mayor and one of the men who started the Sandersville Railroad.

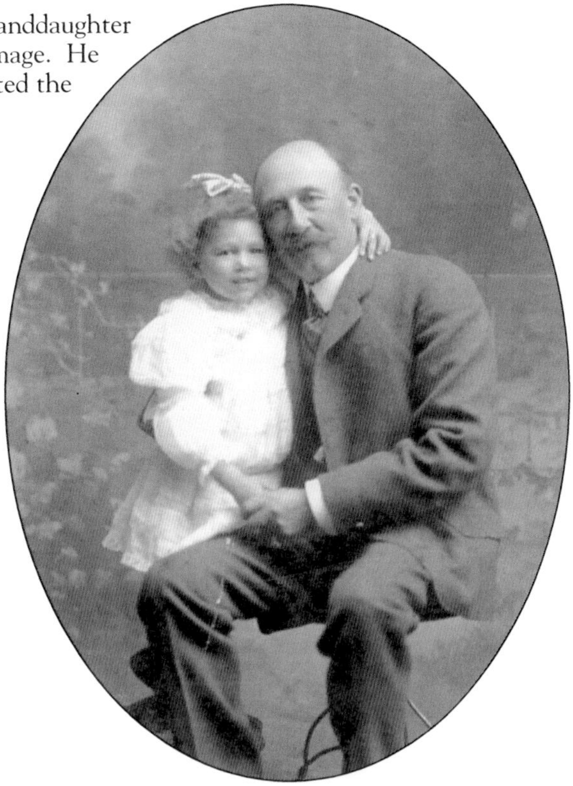

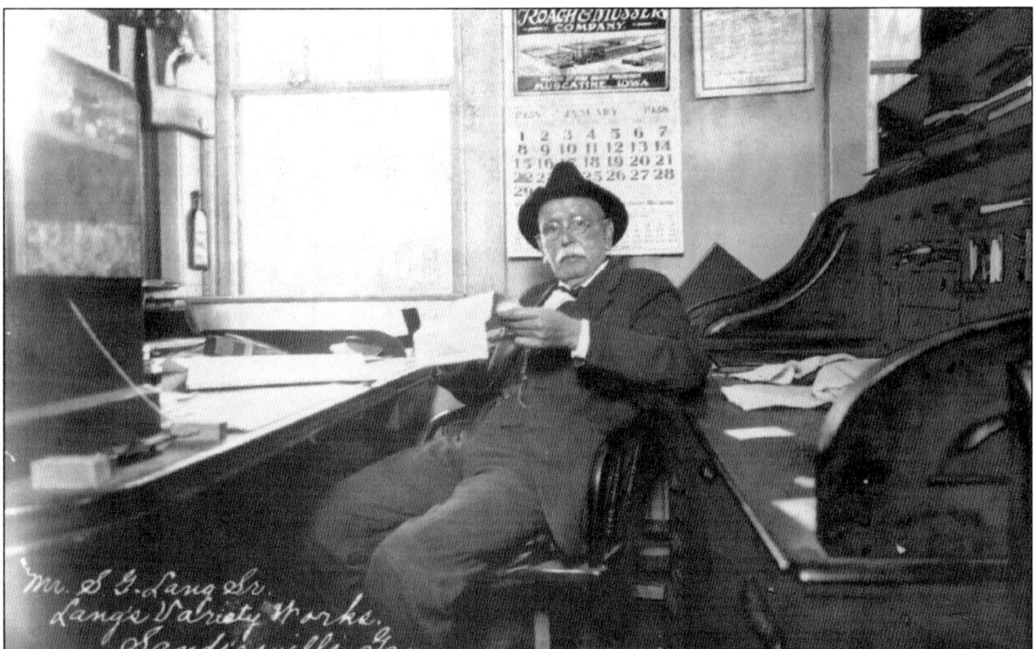

S.G. Lang Sr. works in his office at Lang's Variety Works in 1928. Operated by the Lang family, the Variety Works was responsible for much of the fancy millwork that decorates many Sandersville homes.

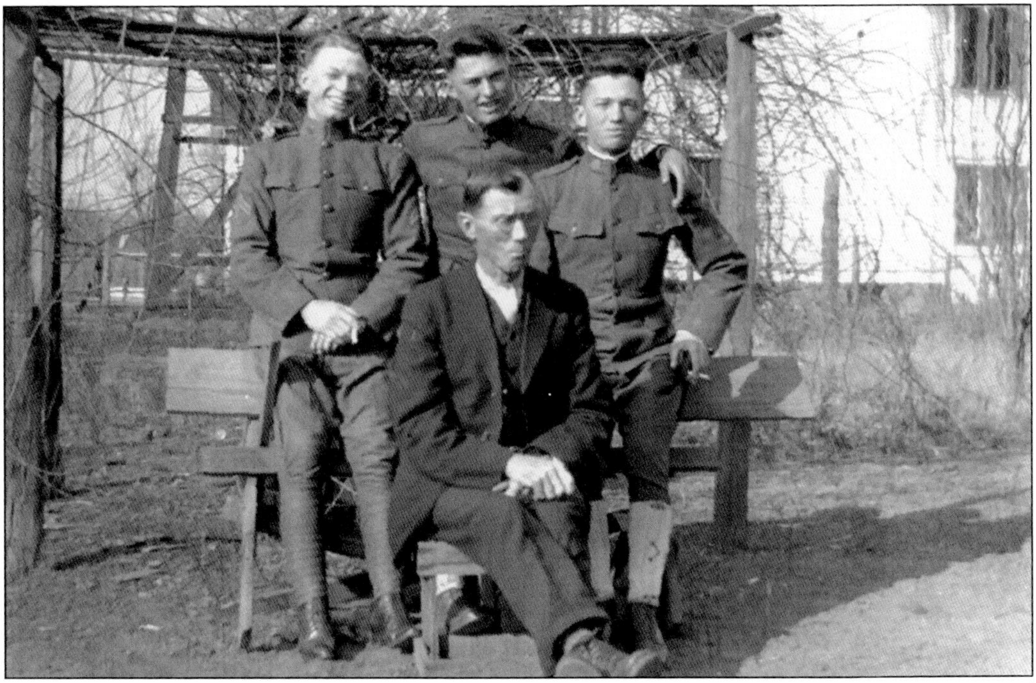

These three World War I soldiers were happy to be home and reunited with their father, seated in front.

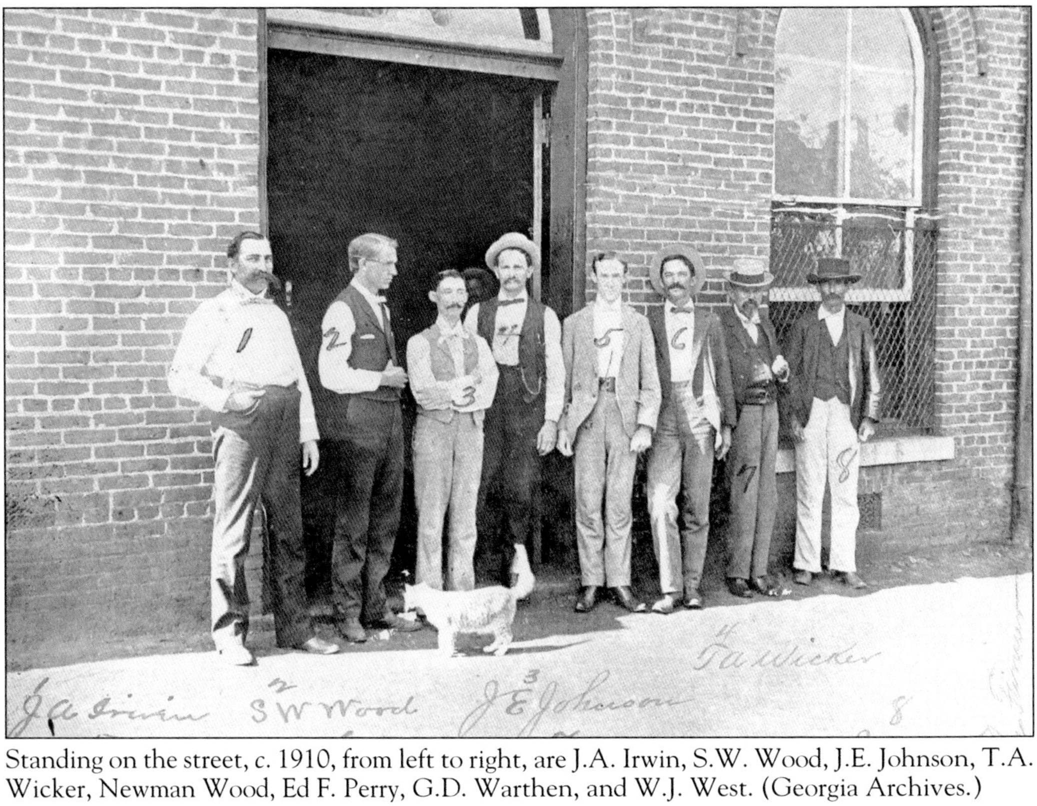

Standing on the street, c. 1910, from left to right, are J.A. Irwin, S.W. Wood, J.E. Johnson, T.A. Wicker, Newman Wood, Ed F. Perry, G.D. Warthen, and W.J. West. (Georgia Archives.)

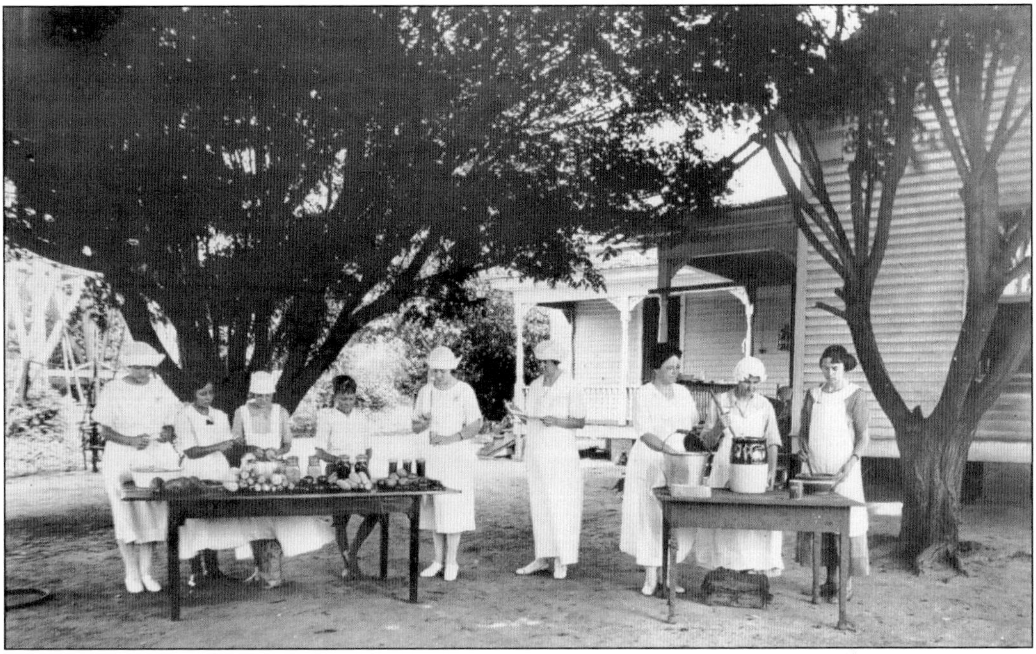

The 4-H Club and Sisters Community Club met for demonstrations on canning and butter-making at the home of Mrs. Ben Tanner, c. 1921. Attending were Kathryn Tanner, Gladys Tanner, Florence Grimes, Leonard Grimes, Frances Champion, Mrs.J.L. Champion, and county agent Ruby Thompson. (Georgia Archives.)

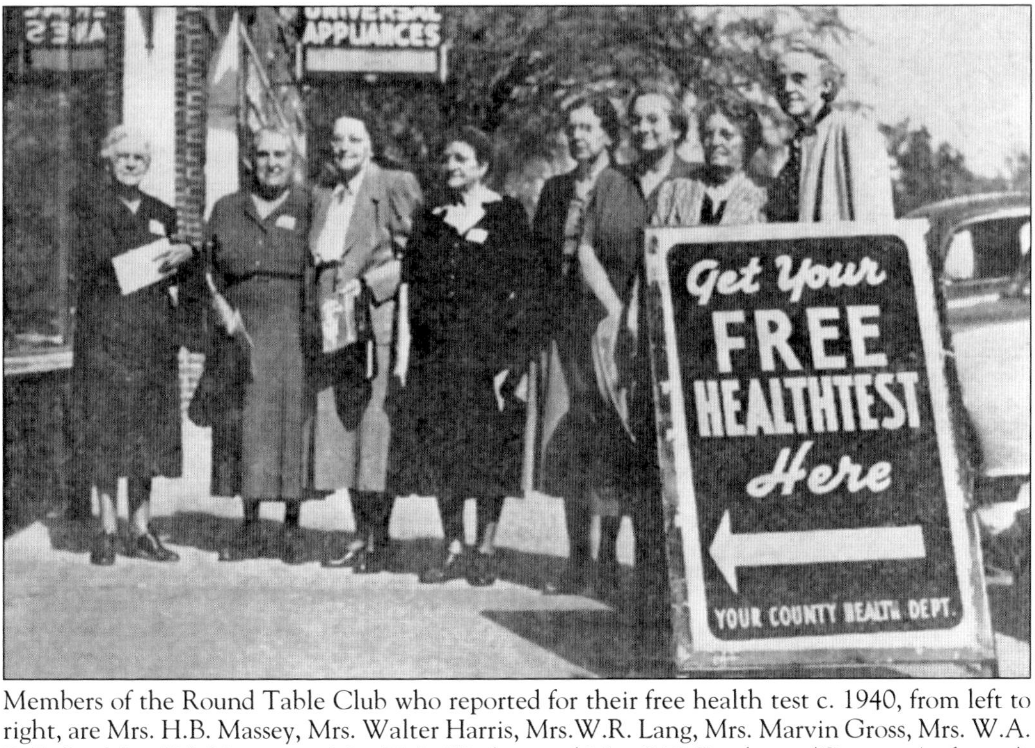

Members of the Round Table Club who reported for their free health test c. 1940, from left to right, are Mrs. H.B. Massey, Mrs. Walter Harris, Mrs.W.R. Lang, Mrs. Marvin Gross, Mrs. W.A. Bell, Sr., Mrs. J.N. Newsome, Mrs. T.A. Wicker, and Mrs. B.T. Rawlings. (Georgia Archives.)

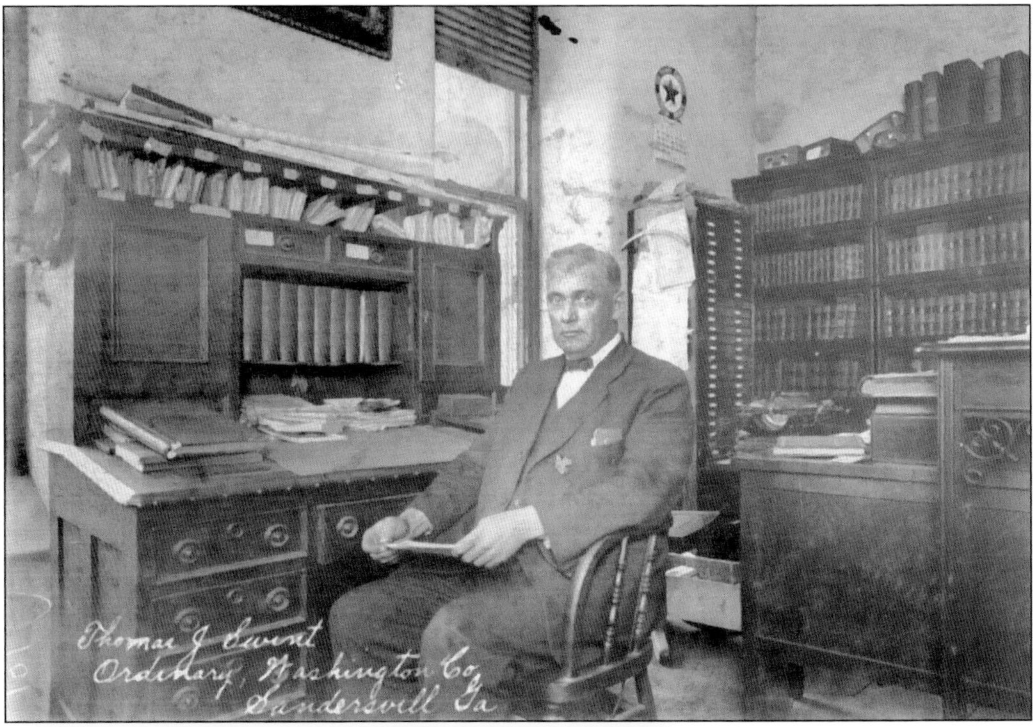

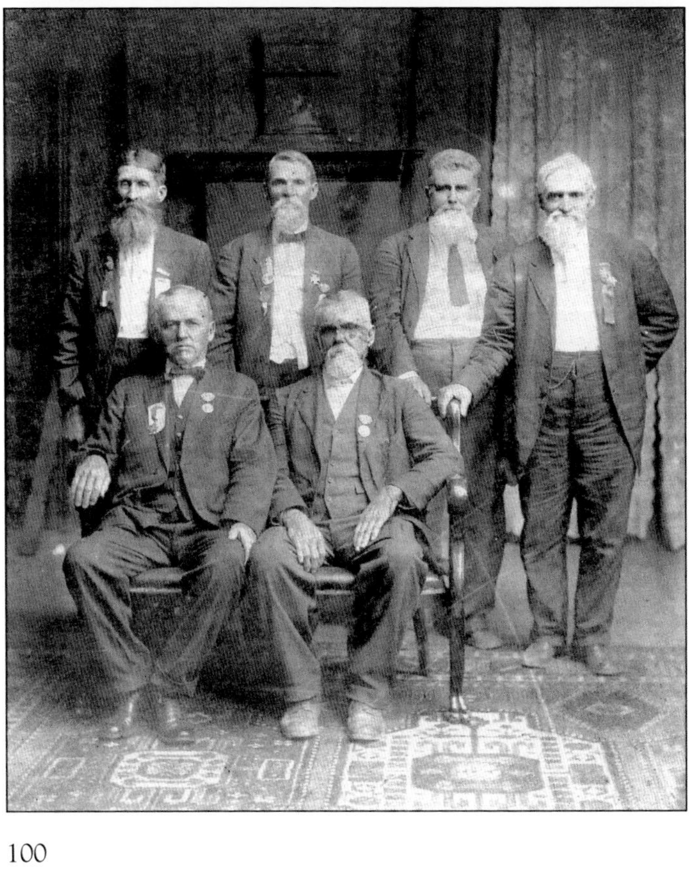

Thomas J. Swint Jr. served as Washington County Ordinary from May 1941 to April 1977. The desk he is using is now at the Historical Society Genealogical Research Museum.

Among those attending the 1916 Civil War Veteran's Reunion, from left to right, are (seated) Newton M. Jordan and G. Hodges. (Georgia Archives.)

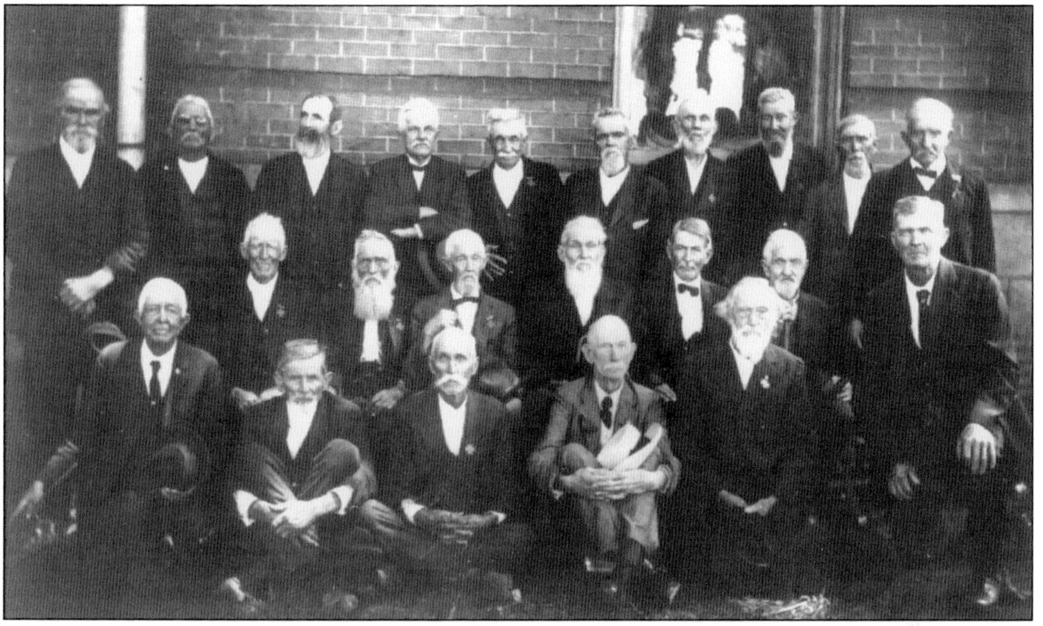

This Civil War Veterans reunion was held about 1920. The fifth person from the left in the second row is John William West, great-grandfather of former Historical Society president Lewis West, and the third person from the left in the back row is Robert Young, grandfather of Lewis's wife, Anita Tanner West. Young was the last surviving Civil War Veteran. Born in 1847, he lived until 1941.

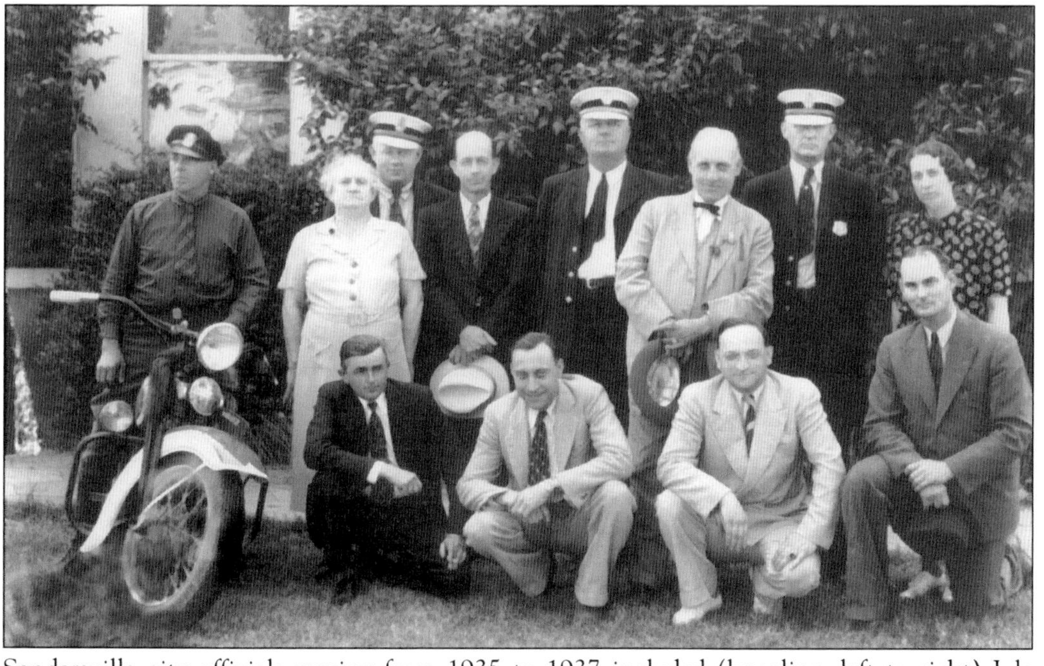

Sandersville city officials serving from 1935 to 1937 included (kneeling, left to right) Jule Evans*, J.B. "Bennie" Wall*, Minus Goodrich*, and Ralph Roughton*; (standing, left to right) Oscar Riner, Mrs. W.G. Gaines*, Arthur Giles, Charlie Will Rawlings, W.E.Garrard, Mayor George Mayo, Leo Scarborough and Leo Rawlings, 1935–1940 (* denotes council members.)

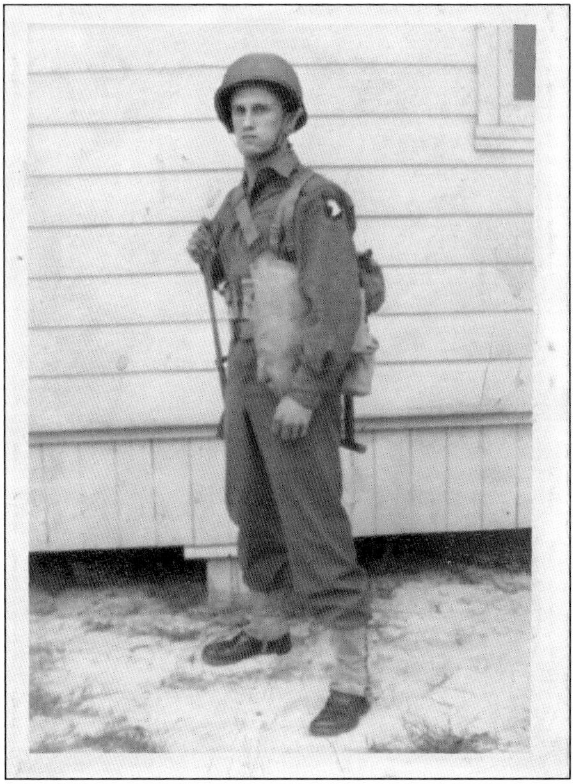

Ralph L. Taylor, Jr., 101st Airborne during World War II, was killed in action.

Men who were prominent in Sandersville during the 1940s were B.J. Tarbutton, Joe Page, Euree Curry, Dr. O.L. Rogers, William Bell, Dr. N.J. Newsom, and A.W. Smith.

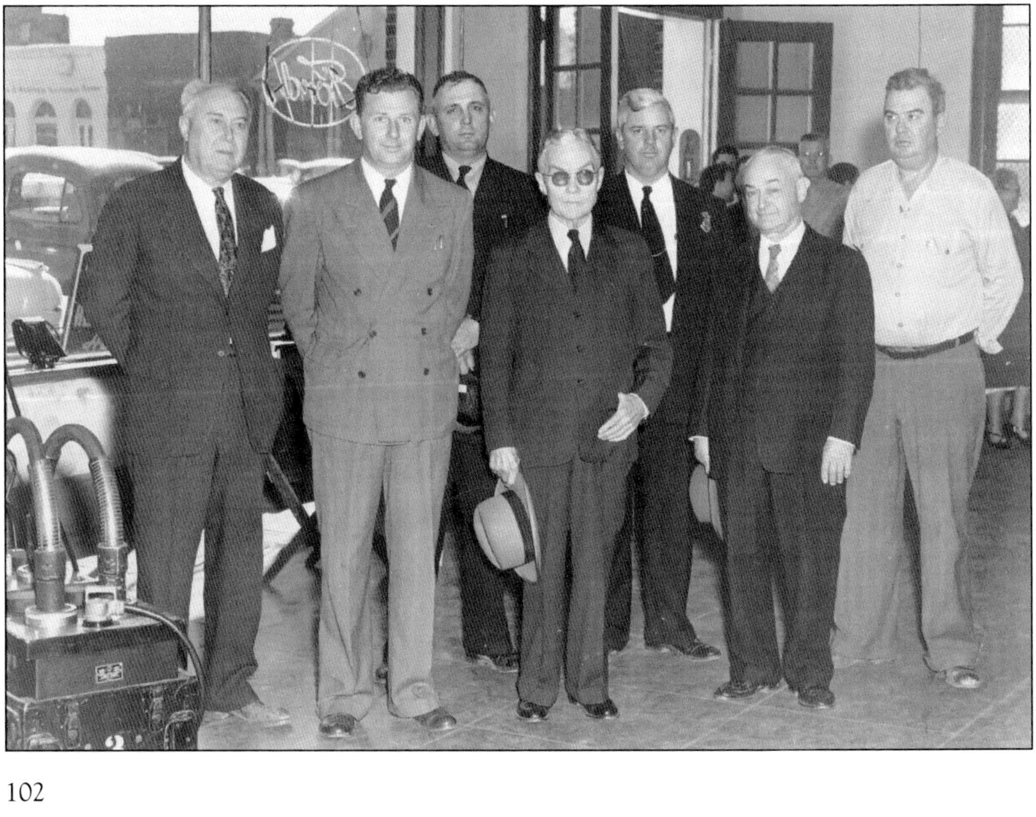

Eight

Time Out for Pictures

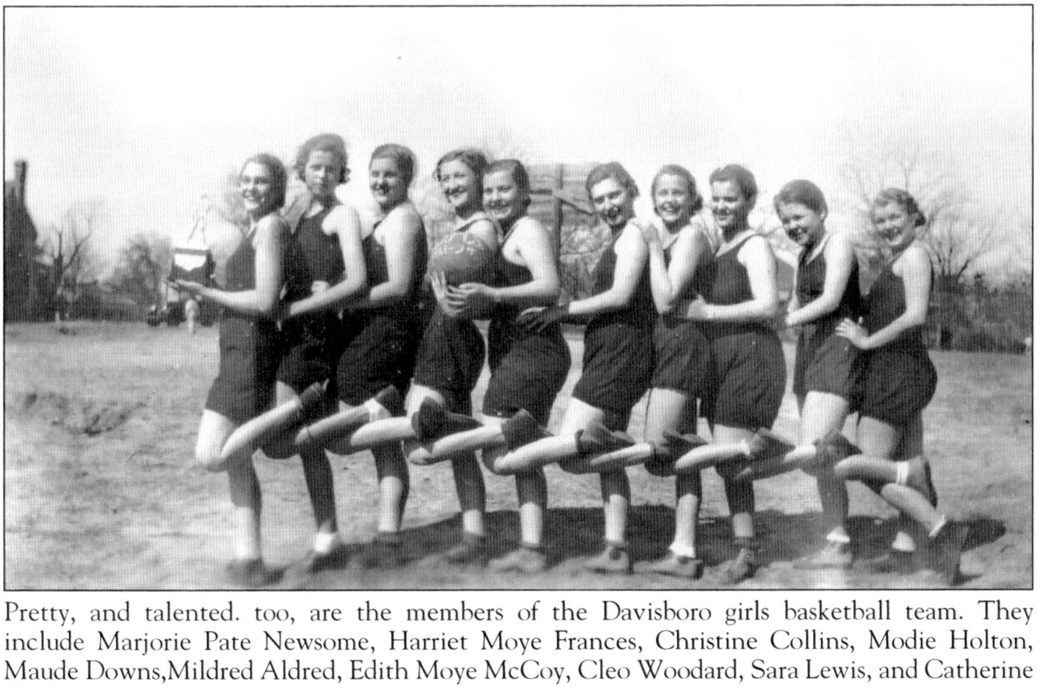

Pretty, and talented. too, are the members of the Davisboro girls basketball team. They include Marjorie Pate Newsome, Harriet Moye Frances, Christine Collins, Modie Holton, Maude Downs,Mildred Aldred, Edith Moye McCoy, Cleo Woodard, Sara Lewis, and Catherine Taylor Dixon.

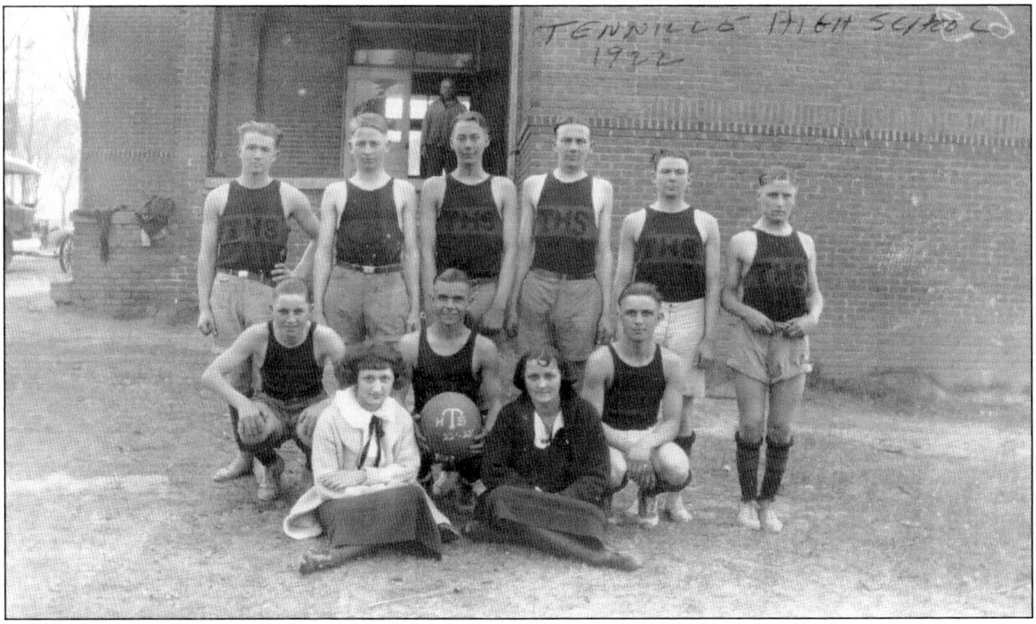

Two girls served as managers for the Tennille High basketball team in 1922.

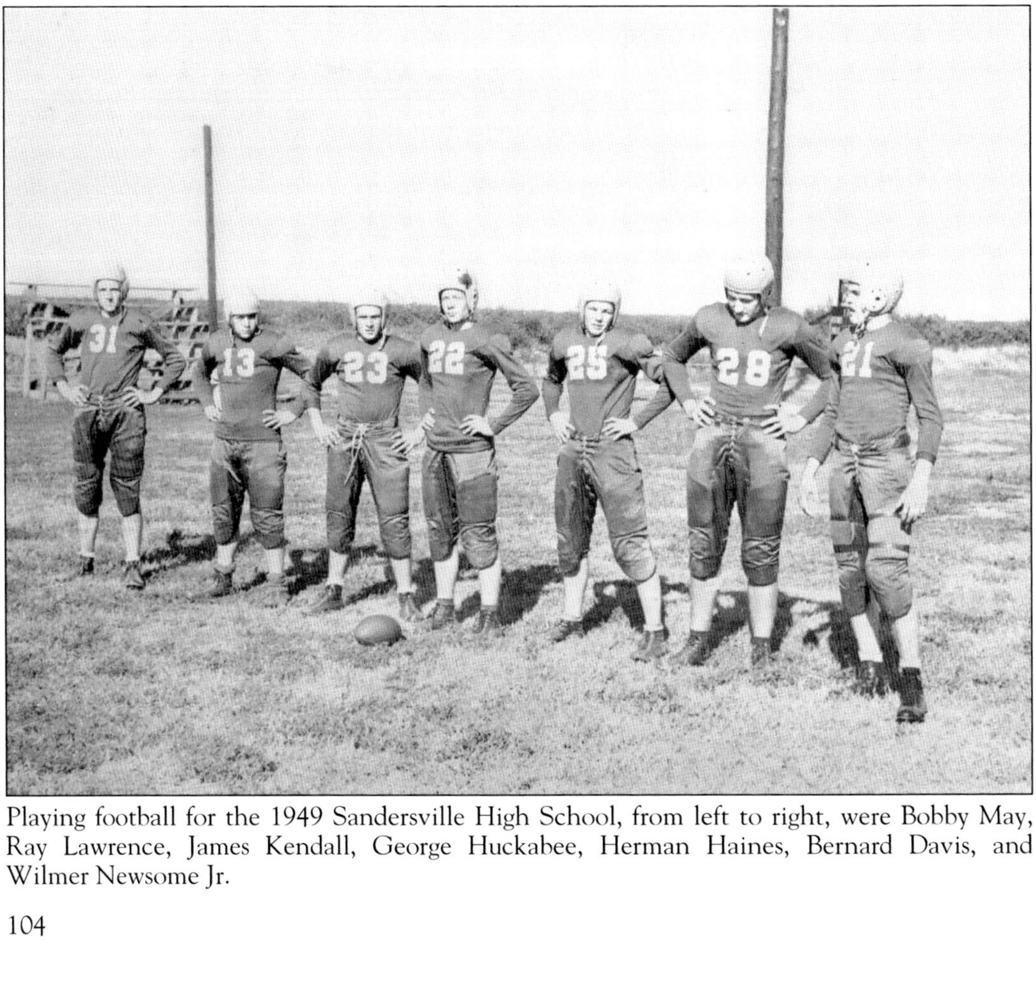

Playing football for the 1949 Sandersville High School, from left to right, were Bobby May, Ray Lawrence, James Kendall, George Huckabee, Herman Haines, Bernard Davis, and Wilmer Newsome Jr.

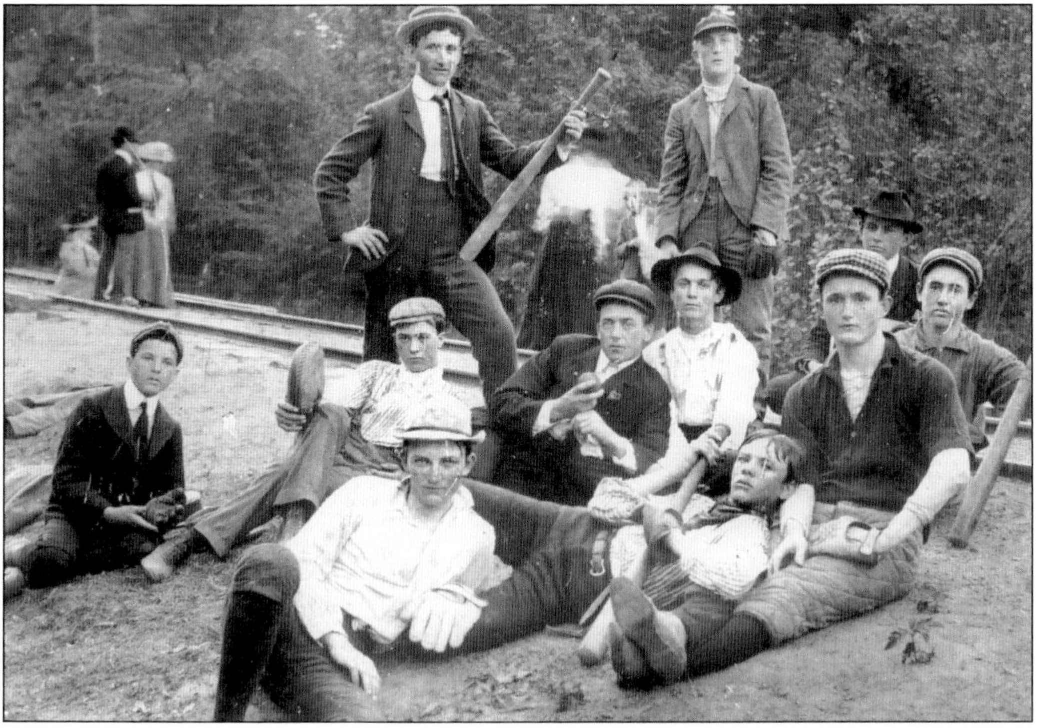

Baseball was serious business for this 1903 Tennille Baseball Club.

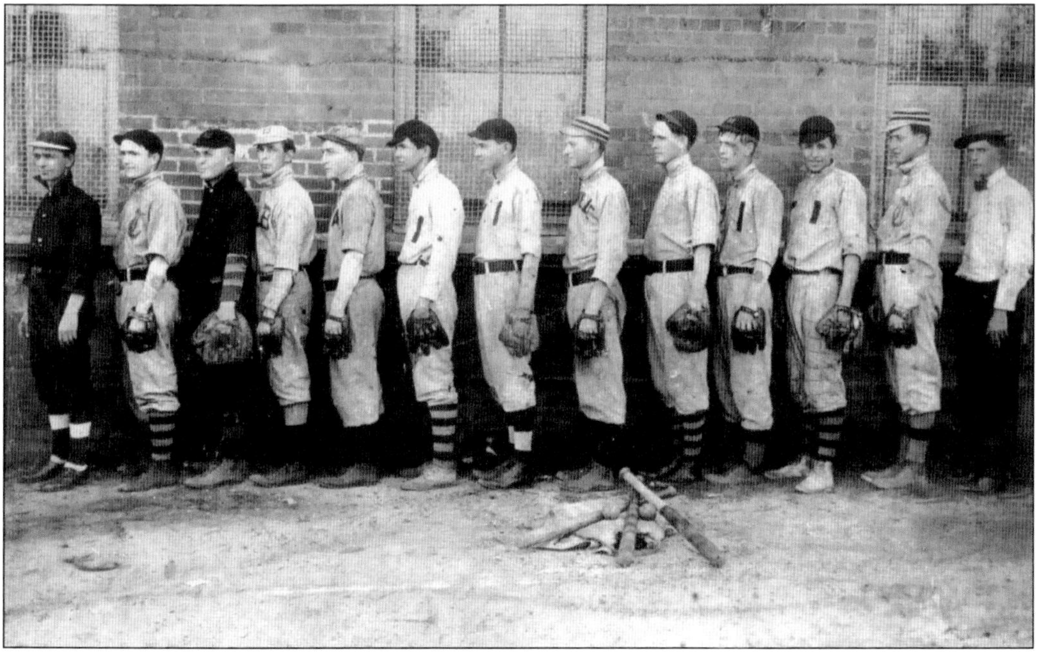

The roster on the 1905 Tennille team included, from left to right, manager Mose Herman, Charlie Pritchard, Wilbur Smith, Pat Murphy, Roy Smith, Horace Sheppard, Clem Brown, Albert Dunham, C.Y. Smith, Beurne Smith, John D. Voss, Tom Hartley, and Claude Carroll, scorekeeper.

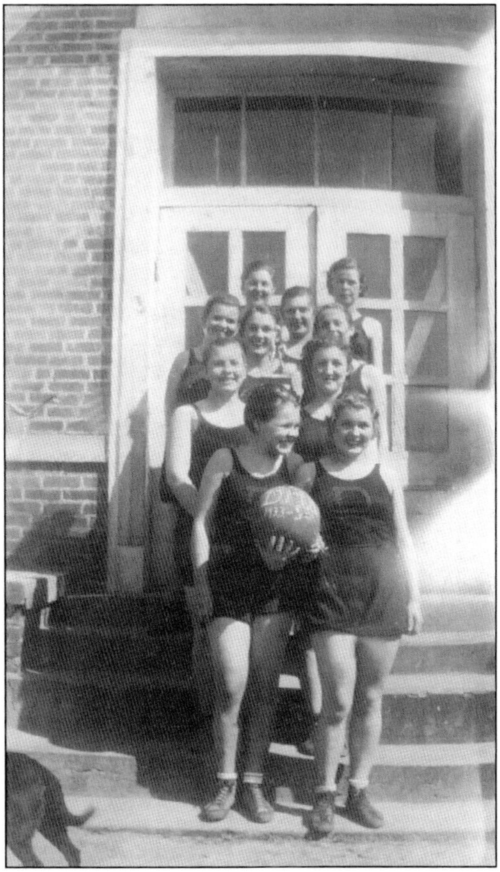

The Davisboro girls basketball team in 1933–1934, from left to right, included (first row) Sara Lewis and Katherine Taylor; (second row) two unidentified girls; (third row) Majorie Pate and Edith Moye; (fourth row) Cleo Woodard and unidentified; (back) unidentified and Harriett Moye.

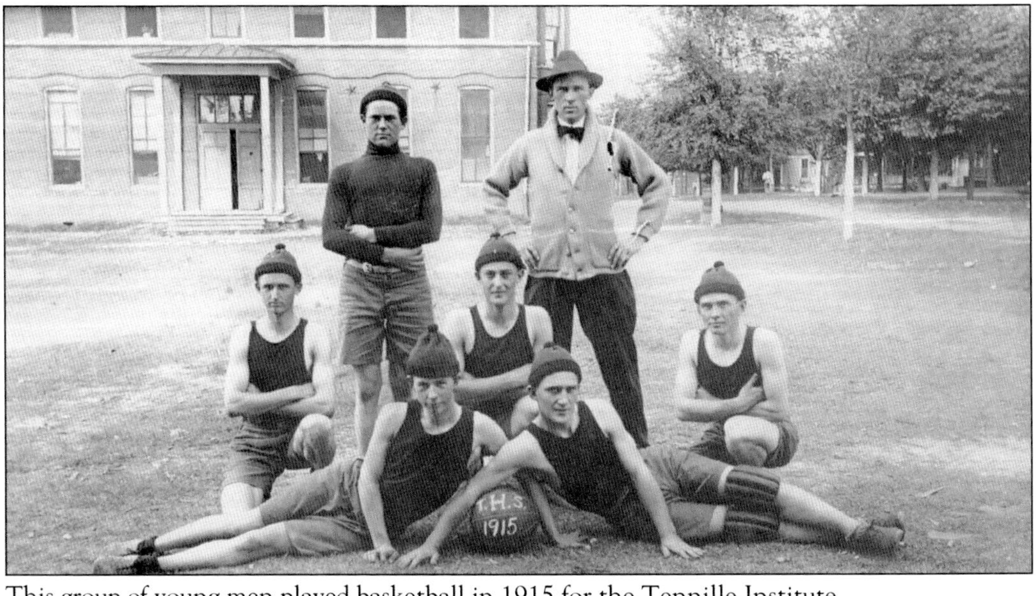

This group of young men played basketball in 1915 for the Tennille Institute.

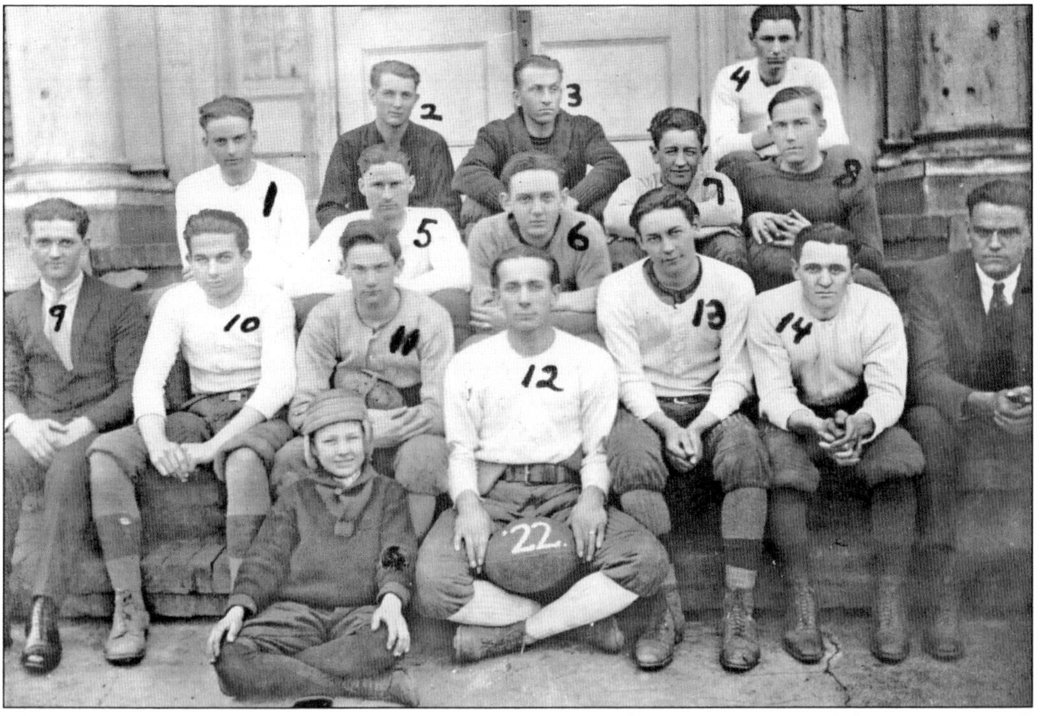

Playing on the 1922 Sandersville High School Football Team were (1) Joiner, guard; (2) Young, half-back; (3) Frost, full-back; (4) Mills, end; (5) Francis Joiner, end; (6) Brinson, guard; (7) Lindsey, lineman; (8) Winston West, tackle; (9) Ivy, linesman (10) Smith, center; (11) Edward T. Averett, tackle; (12) Louis Lockhart, quarter-back and captain; (13) Alford, half-back; (14) John Henry Tyler, half back; (15) E.A. Edwards, coach; and (16) Armstrong, mascot.

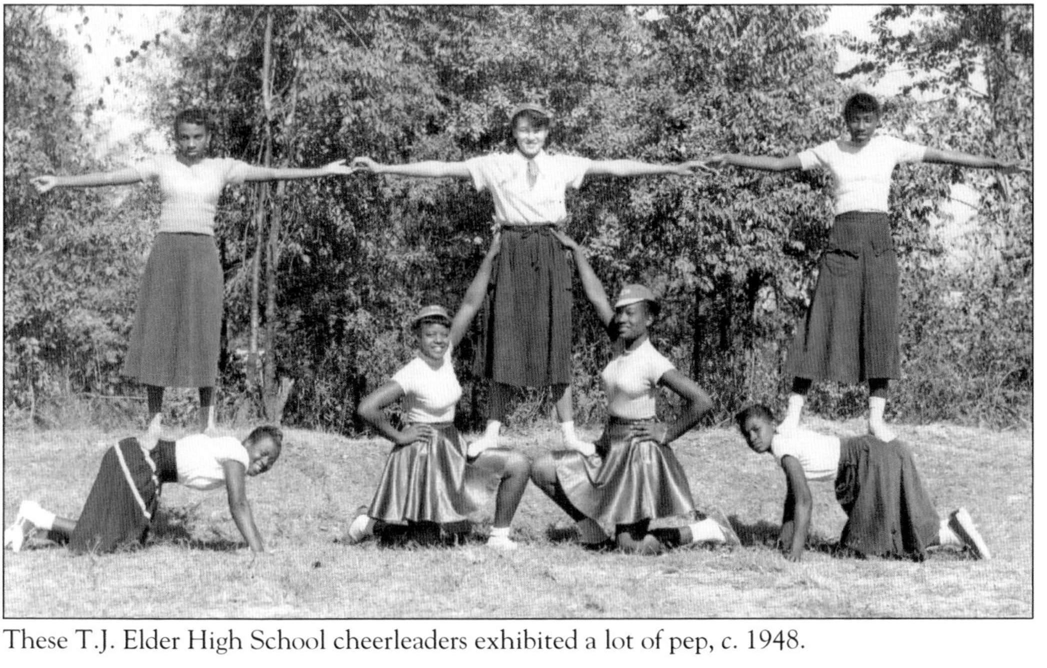

These T.J. Elder High School cheerleaders exhibited a lot of pep, c. 1948.

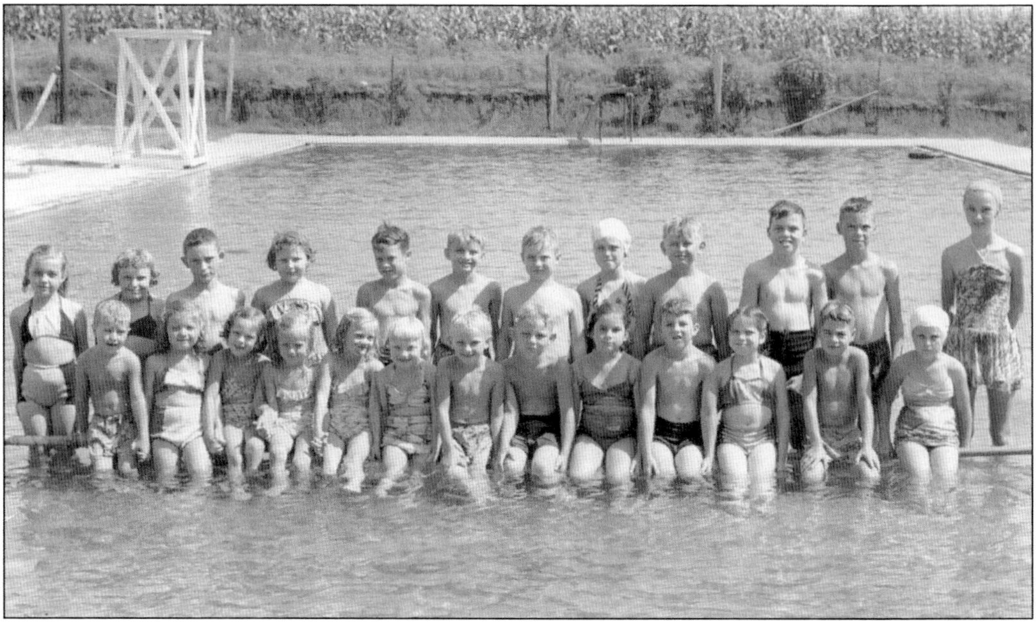

Swimming at the Sandersville City Pool was a popular summer activity. Some of the students in this swimming class are Tommy Walker, Nina Goodrich, Larry Mathis, Jack Taylor, Cynthia Taylor McCaskill, Joann Walden Marshall, and Jewell Turner.

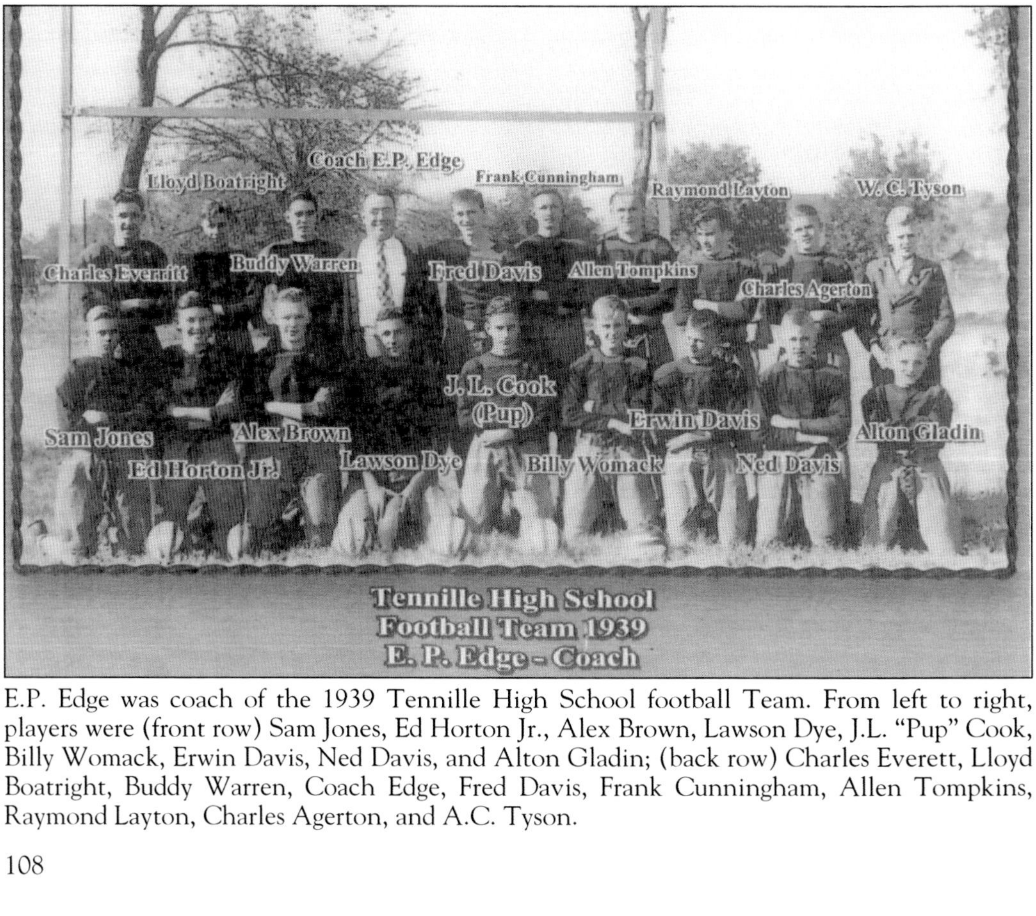

E.P. Edge was coach of the 1939 Tennille High School football Team. From left to right, players were (front row) Sam Jones, Ed Horton Jr., Alex Brown, Lawson Dye, J.L. "Pup" Cook, Billy Womack, Erwin Davis, Ned Davis, and Alton Gladin; (back row) Charles Everett, Lloyd Boatright, Buddy Warren, Coach Edge, Fred Davis, Frank Cunningham, Allen Tompkins, Raymond Layton, Charles Agerton, and A.C. Tyson.

Nine

Parade Time

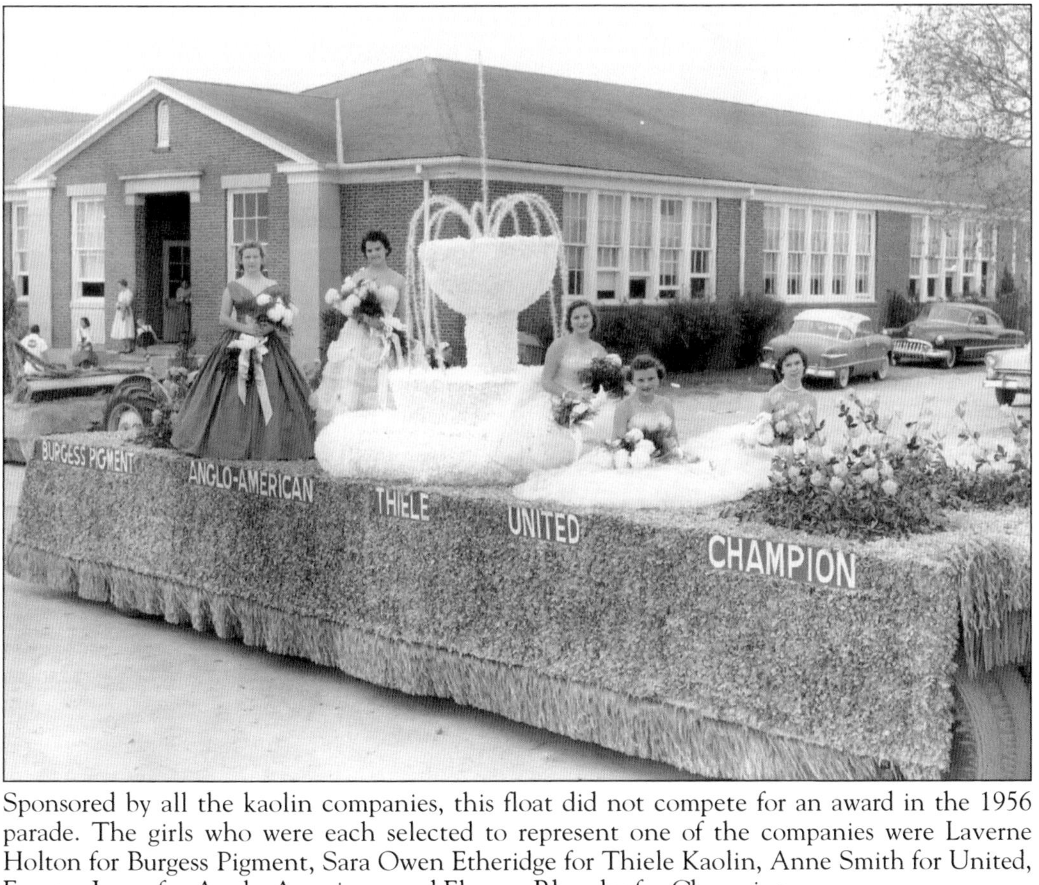

Sponsored by all the kaolin companies, this float did not compete for an award in the 1956 parade. The girls who were each selected to represent one of the companies were Laverne Holton for Burgess Pigment, Sara Owen Etheridge for Thiele Kaolin, Anne Smith for United, Frances Jones for Anglo-American, and Eleanor Rhoades for Champion.

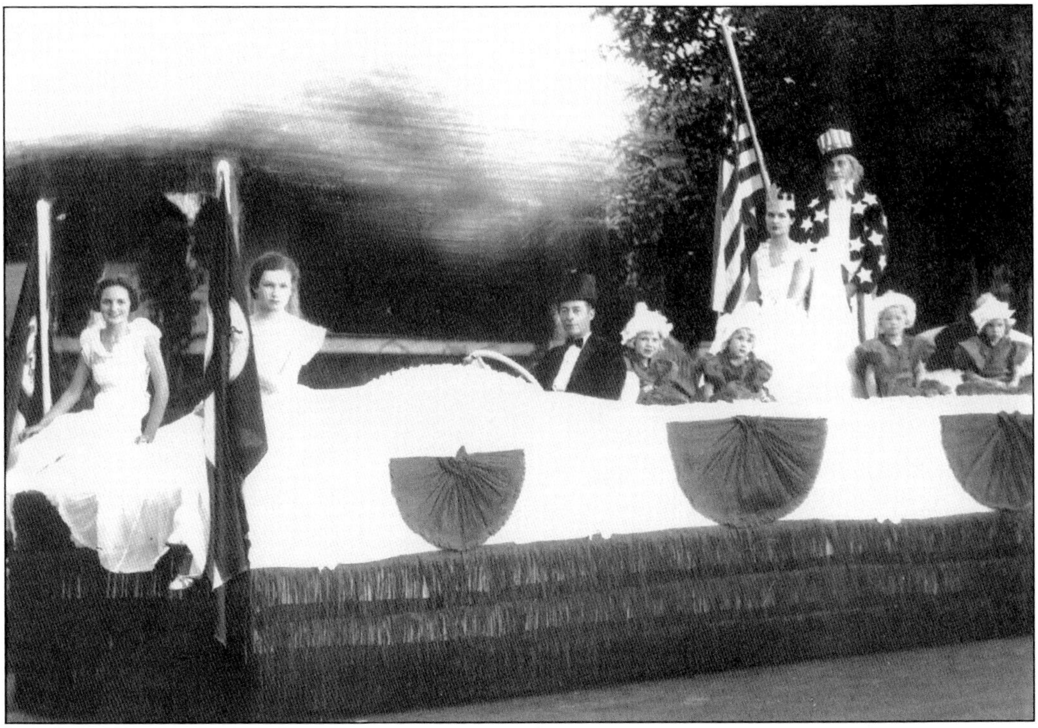

Appearing on this float in 1933 are Ruth Sears Martin, Miss Wilson, Driver Luke West, Nonie Rawlings as the Queen, and Bennie Wall as Uncle Sam.

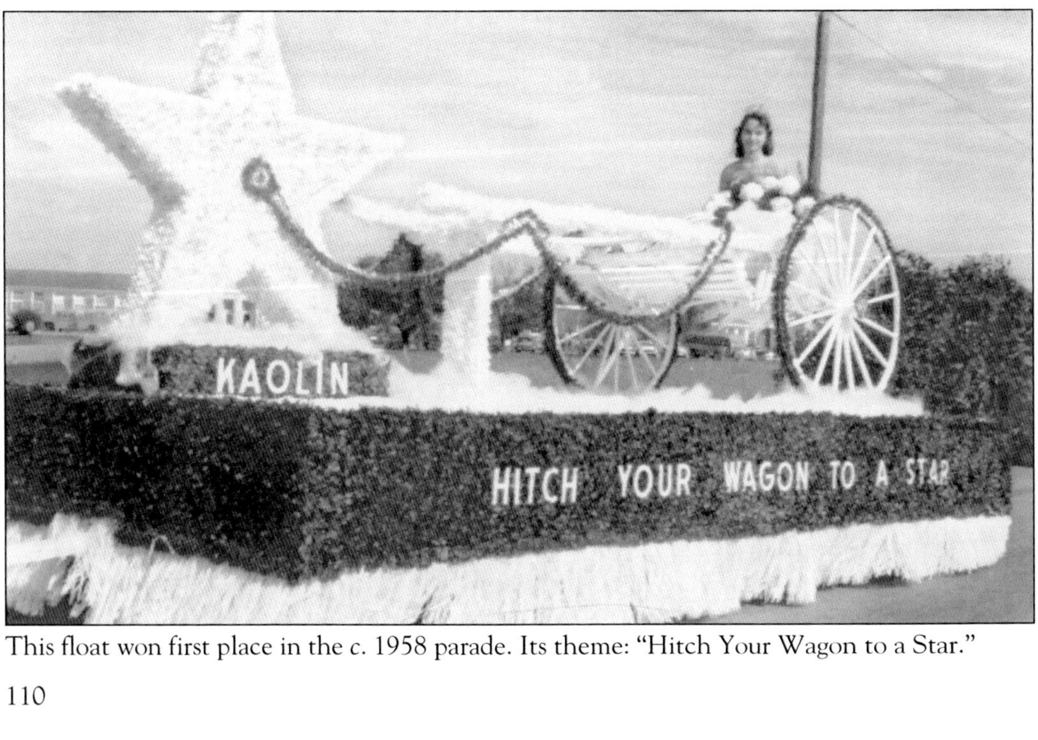

This float won first place in the c. 1958 parade. Its theme: "Hitch Your Wagon to a Star."

The Transylvania Club entered this float in the Kaolin Festival Parade *c.* 1957.

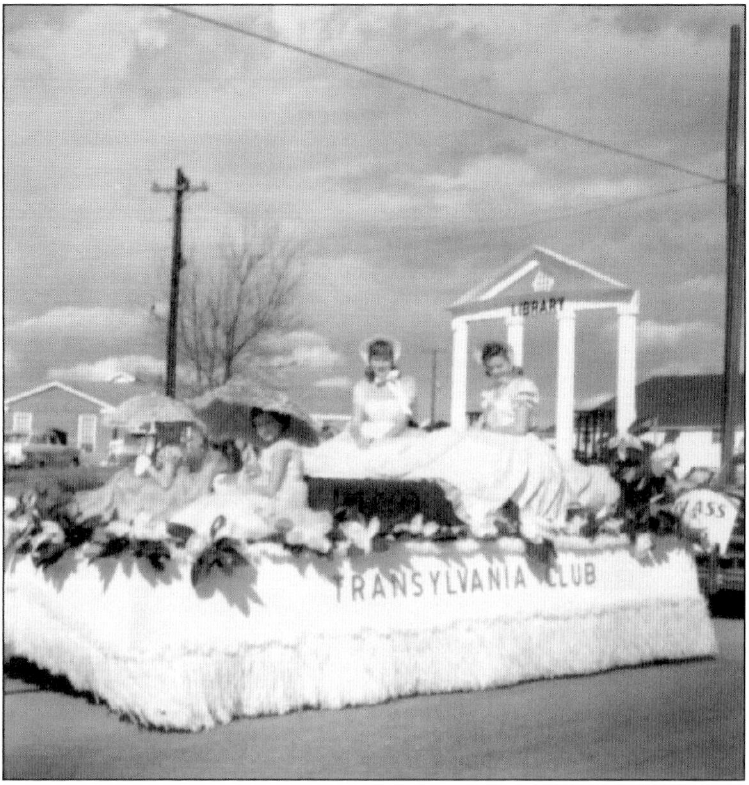

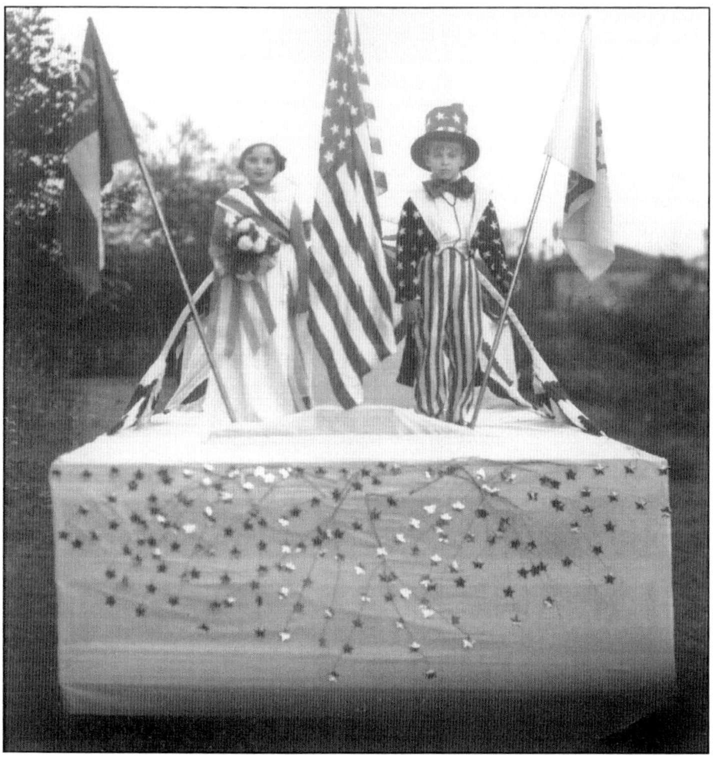

Mary Jane McElrath and Ben Tarbutton Jr. ride on this float in the 1939 Fourth of July parade.

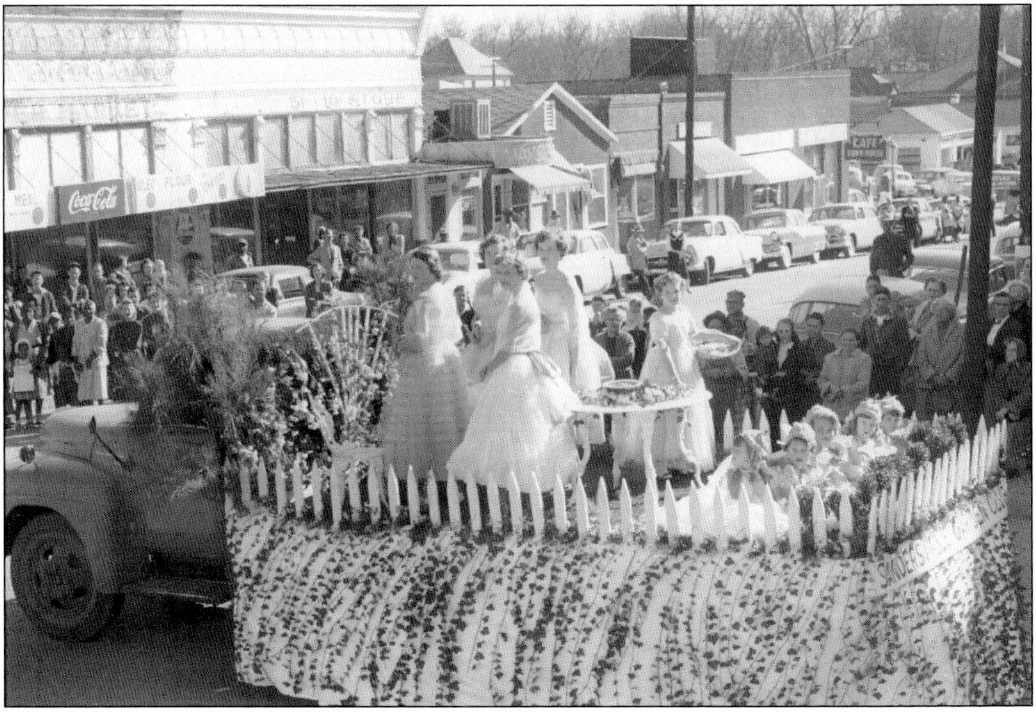

This c. 1956 Sandersville Garden Club float features ivy and flowers and beautiful young ladies.

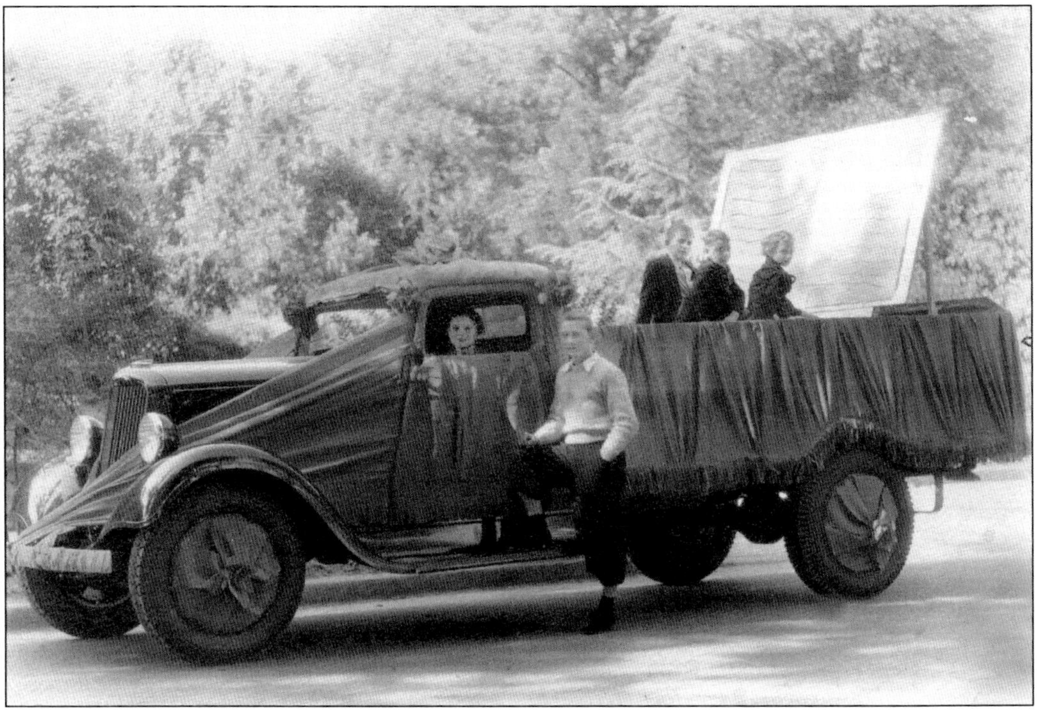

Nelle Cooley Hudson drives this decorated truck c. 1933 with O.E. "Dick" Hudson standing at the door, and Bill Helton, Bill Harrell, and Levi Hill riding in back.

Brenda Rice was the Elder High School Homecoming Queen in 1970. Note how her dress becomes the float.

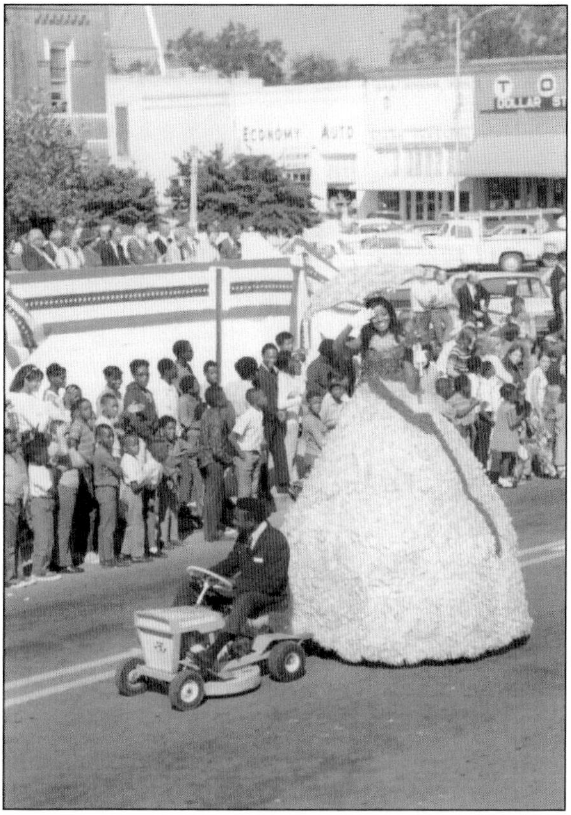

A bevy of angels adorn this 1956 float. That was the year of the first Kaolin Festival event.

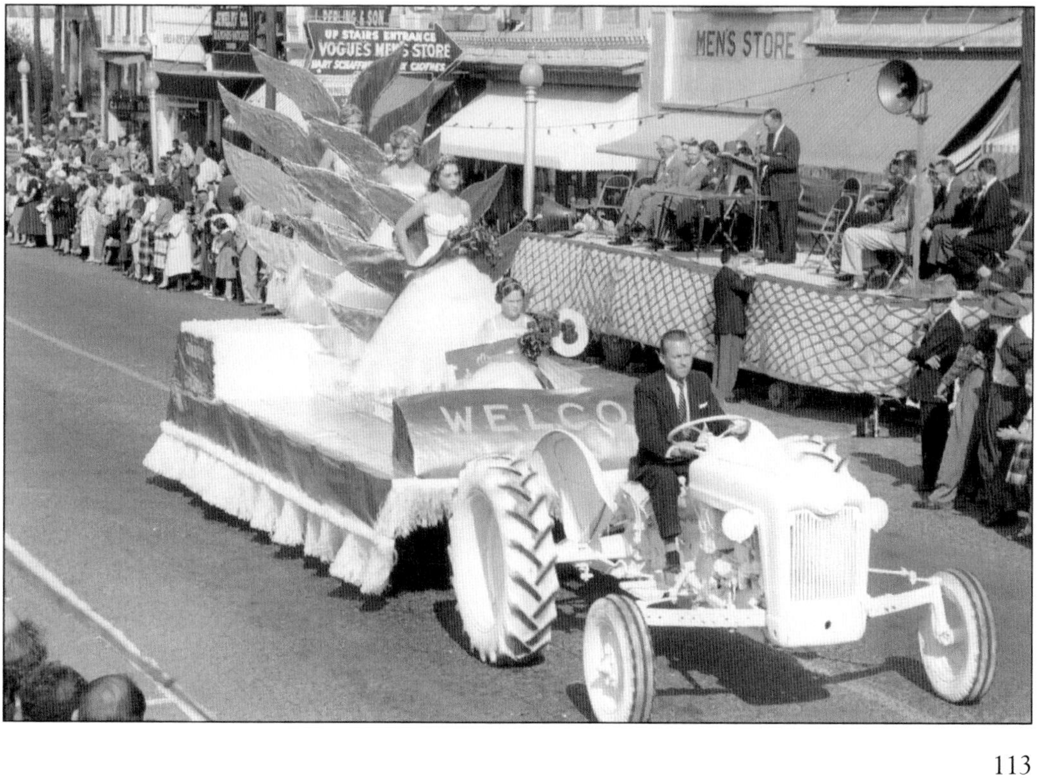

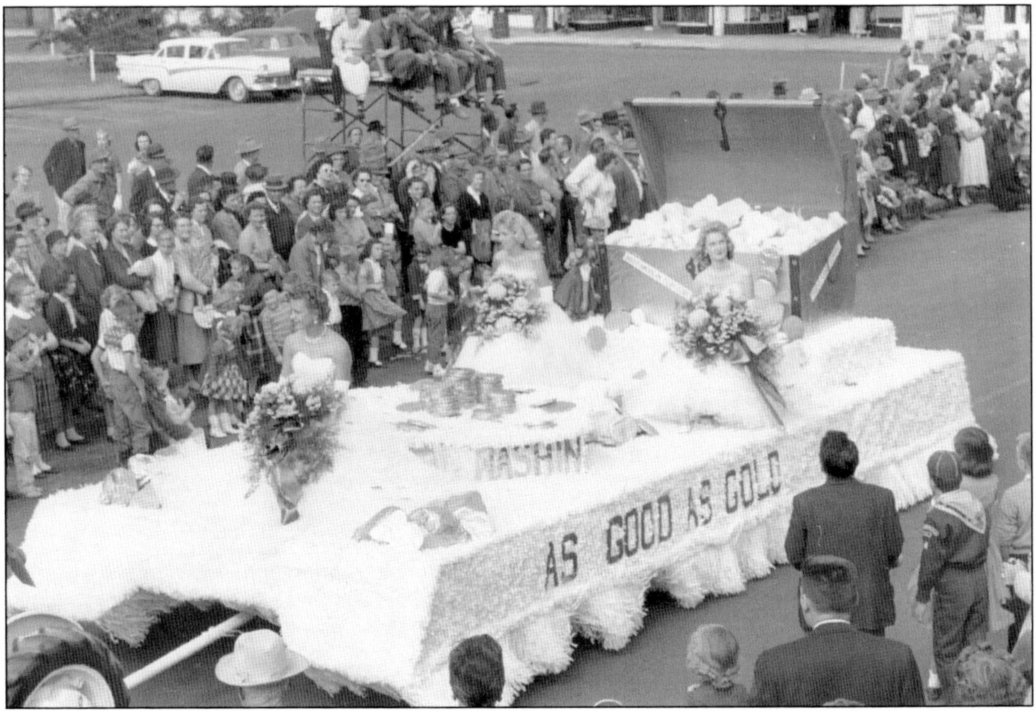

"As Good As Gold" was the theme for this first prize-winning float submitted by the Tennille Fine Arts Club in the November 1958 Kaolin Parade. They won in the club division.

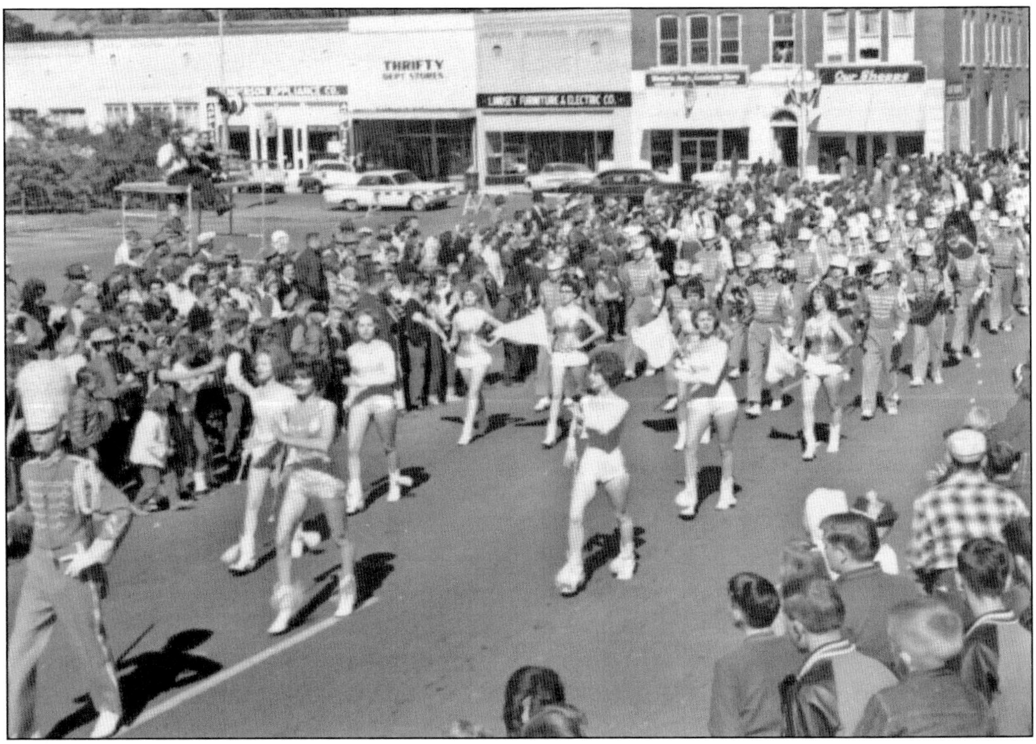

Not everyone was in step in this band in the 1962 parade.

Ten

Other Times and Places

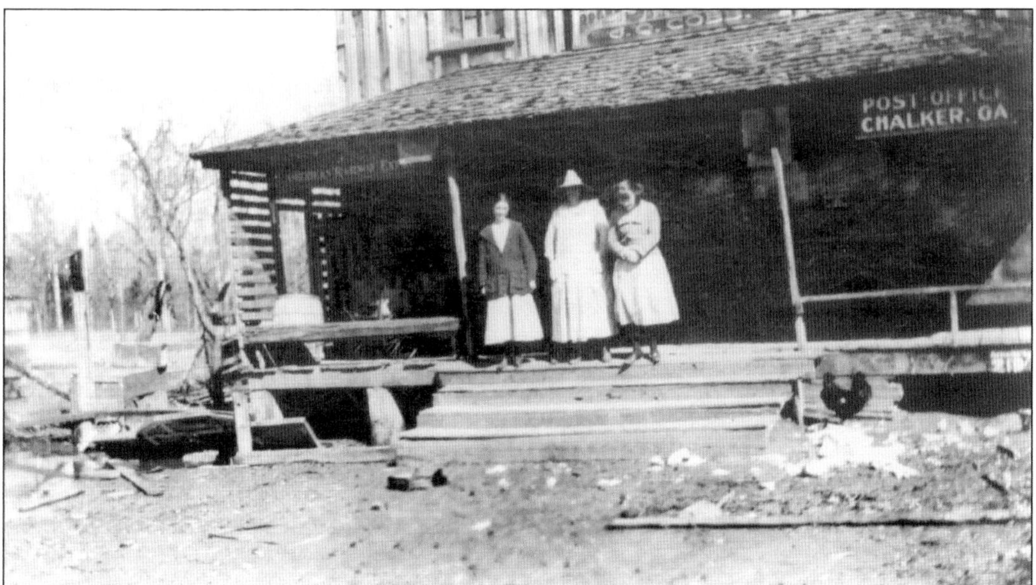

Chalker was a busy town from the 1880s until the 1930s, with a saw mill, a brick factory, a pottery maker, and this post office. Nothing remains of the community.

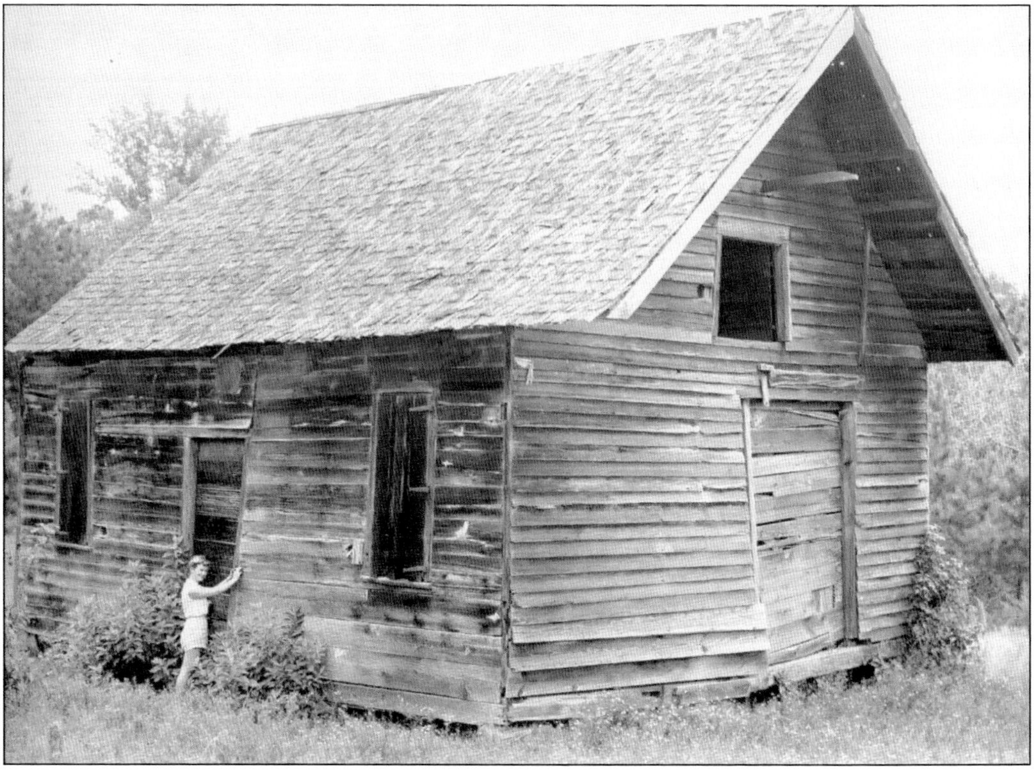

Still standing in 1955, this store and post office near Fenn's Bridge was doing business during the Civil War. (Georgia Archives.)

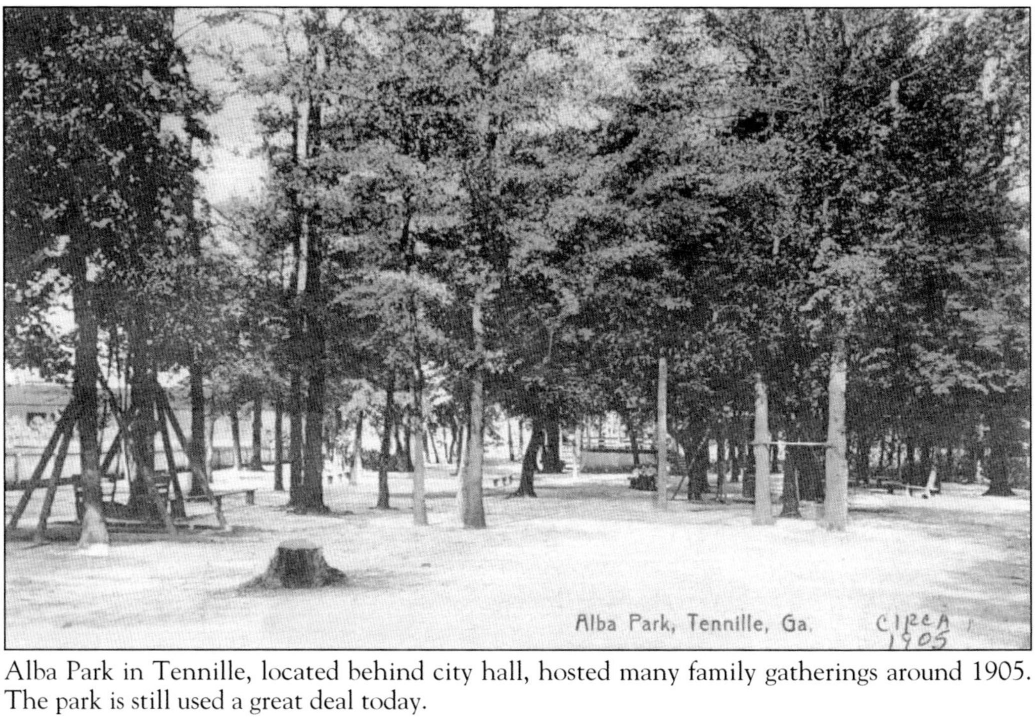

Alba Park in Tennille, located behind city hall, hosted many family gatherings around 1905. The park is still used a great deal today.

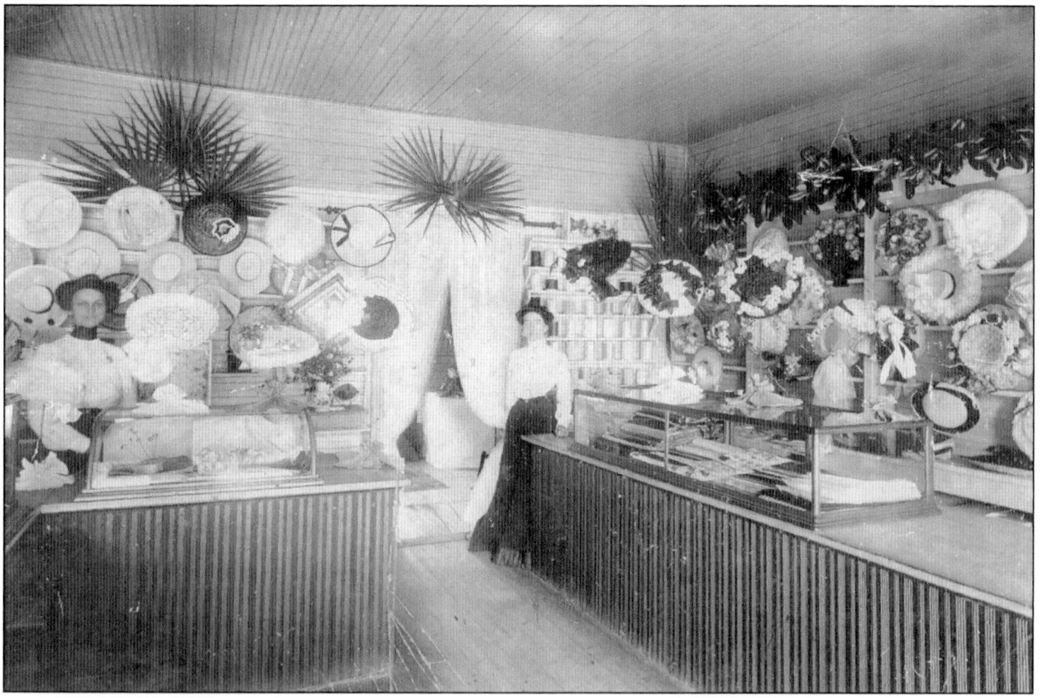

The finest hats were available in Davisboro at Bessie Sheppard's Hat Shop, c. 1895.

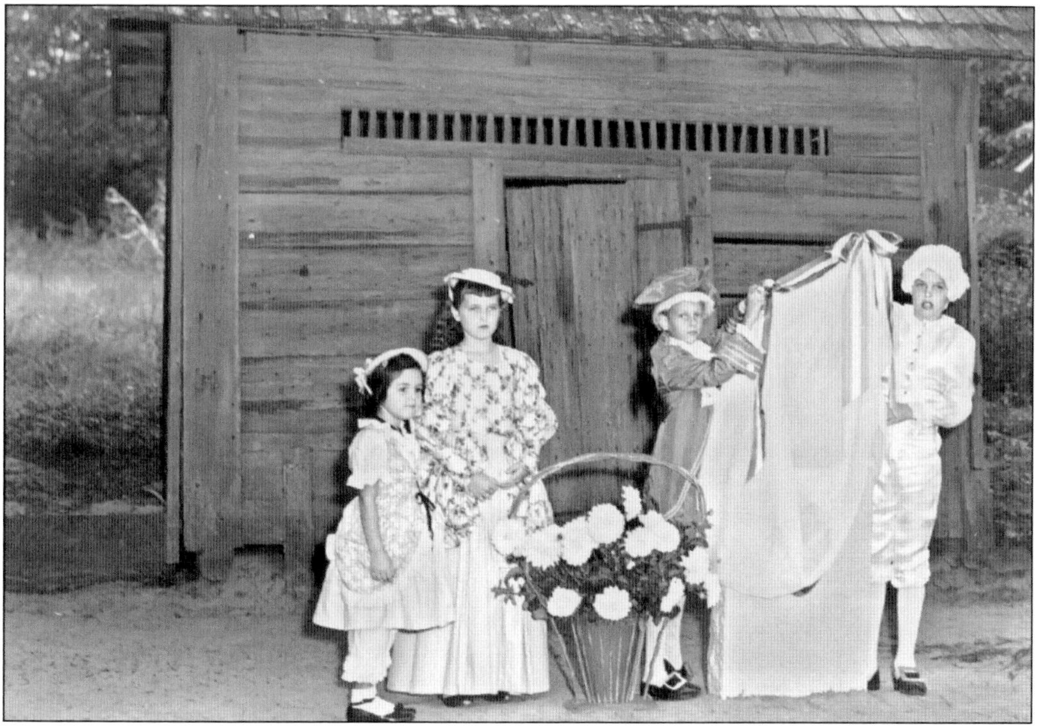

Participating in the 1949 unveiling ceremony of the DAR marker at the Log Jail in Warthen, from left to right, are Suzanne Warthen, Elizabeth Turner Wolfe, Jack Candler, and Jewell Turner Jr.

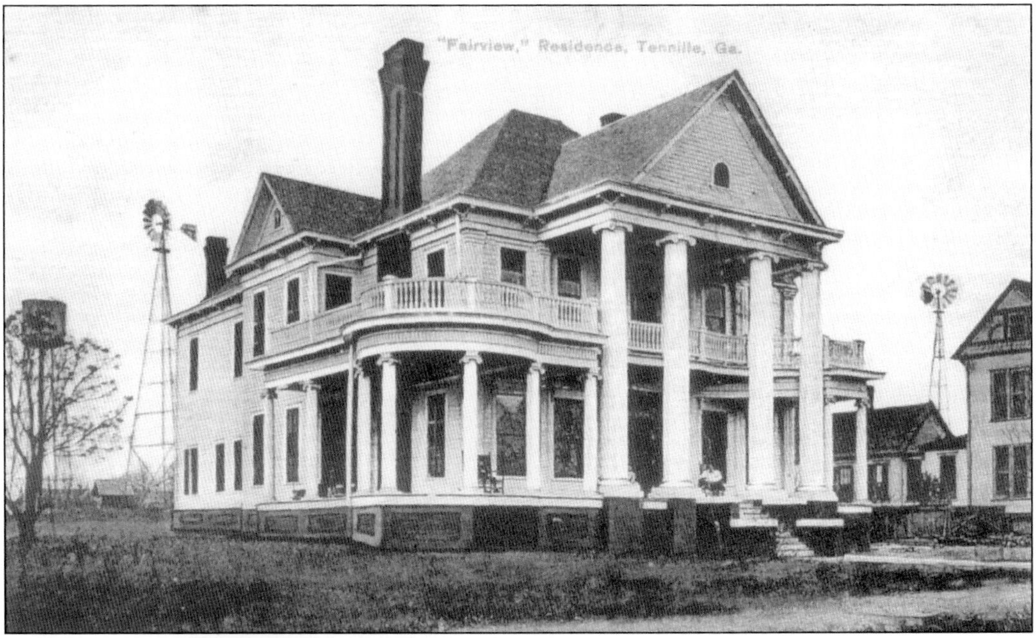

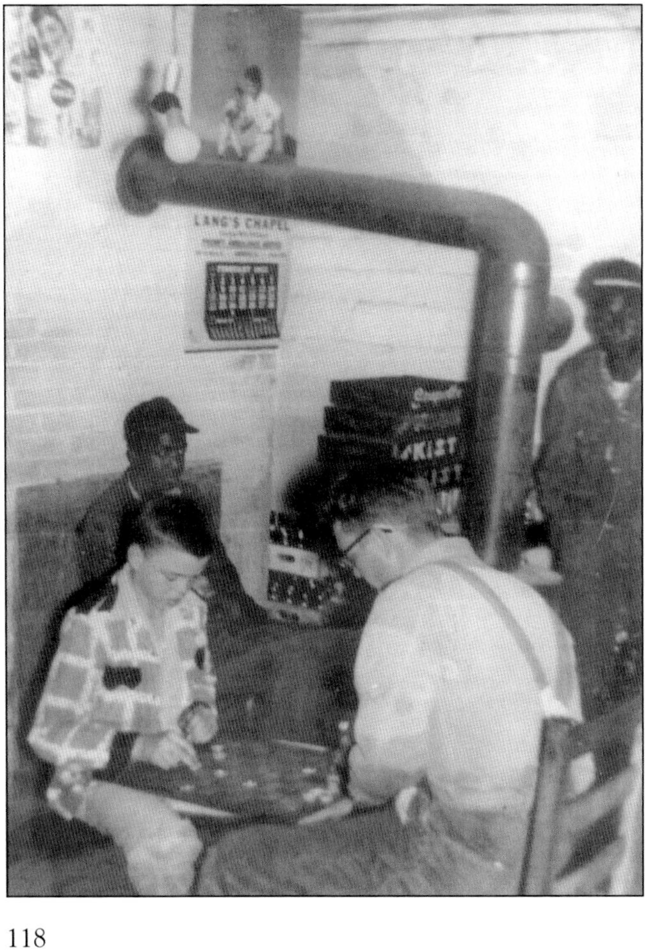

Fairview was the Tennille home of the Bashinski family. Note the windmills and the water storage tank behind this Main Street residence. This house is still standing although the classic porches and columns have been removed.

Jewell Turner plays checkers in 1952 at Lamar Brown's filling station in Warthen with Albert Brown. Seated on the left is James Miles and standing on the right is Bemon "Pap" Lymon.

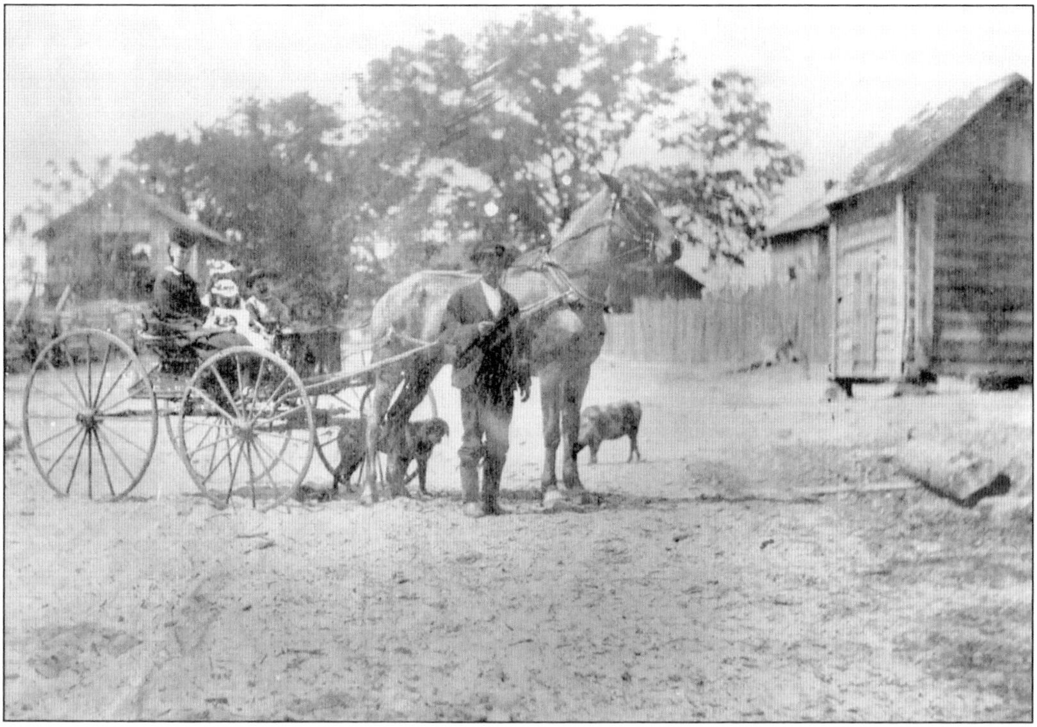

This family paused for the photographer near the Old Warthen Jail, located on the right, c. 1895.

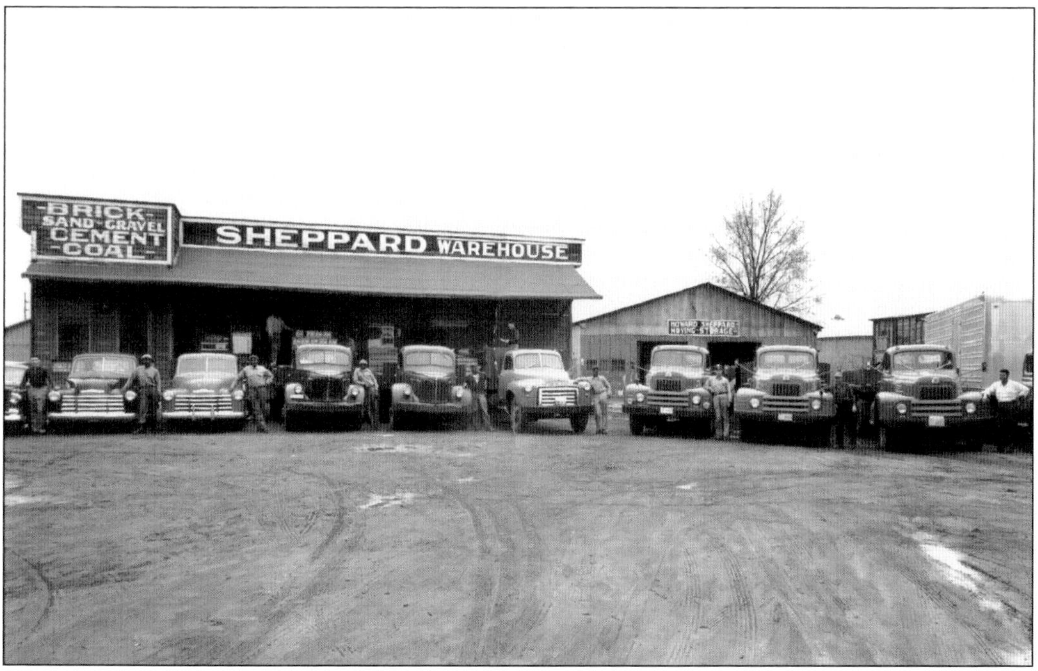

Howard Sheppard was a successful businessman in the 1940s, supplying construction materials to the area, as well as providing moving and trucking facilities.

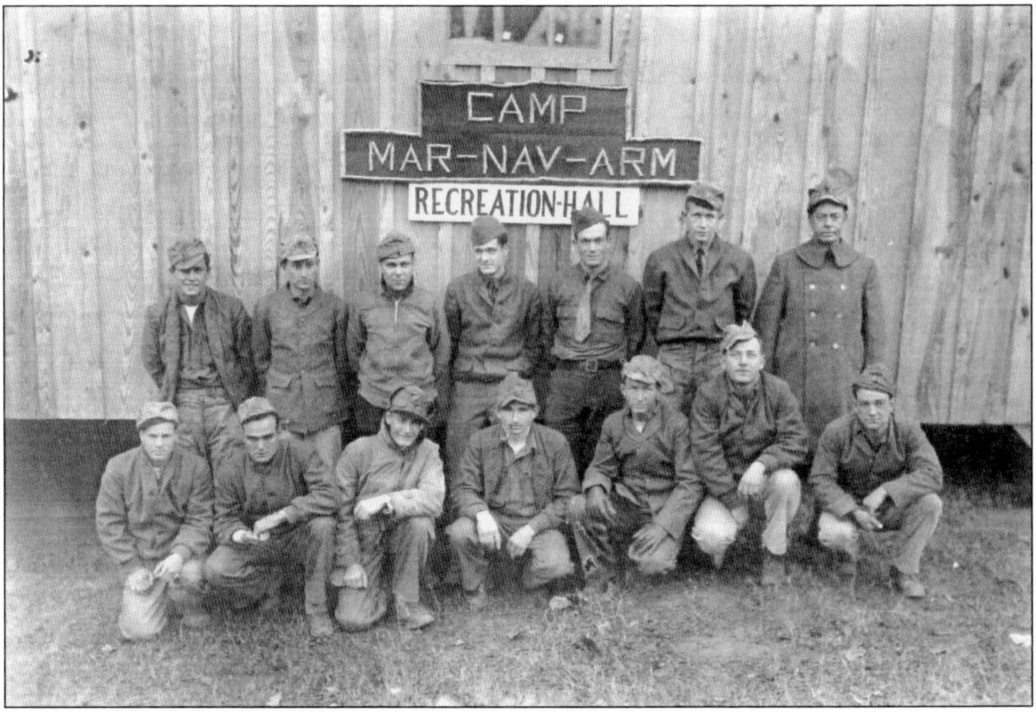

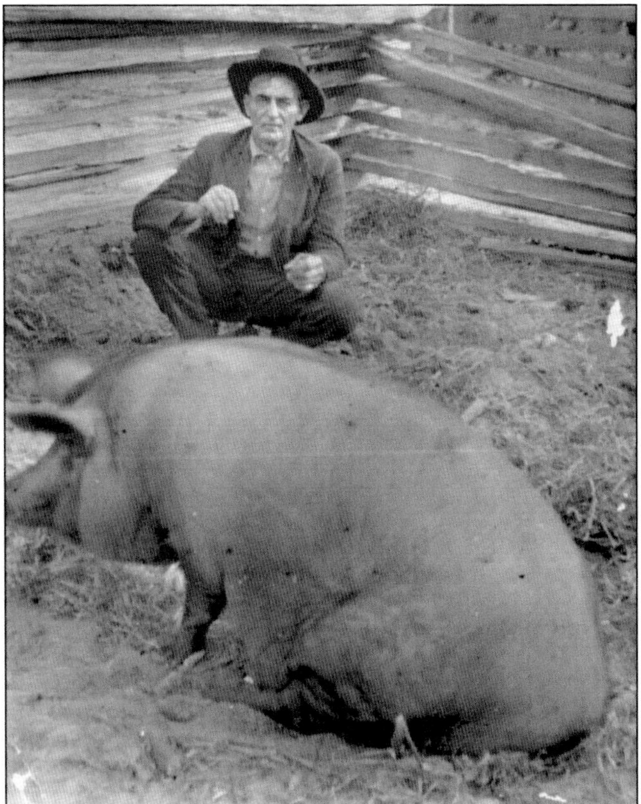

During the Depression years of the 1930s when jobs were scarce, men worked for the government program, Civilian Conservation Corps. Raymond Samson Smith kneels at the center, front.

A farmer is proud of his prize hog, c. 1920. Split rail fences were very common during that era.

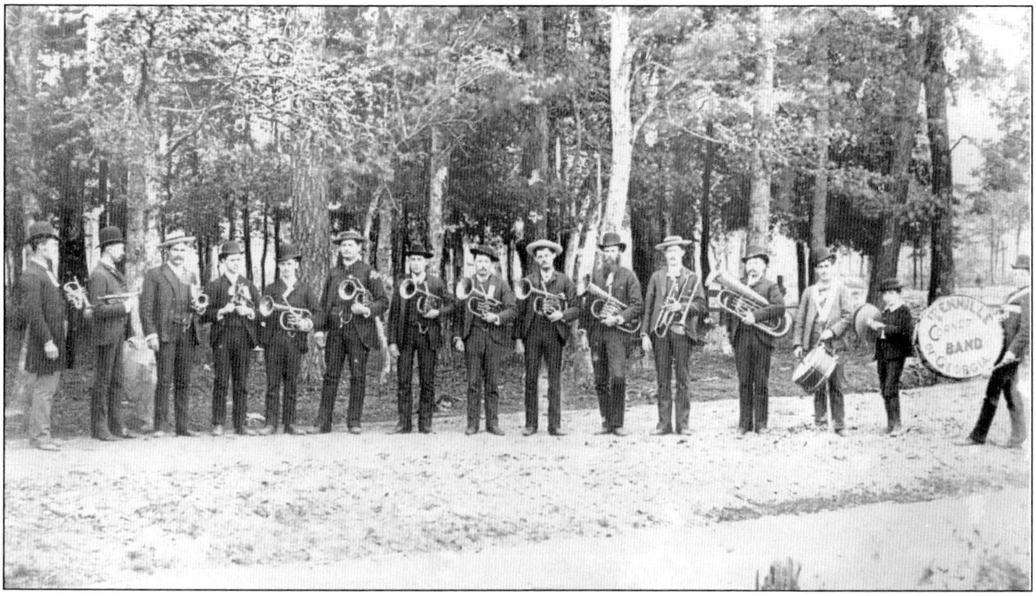

Professor Weinbhodt was in charge of the Silver Cornet Band of Tennille. Revived in June 1899, members, from left to right, are Harry Bashinski, H.L. Pritchard, Lawson Pritchard, Charlie Pritchard, Horace Walker, George Duggan, Lonnie Adams, Mose Herman, Jeff Gilbert, Nesbitt Kendrick, Abe Bashinski, Dorsey Franklin, Sam Franklin, and Morris Watkins.

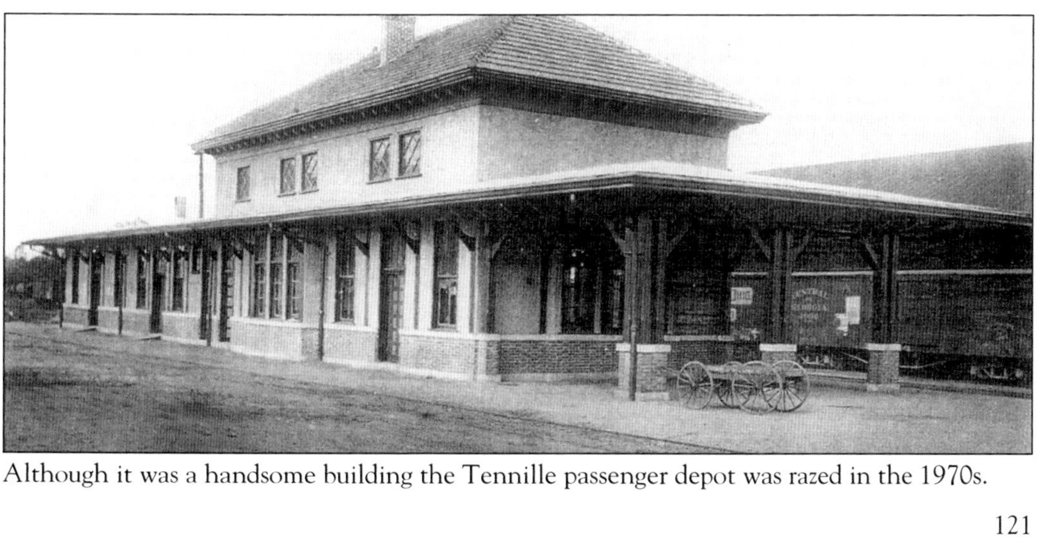

Although it was a handsome building the Tennille passenger depot was razed in the 1970s.

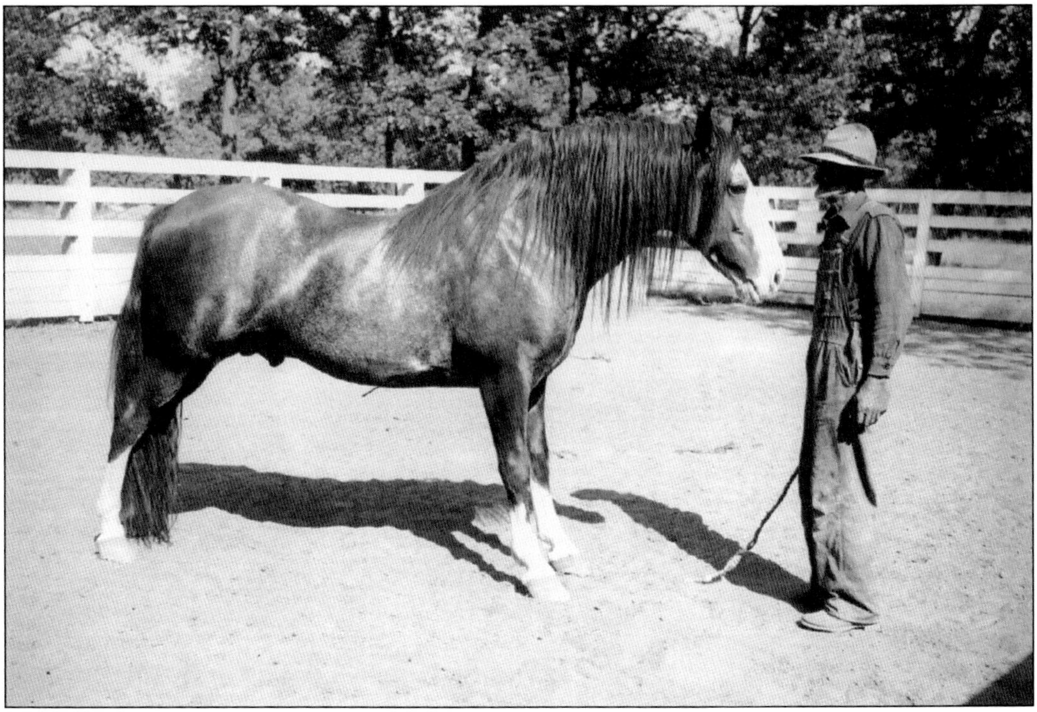

"Blue Boy" was a registered Tennessee Walking Horse owned by Tom C. Wylly, shown with Alex, his handler, in 1948.

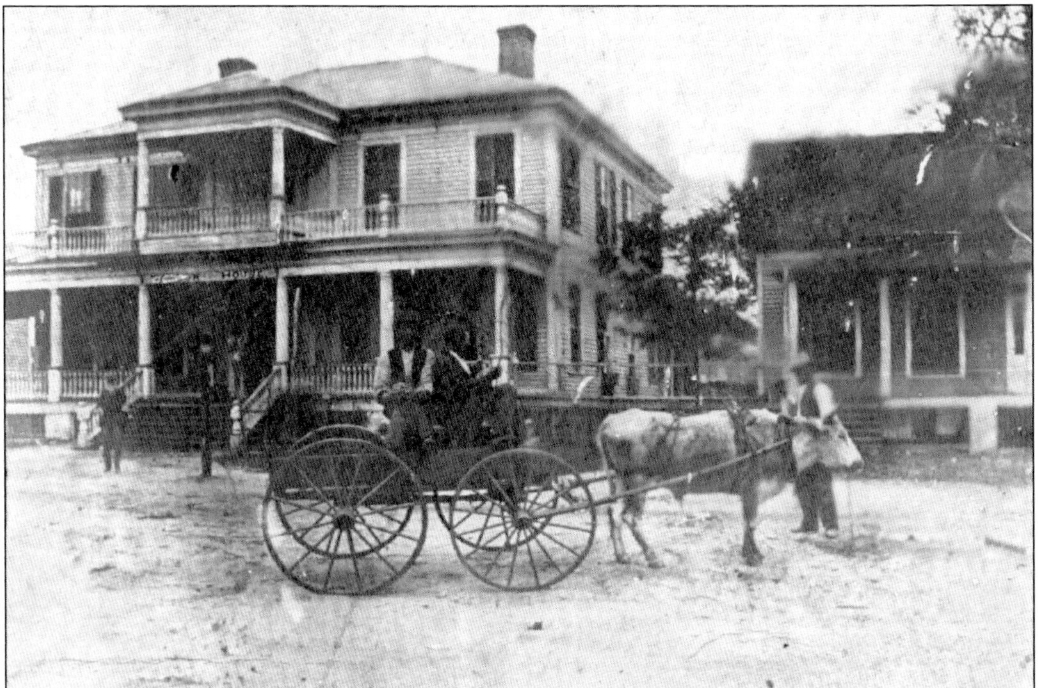

The Tennille home of the S.O. Franklin family was located south of the Central of Georgia Railroad. This photo was taken before it burned about 1892.

J.M. Gilbert, pictured c. 1923, is proud of his 1921 Model-T automobile.

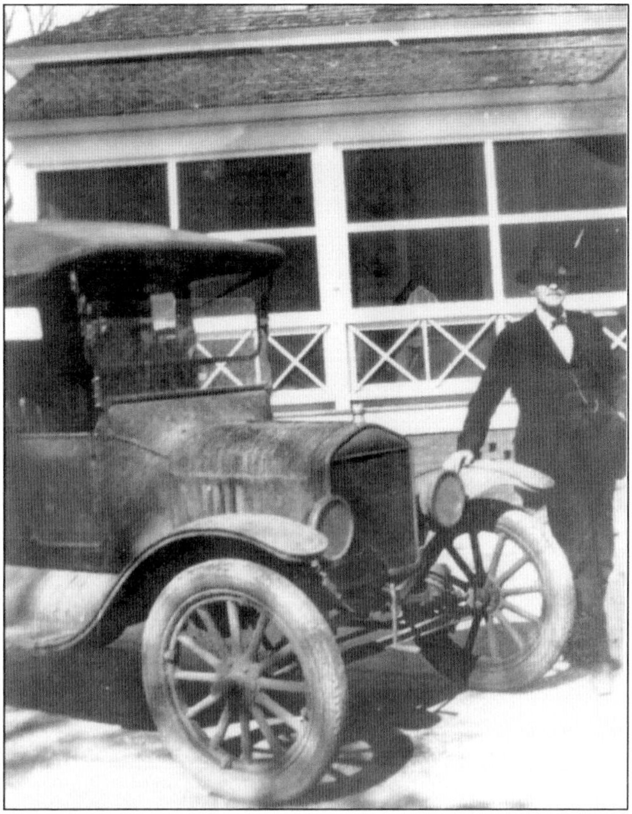

The Pritchard Hotel, south of the railroad tracks in Tennille, welcomed many a passenger for a meal and lodging. It was built by Harley and Lawson Pritchard in 1900 and torn down about 1983.

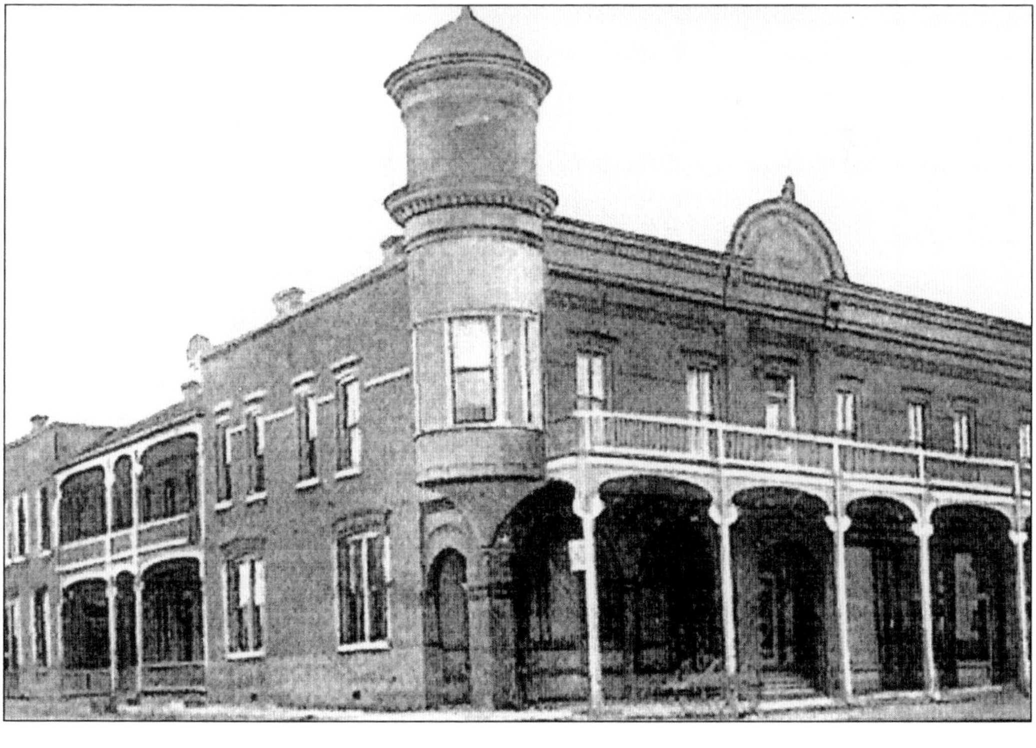

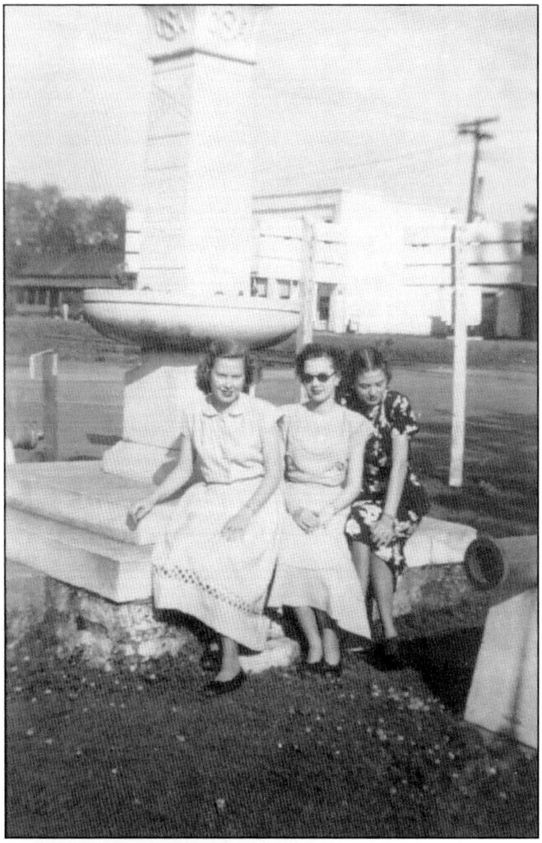

Enjoying the original fountain in Tennille in 1945, from left to right, are Marjorie Sessions, Odessie Cooper, and Patricia Sessions.

The Sandersville High School domestic science building, shown *c.* 1905, later became the Goodrich Hotel. (Georgia Archives.)

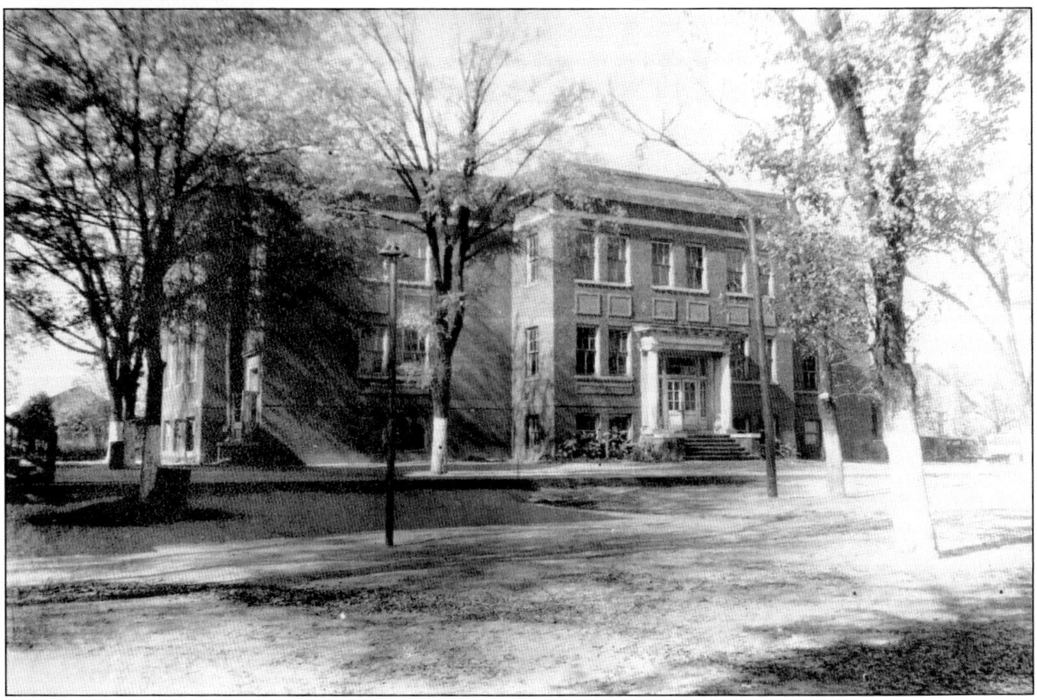

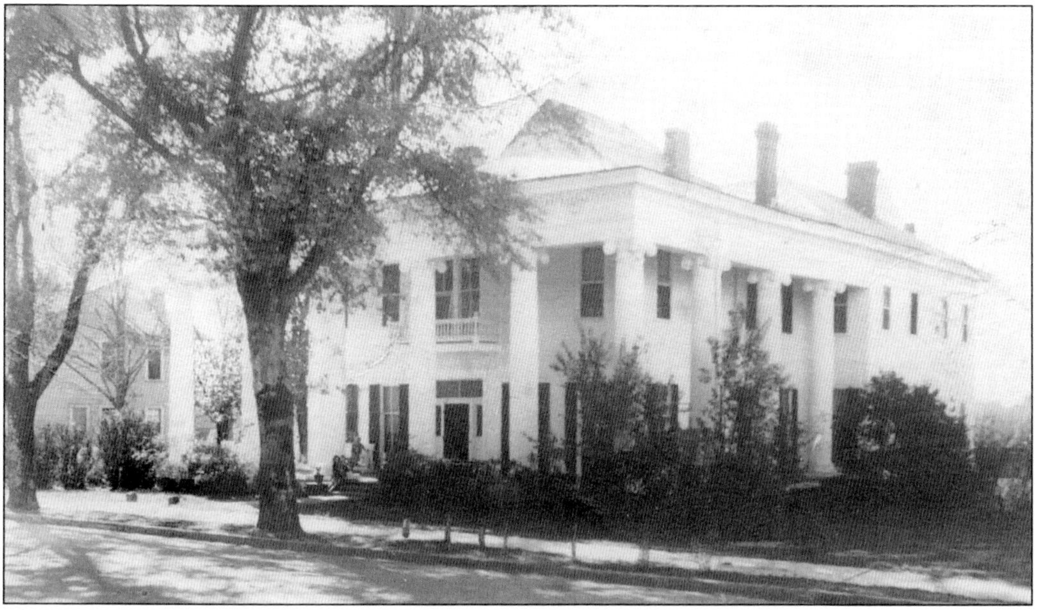

The McCarty House, located at the southwest corner of North Harris and McCarty Streets, was built around the time of the Civil War. Owners included the Newsoms, Adams and McCool families (one family). A park now replaces the house.

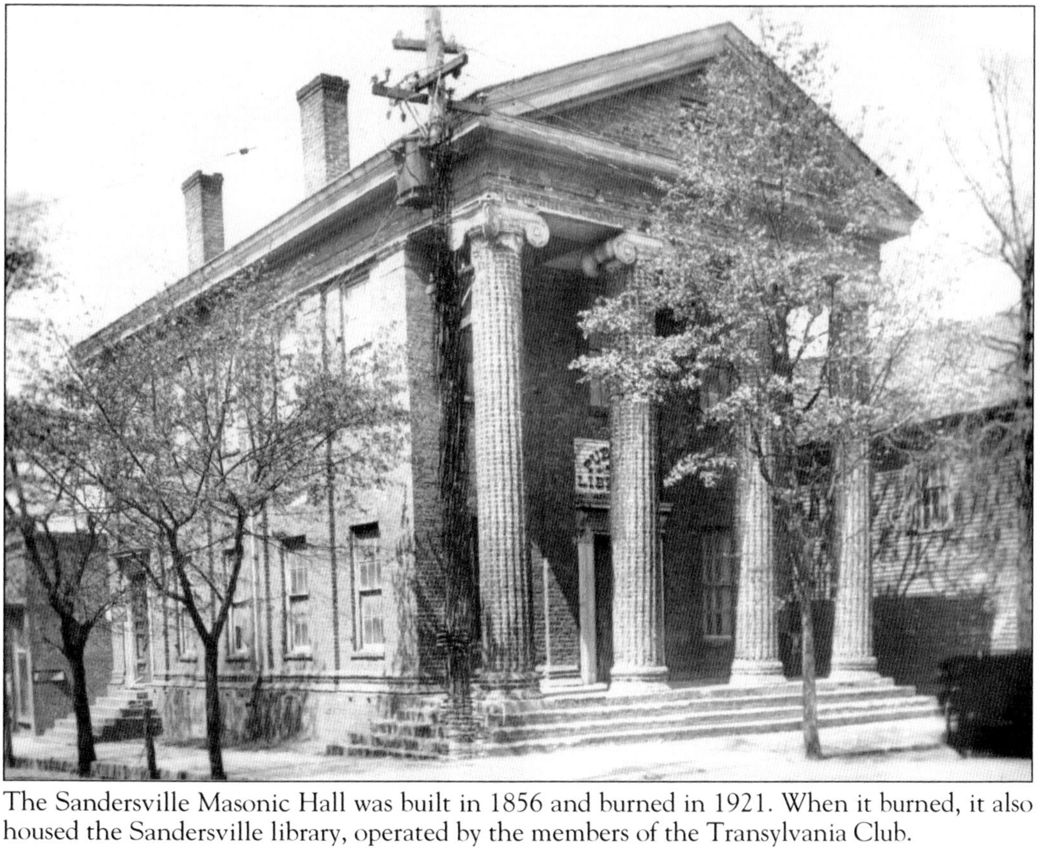

The Sandersville Masonic Hall was built in 1856 and burned in 1921. When it burned, it also housed the Sandersville library, operated by the members of the Transylvania Club.

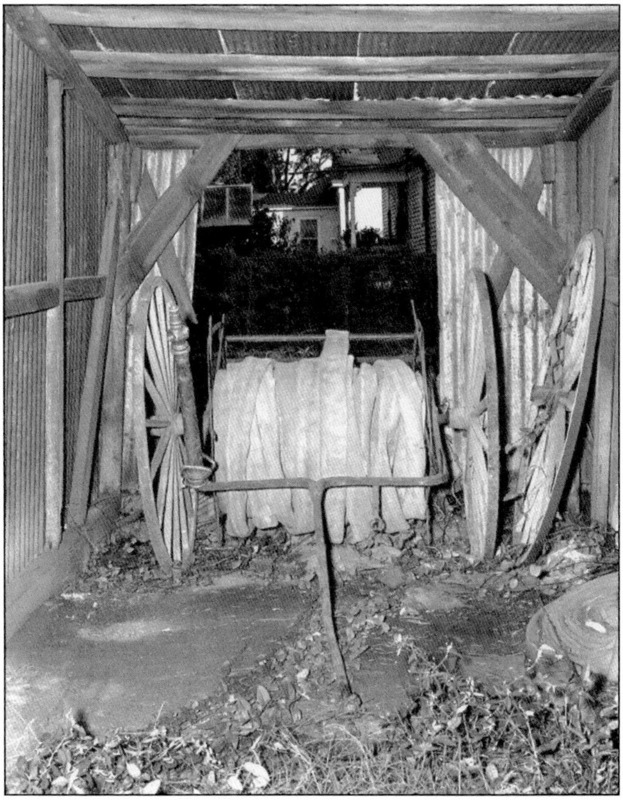

Before Tennille acquired their first fire truck, the hoses traveled to the fire on this reel, which was attached to an automobile.

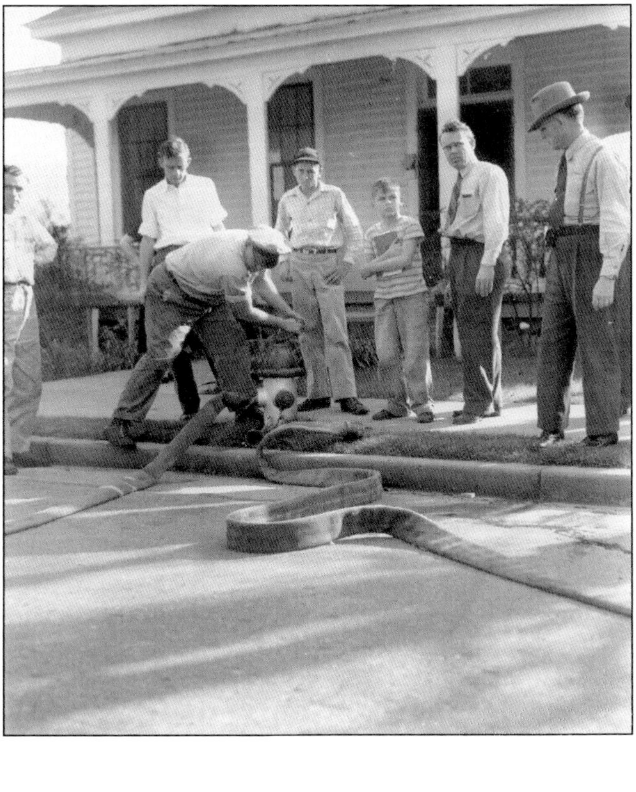

It had been nine months since these fire hoses had last been used. A Tennille fireman attaches the hose to the hydrant.

Tennille volunteer fire fighters stretch the fire hose to the barn fire.

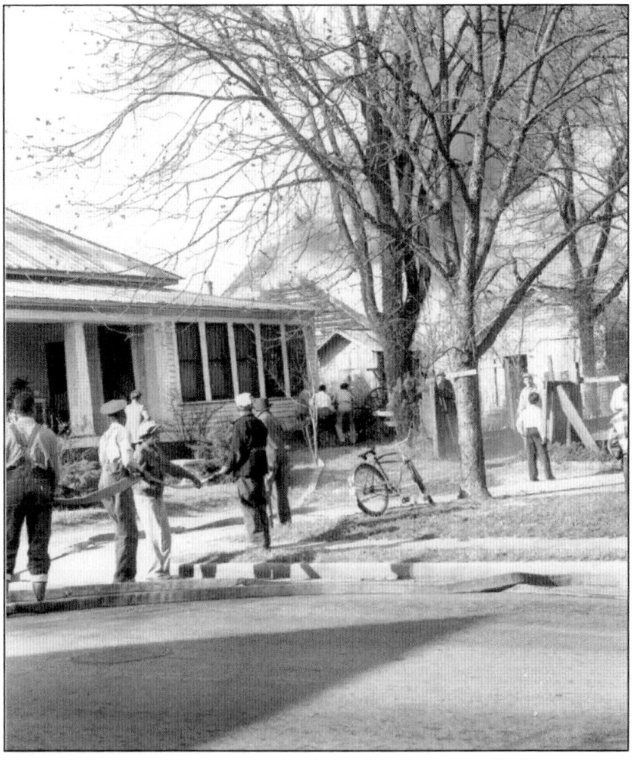

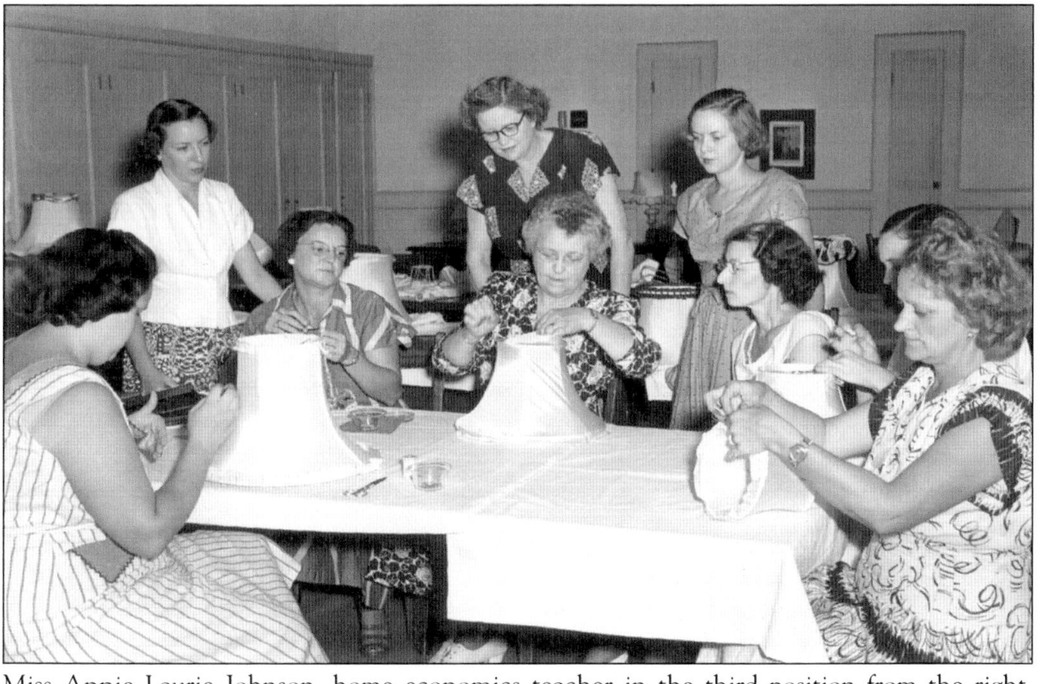

Miss Annie Laurie Johnson, home economics teacher in the third position from the right, organized a two-day workshop for covering lampshade frames. Working on the shades in August 1949, from left to right are Jessie Tanner Fawcett, Helen McElreath, Agnes Orr, Anita West, Kitty Fuquae, and others.

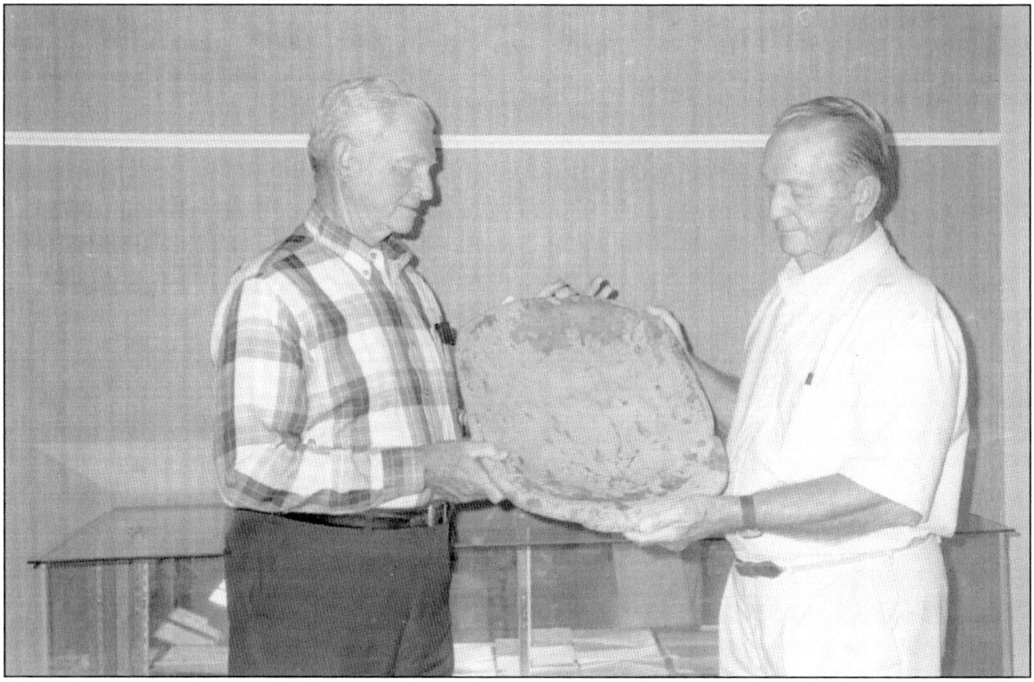

Harold Sheppard and J. Warren Newman examine a biscuit tray, also called a dough tray. Newman believes his ancestor Maj. Mark Newman brought the tray with him when he emigrated from Poland in 1846.

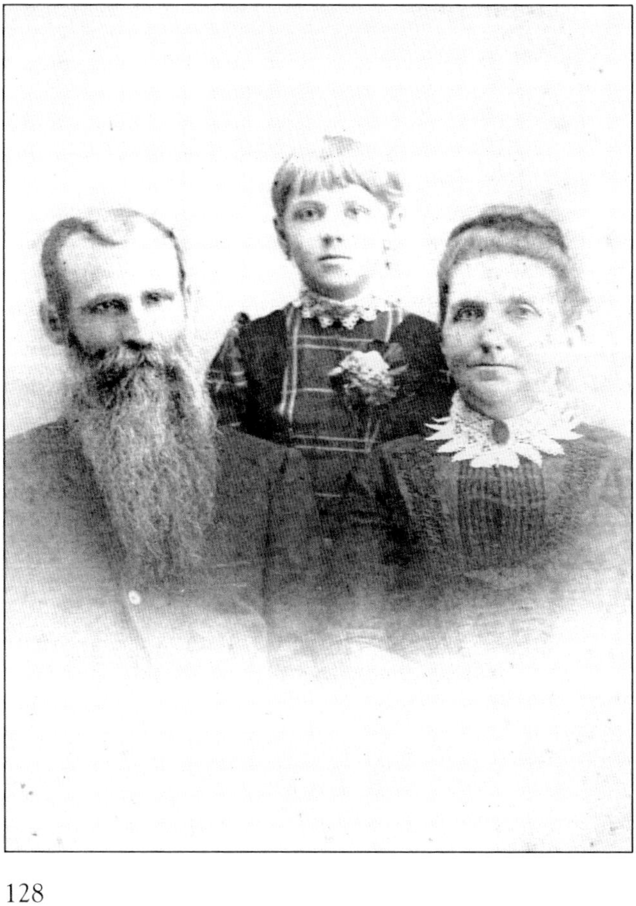

Dr. and Mrs. Ben Smith are pictured with Dumphie Smith, center. Dr. Smith graduated from Augusta Medical School in 1853. He also served as the minister at Bethany Church in Tennille.